WOMEN'S BIRTHING BODIES AND THE LAW

This is the first book to unpack the legal and ethical issues surrounding unauthorised intimate examinations during labour. The book uses feminist, socio-legal and philosophical tools to explore the issues of power, vulnerability and autonomy. The collection challenges the perception that the law adequately addresses different manifestations of unauthorised medical touch through the lens of women's experiences of unauthorised vaginal examinations during labour. The book unearths several broader themes that are of huge significance to lawyers and healthcare professionals such as the legal status of women and their bodies.

The book raises questions about women's experiences during childbirth in hospital settings. It explores the status of women's bodies during labour and childbirth where too easily they become objectified, and it raises important issues around consent. The book highlights links to the law on sexual offences and women's loss of power under the medical gaze.

The book includes contributions from leading feminist philosophers, medical professionals, and academics in medicine and law, and offers pioneering analysis relevant to lawyers and healthcare professionals with an interest in medical law and ethics; feminist theory; criminal law; tort law; and human rights law.

Women's Birthing Bodies and the Law

Unauthorised Intimate Examinations, Power and Vulnerability

Edited by
Camilla Pickles
and
Jonathan Herring

·HART·
OXFORD · LONDON · NEW YORK · NEW DELHI · SYDNEY

HART PUBLISHING

Bloomsbury Publishing Plc

Kemp House, Chawley Park, Cumnor Hill, Oxford, OX2 9PH, UK

1385 Broadway, New York, NY 10018, USA

HART PUBLISHING, the Hart/Stag logo, BLOOMSBURY and the Diana logo are
trademarks of Bloomsbury Publishing Plc

First published in Great Britain 2020

A catalogue record for this book is available from the British Library.

Library of Congress Cataloging-in-Publication data

Names: Pickles, Camilla, editor. | Herring, Jonathan, editor.

Title: Women's birthing bodies and the law : unauthorised intimate examinations, power
and vulnerability / edited by Camilla Pickles and Jonathan Herring.

Description: Oxford, UK ; New York, NY : Hart Publishing, an imprint of
Bloomsbury Publishing, 2020. | Includes bibliographical references and index.

Identifiers: LCCN 2020027402 (print) | LCCN 2020027403 (ebook) |
ISBN 9781509937578 (hardback) | ISBN 9781509937585 (ePDF) | ISBN 9781509937592 (Epub)

Subjects: LCSH: Informed consent (Medical law) | Pregnant women—Legal status, laws, etc. |
Medical examinations. | Obstetrics—Law and legislation. | Physician and patient. | Childbirth.

Classification: LCC K3611.I5 W66 2020 (print) | LCC K3611.I5 (ebook) | DDC 344.04/382—dc23

LC record available at https://lccn.loc.gov/2020027402

LC ebook record available at https://lccn.loc.gov/2020027403

ISBN: HB: 978-1-50993-757-8
        ePDF: 978-1-50993-758-5
        ePub: 978-1-50993-759-2

Typeset by Compuscript Ltd, Shannon

ACKNOWLEDGEMENTS

The editors would like to express our sincerest gratitude to everyone who made this book possible. We would like to thank all the contributors for sharing their knowledge and insights, and for their open and honest debates on this challenging subject. We thank Marthe Goudsmit for her research assistance and reliable support throughout the project. Her attention to detail saved the day! Special thanks are due to the four women who bravely shared their lived experiences of unauthorised vaginal examinations at the seminar. Their insights and expertise on the subject contributed immensely to this collection. They exposed the devastating consequences of obstetric violence and its complexity, and their participation underscores women's strength and ability to reject and challenge this form of violence and abuse. We owe a special debt to them. We are grateful for the support of our funders, the British Academy and the Oxford University Faculty of Law's Research Support Fund for funding our seminar. The generous funding enabled meaningful and exciting exchange of ideas at a seminar and this undoubtedly makes this a better collection. Thank you to Exeter College for hosting our seminar and to all the administrative staff in the Oxford University Faculty of Law who provided invaluable assistance throughout the project. Finally, we are so grateful to all at Hart who were instrumental in bringing this collection to print.

CONTENTS

LIST OF CONTRIBUTORS

Rebecca Brione is the Research and Partnerships Officer at Birthrights

Elsa Montgomery is a Senior Lecturer in Midwifery in the Florence Nightingale Faculty of Nursing, Midwifery and Palliative Care, King's College London

Neda Taghinejadi is a specialist registrar in community sexual and reproductive health and Academic Clinical Fellow at the University of Oxford

Brenda Kelly is a Consultant Obstetrician and Subspecialist in Fetal Medicine at John Radcliffe Hospital and an Honorary Clinical Fellow and Nuffield Department of Obstetrics and Gynaecology, University of Oxford

Stella Villarmea is a Professor of Philosophy at University of Alcalá and an ERC Marie Curie Fellow at University of Oxford.

Charles Foster is a Visiting Professor of Law and a Fellow of Green Templeton College at the University of Oxford

Camilla Pickles is an Assistant Professor of Biolaw at Durham University

Catarina Sjölin sits as a Circuit Judge in Crime on the Midland Circuit

Jonathan Herring is a Professor of Law at the University of Oxford and the DM Wolfe-Clarendon Fellow at Exeter College

Claire Murray is a lecturer in Law at University College Cork

Andrea Mulligan is an Assistant Professor of Law at Trinity College Dublin

Christina Zampas is an international human rights lawyer and a Reproductive and Sexual Health Law Fellow at the University of Toronto

TABLE OF CASES

1

Introduction

CAMILLA PICKLES AND JONATHAN HERRING

Vaginal examinations are generally regarded as routine procedures during facility-based childbirth. It is a given that these examinations form an intrinsic part of maternity care: the plethora of clinical guidelines support this contention and self-help books for pregnant women tell women to expect these examinations to happen on a regular basis.[1] Reasons for vaginal examinations include the need to establish labour progression and foetal position.[2] Depending on the jurisdiction, clinical indication and available resources,[3] one woman can expect to be examined every four hours during early labour, and hourly as she progresses through to the later stages of labour and nears childbirth.[4] Further, studies demonstrate that some women are subjected to more examinations than recommended by the relevant guidelines.[5] These diverging approaches between jurisdictions and healthcare facilities reveal that this procedure is shaped by broader contexts rather than by the individual needs of the women being examined.

Despite its routine character and its pervasive use within a facility settings, for women on the receiving end of this type of examination it can be particularly painful, distressing and invasive as it involves penetration into women's

---

[1] See Chapter 2 in this volume, R Brione, 'Non-Consented Vaginal Examinations: The Birthrights and AIMS Perspective'. For an example of the approach taken in self-help books, see M Blott, *The Day-by-Day Pregnancy Book* (London, Dorling Kindersley, 2009); H Murkoff et al, *What to Expect When You're Expecting*, 3rd edn (London, Pocket Books, 2002).

[2] Brione (n 1).

[3] The capacity to subject women to regular vaginal examinations is dependent on staff-patient ratios and sufficiently resourced maternity care contexts. In under-resourced contexts, some women may be admitted into maternity wards, but they may not be attended to (or examined) because of inappropriate staff-patient ratios. In these contexts, women tend to birth alone without professional support because staff simply do not have the capacity to meet the demand for care. For instance, see K Shimoda et al, 'Midwives' Respect and Disrespect of Women during Facility-Based Childbirth in Urban Tanzania: A Qualitative Study' (2018) 15 *Reproductive Health* 8; R Chadwick et al, 'Narratives of Distress about Birth in South African Public Maternity Settings: A Qualitative Study' (2014) 30(7) *Midwifery* 862.

[4] Brione (n 1) considers these in detail in her contribution to this volume.

[5] See, for instance, M Maaita et al, 'Jordanian Women's Feelings, Opinions and Knowledge of Vaginal Examination during Child Birth' (2017) 102 *Journal of the Royal Medical Services* 1.

vaginas during an especially physically and psychologically demanding time. The extent of the invasion will be far greater when healthcare professionals perform vaginal examinations without women's consent, with force or without regard for their individual histories, personal needs, autonomy, privacy and human dignity. Outside the medical context and without consent, the acts involved in a vaginal examination would constitute an extremely serious criminal offence and represent a major invasion of human rights.

The edited collection explores this issue: vaginal examinations during labour without women's comprehensive and voluntary consent. The chapters contained herein do not question whether unauthorised examinations happen. The contributors accept that unauthorised vaginal examinations do happen in the maternity care context and we are confident of this position for two reasons: individual women have shared their diverse and complex experiences with those who have contributed to this collection,[6] and because literature from across the globe records this as a relatively prevalent practice.[7] Confirmation of its global prevalence is confirmed by the fact that unauthorised vaginal examinations featured as a human rights violation of concern in the Special Rapporteur on Violence against Women's thematic report on mistreatment and violence against women in reproductive health services with a focus on childbirth and obstetric violence.[8] Despite regular reports, it is not entirely clear how many women experience vaginal examinations without fully informed and comprehensive consent. This issue has not been quantified in any country. Regrettably, quantification may not be possible because some women are not aware that this is a procedure that requires consent, or because it is perceived to be 'normal' part of childbirth. Statements by women in relation to their experiences of vaginal examinations while receiving maternity

---

[6] This edited collection is the outcome of a closed seminar held at the University of Oxford, Faculty of Law at the start of 2019. The seminar was used as a platform to bring together women with lived experiences of unauthorised vaginal examinations, civil society organisations dedicated to promoting and protecting women's rights during childbirth, lawyers, philosophers, obstetricians and gynaecologists, and midwives. Together, we listened to women on a 'Lived Experiences Panel' and their experiences shaped and moulded the contributions published herein. Some contributors were not able to attend the seminar in person and not all who attended contributed to the book.

[7] For instance, see M Bohren et al, 'How Women are Treated during Facility-Based Childbirth in Four Countries: A Cross-Sectional Study with Labour Observations and Community-Based Surveys' (2019) 394 *The Lancet* 1750; S Hussein et al, 'Women's Experiences of Childbirth in Middle Eastern Countries: A Narrative Review' (2018) 59 *Midwifery* 100; C Beck, 'A Secondary Analysis of Mistreatment of Women during Childbirth in Health Care Facilities' (2018) 47 *Journal of Obstetric, Gynecologic & Neonatal Nursing* 94; R Reed et al, 'Women's Descriptions of Childbirth Trauma Relating to Care Provider Actions and Interactions' (2017) 17(1) *BMC Pregnancy Childbirth* 21; Maaita et al (n 5); S Hassan et al, 'The Paradox of Vaginal Examination Practice during Normal Childbirth: Palestinian Women's Feelings, Opinions, Knowledge and Experiences' (2012) 9 *Reproductive Health* 16; C Lai and V Levy, 'Hong Kong Chinese Women's Experiences of Vaginal Examinations in Labour' (2002) 18 *Midwifery* 296.

[8] United Nations General Assembly, 'Report of the Special Rapporteur on Violence Against Women, its Causes and Consequences on a Human Rights-Based Approach to Mistreatment and Violence Against Women in Reproductive Health Services with a Focus on Childbirth and Obstetric Violence', UN Doc A/74/137 (2019).

care in Hong Kong are particularly telling: 'I can tolerate it … there is no other way round, labour is like this' and '[t]his is a very natural and normal event … it is ok and I can accept this'.[9] Similarly healthcare professionals assume consent is present and are often unaware that there is no consent. So simply asking women or healthcare professionals whether they have experienced unwanted vaginal examinations will not reveal the extent of the problem.

Instead of asking if unauthorised vaginal examinations *really* happen, we take on the challenge of exploring and understanding how this violation happens and why; and we interrogate the law relevant to this issue. While unauthorised vaginal examinations are its focal point, the book uses this violation as a strategic lens to expose the broader issues surrounding women's experiences of violence and abuse during childbirth around the world and the inadequacies of the law to address these broader issues.

The cover of the book deserves special mention here. First, it offers a visual demonstration of the deeply destructive consequences of abuse and violence during labour and childbirth.[10] Antje Horsch and Susan Garthus-Niegel explain that women with post-traumatic stress disorder report feeling a loss of identity and self-esteem, and women report experiencing high levels of distress, panic, anxiety, grief, anger and tearfulness.[11] Women have reported having suicidal thoughts and ideations; shared thoughts of harming their babies; decided not to have further children; or developed an extreme fear of any subsequent pregnancy and childbirth.[12] Traumatic memories can stay with women for years, causing a 'black hole' of 'endless pain'.[13] The disorder can negatively impact the family unit and the mother-baby relationship can be shaped in part by emotional detachment: 'Mechanically I would go through the motions of being a good mother. Inside I felt nothing'.[14] Violations during childbirth have the power to break open women's lives and these damaging consequences must be recognised from the onset.

Second, and going beyond the lived harms, the cracked concrete image offers a visual representation of the purpose of this book. We aim to contribute towards

---

[9] Lai and Levy (n 7) 299. These experiences mirror some of the experiences reported by Birthrights and AIMS in this volume. For more on women's inability to recognise abusive interactions, see L Freedman et al, 'Eye of the Beholder? Observation versus Self-Report in the Measurement of Disrespect and Abuse during Facility-Based Childbirth: Implications for a Human-Rights Based Approach to Maternal Health' (2018) 26 *Reproductive Health Matters* 107.

[10] A Horsch and S Garthus-Niegel, 'Post-traumatic Stress Disorder Following Childbirth' in C Pickles and J Herring (eds), *Childbirth, Vulnerability and Law: Exploring Issues of Violence and Control* (Abingdon, Routledge, 2019) 49; Reed et al (n 7); M Simpson and C Catling, 'Understanding Psychological Traumatic Birth Experiences: A Literature Review' (2016) 29 *Women and Birth* 203; Ziba Taghizadeh et al, 'Iranian Mothers' Perception of the Psychological Birth Trauma: A Qualitative Study' (2014) 9 *Iranian Journal of Psychiatry* 31; C Beck, 'Birth Trauma: In the Eye of the Beholder' (2004) 53 *Nursing Research* 28.

[11] Horsch and Garthus-Niegel (n 10) 55.

[12] ibid.

[13] ibid.

[14] ibid, 55 citing S Ayers et al, 'The Effects of Childbirth-Related Post-Traumatic Stress Disorder on Women and Their Relationships: A Qualitative Study' (2006) 11 *Psychology, Health & Medicine* 389.

and support continued efforts to expose and interrogate cracks in the maternity care system and in the laws that regulate violations during childbirth. The cracks illustrate the vulnerability that is commonly associated with childbirth and which represent a repeated feature of the description of unauthorised vaginal examinations. We will consider these issues separately because each is deserving of detailed analysis.

I. Cracks in the System: Violence and Abuse during Maternity Care

Unauthorised vaginal examinations must be situated within the broader context of disrespect and abuse of women during labour and childbirth while accessing formal maternity care. That is, these unauthorised procedures constitute one manifestation of a broad spectrum of issues that women are subjected to when they give birth in healthcare facilities, and these are typically framed as mistreatment,[15] disrespect and abuse[16] or obstetric violence.[17] While different terms are used by different stakeholders,[18] there is a measure of overlap regarding the sorts of issues that these terms attempt to capture and there is agreement that 'testimonies from women have shown that mistreatment and violence during childbirth is widespread and ingrained in the health system'.[19]

Abuse and violence during facility-based childbirth can take several forms and range from interpersonal violence, abuse and mistreatment[20] to systemic failures and structural forms of violence and abuse.[21] Typical examples of interpersonal violence and abuse include verbal and physical abuse, treatment without consent and the use of coercive control to gain compliance with hospital protocols and

---

[15] Bohren et al (n 7).

[16] G Sen et al, 'Beyond Measurement: The Drivers of Disrespect and Abuse in Obstetric Care' (2018) 26 *Reproductive Health Matters* 6

[17] C Williams et al, 'Obstetric Violence: A Latin American Legal Response to Mistreatment during Childbirth' (2018) 125 *BJOG: An International Journal of Obstetrics & Gynaecology* 1208.

[18] Compare the different positions taken in J Vogel et al, 'Promoting Respect and Preventing Mistreatment during Childbirth' (2016) 123 *BJOG: An International Journal of Obstetrics & Gynaecology* 671; Sen et al (n 16); M Sadler et al, 'Moving Beyond Disrespect and Abuse: Addressing the Structural Dimensions of Obstetric Violence' (2016) 24 *Reproductive Health Matters* 51.

[19] United Nations General Assembly (n 8) [16].

[20] Interpersonal violence concerns direct manifestations of violence. These actions are visible, commonly recognisable and generally involve the commission or omission of an act that causes a violation of a person's integrity. See H Fraser and K Seymour, *Understanding Violence and Abuse: An Anti-Oppressive Practice Perspective* (Halifax, Fernwood Publishing, 2017) 21; V Bufacchi, *Violence and Social Justice* (Basingstoke, Palgrave Macmillian, 2007).

[21] Fraser and Seymour explain that structural violence is an indirect form of violence and it 'refers to "social arrangements" that are "embedded in the political and economic organization of our social world" … which advantage some individuals and groups and not others via, for example, access to goods, resources and opportunities including political power / agency, education, health care and legal status' (Reference omitted.) ibid 22.

medical advice.[22] Systemic failures include inadequate provision of resources, inappropriate and disrespectful hospital policies that lack an evidence base, and poorly designed maternity wards that do not offer enough privacy to individual women using them.[23] Structural violence and abuse include gender inequality and discrimination based on women's sociodemographic characteristics and health status.[24] These issues frustrate effective communication among healthcare professionals and between healthcare professionals and birthing women, and they create unsupportive birthing environments. These conditions result in the violation of women's rights to privacy, bodily and psychological integrity, dignity and autonomy.[25] Conditions such as these render women strangers to their own birth processes. They are reduced to a mechanical role in the birth and used instrumentally to produce a healthy baby. Women's health and wellbeing are compromised, and in some cases these conditions cost women and newborns their lives.[26]

Recently, the Special Rapporteur on Violence against Women recognised a range of medical processes as forms of violence against women.[27] These procedures and interventions were specific concerns highlighted in the 128 reports submitted from around the world in response to the Rapporteur's call for submissions on mistreatment and violence against women during childbirth.[28] The reports confirm the global and embedded nature of this phenomenon. Recognised instances of abuse and violence include failures to provide out-of-hospital birth support, symphysiotomies without informed consent, forced and coerced sterilisations, physical restraint of incarcerated women during facility-based childbirth, and detention of women and their newborns because of women's inability to settle hospital bills related to care during childbirth.[29] The Special Rapporteur also labelled the routine provision of caesarean section surgeries, overuse of episiotomies, 'husband stitches', suturing vaginal tears or episiotomies without pain relief medication, and overuse of synthetic oxytocin as forms of violence and abuse.[30]

---

[22] Bohren et al (n 7).

[23] ibid.

[24] Sadler et al (n 18); R Jewkes and L Penn-Kekana, 'Mistreatment of Women in Childbirth: Time for Action on the Important Dimension of Violence against Women' (2015) 12 *PloS Med e1001849*; L Dixon, 'Obstetrics in a Time of Violence: Mexican Midwives Critique Routine Hospital Practices' (2015) 29 *Medical Anthropology Quarterly* 437.

[25] United Nations General Assembly (n 8); E Prochaska, 'Human Rights Law and Challenging Dehumanisation in Childbirth: A Practitioner's Perspective' in Pickles and Herring (n 10); Bohren et al (n 7); R Khosla et al, 'International Human Rights and the Mistreatment of Women during Childbirth' (2016) 18 *Health and Human Rights* 131.

[26] World Health Organization, *WHO Recommendations: Intrapartum Care for a Positive Childbirth Experience* (Geneva, WHO, 2018) at www.who.int/reproductivehealth/publications/intrapartum-care-guidelines/en.

[27] United Nations General Assembly (n 8).

[28] For a list of all submissions, see United Nations Human Rights, Office of the High Commission 'Call for Submissions: Mistreatment and Violence against Women during Reproductive Health with a focus on Childbirth' (2019) at www.ohchr.org/EN/Issues/Women/SRWomen/Pages/Mistreatment.aspx.

[29] United Nations General Assembly (n 8) [19]–[23].

[30] ibid [24]–[26].

Other abusive practices included application of the Kristeller manoeuvre, a lack of choice regarding position during childbirth, and the Rapporteur noted extensive reports of verbal abuse, sexist remarks, and threats of violence for non-compliance with medical direction.[31]

Unauthorised vaginal examinations can be located within this long list of violence and abuse against women; where women are examined in ways that undermine their privacy, dignity and autonomy' and where they are treated as mere training objects.[32] Indeed, the very fact that vaginal examinations, which in other circumstances would constitute a serious assault, are often treated as routine and not requiring specific consent, is revealing. In the context of childbirth any act done to the woman which can be seen as facilitating the delivery of a healthy baby is taken as justified and consented to.

Many more instances of violence and abuse have been reported by relevant stakeholders and by women themselves on various social media platforms. Not all of these can be explored here, but they raise key points worthy of emphasis here. First, the Special Rapporteur *confirms* that these various incidents of abuse in healthcare facilities amount to gender-based violence:

> [T]he Special Rapporteur points out that the following definition of violence against women, as enshrined in article 1 of the Declaration on the Elimination of Violence against Women, *is applicable to all forms of mistreatment and violence against women in reproductive health services and childbirth*: 'any act of gender-based violence that results in, or is likely to result in, physical, sexual or psychological harm or suffering to women, including threats of such acts, coercion or arbitrary deprivation of liberty, whether occurring in public or in private life'. General recommendation 19 of the Committee on the Elimination of Discrimination against Women defines gender-based violence against women as 'violence which is directed against a woman because she is a woman or that affects women disproportionately' (emphasis added).[33]

A gender-based violence framing is in line with the position taken by many others around the world in the years preceding the release of this report.[34] A declaration of this kind is particularly powerful because it authoritatively links routine facility-based practices and interventions to current constructions of violence

---

[31] ibid [27], [29]–[31].

[32] ibid [28].

[33] United Nations General Assembly (n 8) [11].

[34] See for instance, Williams et al (n 17); F Diaz-Tello, 'Invisible Wounds: Obstetric Violence in the United States' (2017) 24 *Reproductive Health Matters* 56; C Vacaflor, 'Obstetric Violence: A New Framework for Identifying Challenges to Maternal Healthcare in Argentina' (2017) 24 *Reproductive Health Matters* 65; S Cohen Shabot, 'Making Loud Bodies "Feminine": A Feminist-Phenomenological Analysis of Obstetric Violence' (2016) 39 *Human Studies* 231; Sadler et al (n 18); S Sánchez, *Obstetric Violence: Medicalization, Authority Abuse and Sexism within Spanish Obstetric Assistance: A New Name for Old Issues?* (MS thesis, Utrecht University, 2014); Dixon (n 24); S Charles, 'Obstetricians and Violence against Women' (2012) 11 *The American Journal of Bioethics* 51; R Castro and J Erviti, 'Violations of Reproductive Rights during Hospital Births in Mexico' (2003) 7 *Health and Human Rights* 90; A d'Oliveira et al, 'Violence against Women in Health-Care Institutions: An Emerging Problem' (2002) 359 *The Lancet* 1681.

against women and this triggers states' international human rights obligations to actively address this issue. This is not the first time these linkages have been made; Latin American countries and activists are leaders in this context and there is much to learn from their experiences.[35] However, it is the first time a United Nations Special Rapporteur has explicitly confirmed this link on the international stage and established recommendations to tackle the issue under the umbrella of 'obstetric violence' and 'mistreatment'.

A second key point relates to the Special Rapporteurs framing of these different violations as forming 'part of a continuum of the violations that occur in the wider context of structural inequality, discrimination and patriarchy'.[36] Working with the notion of 'continuum' is particularly helpful here. Liz Kelly developed the concept of 'continuum of violence' in the context of sexual violence against women.[37] She uses it to describe the extent and range of the violence that women experience in this context. The 'continuum of violence' helps to reveal the common character that underlies many different events and it emphasises that these are continuous in that they pass into one another and sometimes cannot be readily distinguished.[38] Kelly explains that the continuum does not serve as a statement of the relative seriousness of the different forms of sexual violence, but that it 'enables us to document and name the range of abuse, intimidation, coercion, intrusion, threat and force whilst acknowledging that there are no clearly defined and discrete analytic categories into which men's behaviour can be placed'.[39] This approach too means that a particular act of abuse can take on further meanings and have further significance because of earlier instances of abuse, or because of the wider social meaning that the act has. This explains why any unauthorised vaginal examination has greater significance, than, say, an unauthorised examination of a finger.[40]

In the context of facility-based abuse and obstetric violence, gender inequality and patriarchy serve as the connecting link between violence that occurs at an individual level and structural domains. In this way, it challenges the division

---

[35] For instance, see Grupo de Información en Reproducción Elegida, *Obstetric Violence: A Human Rights Approach* (2015) at gire.org.mx/en/informes/obstetric-violence-a-human-rights-approach-2015/; R D'Gregorio, 'Obstetric Violence: A New Legal Term Introduced in Venezuela' (2010) 111 *International Journal of Gynecology & Obstetrics* 201.

[36] United Nations General Assembly (n 8) [9].

[37] See L Kelly, *Surviving Sexual Violence* (Cambridge, Polity Press, 1988) Chs 4 and 5. She developed this from others' initial use of the term; Kelly cites L Clark and D Lewis, *Rape: The Price of Coercive Sexuality* (Toronto, Women's Press, 1979); J Williams and K Holmes, *The Second Assault: Rape and Public Attitudes* (Westport, Greenwoord Press, 1981); L Gilbert and P Webster, *Bound by Love* (Boston, Beacon Press, 1982); J Marolla and D Scully, 'Rape and Psychiatric Vocabularies of Motive' in E Gomberg and V Franks (eds), *Gender and Disordered Behaviour* (New York, Brunner/Mazel, 1979); M Leidig, 'Violence against Women: A Feminist Psychological Analysis' in S Cox (ed), *Female Psychology: The Emerging Self* (New York, St Martins Press, 1981).

[38] Kelly (n 37) 76.

[39] ibid.

[40] Neda Taghinejadi and Brenda Kelly explore this in Chapter 4 of this volume, 'Female Genital Examination and Autonomy in Medicine'.

between private and public domains.[41] Thinking in terms of a 'continuum' reveals that gender-based violence during facility-based childbirth is shaped and maintained by individuals and institutional structures, and its reach extends from the personal all the way to the international. The impact of the violence also is reinforced by, and reinforces, patriarchal messages about the worth and role of women within society generally. The extent and range of violations against women during facility-based childbirth are vast, with more issues still to be determined, and it would be impossible to offer detailed analysis of all the different ways that women are violated within the maternity care context. However, knowing that there is a continuum of violence within the maternity care sector and that vaginal examinations are located along this continuum, renders our focus on this violation a helpful approach that supports deeper interrogation of broader issues around how and why women are treated this way. The issues raised in this book around consent, feelings of sexual violation, human rights, autonomy, medical authority and coercion, vulnerability, and battery, are all relevant to other manifestations of violence and abuse during facility-based childbirth.

Four chapters in this edited collection expose the cracks in the maternity care system. Rebecca Brione, a member of Birthrights, shares in Chapter 2 women's experiences of unauthorised vaginal examinations while accessing maternity care services in the United Kingdom. These are the experiences of women who have approached the Association for Improvements in the Maternity Services and Birthrights in search of help and support to secure redress. This chapter creates the foundation for the chapters that follow it by providing much needed context. Brione reveals the complexities of women's experiences and she exposes on-the-ground challenges that women and organisations experience when attempting to navigate the maternity care system as it is currently constructed. In this way, Brione challenges the assumptions that vaginal examinations during labour are always done with consent (as one would assume given that clinical guidelines require consent) and that professional regulatory bodies are adequately equipped to deal with complaints in cases where consent was lacking.

Key themes relevant to abuse and violence during childbirth emerge from Brione's chapter on authorised vaginal examinations. First, issues around consent arise. It is apparent that there are serious flaws in the process of obtaining women's informed consent, explaining the right to refuse an examination, and there is an alarming lack of respect of women's refusals. Second, criminal battery and sexual assault are regularly raised in the context of forced medical touch and penetration. This raises questions about the role of the law relevant to the criminal battery and sexual assault and their applicability to unauthorised vaginal examinations and

---

[41] Wenona Giles and Jennifer Hyndman consider this issue in the context of conflict zones, see W Giles and J Hyndman, 'Introduction: Gender and Conflict in a Global Context' in W Giles and J Hyndman (eds) *Sites of Violence: Gender and Conflict Zones* (Berkeley, University of California Press, 2004) 3.

other forms of medical touch. Third, there are inadequate complaints mechanisms and a flawed system to support redress. This theme highlights the urgent need to meaningfully interrogate the mechanics of professional regulation and move beyond the assumption that professional regulatory bodies are the best means available to regulate and address human rights violations within the healthcare context. All the chapters in this collection touch on each of these themes.

Elsa Montgomery also exposes cracks in the maternity care system; her chapter adds to the broader context around consent during labour and childbirth. In Chapter 3, 'Silence, Acquiescence or Consent: Interpreting Women's Responses to Intimate Examinations', Montgomery unpacks the challenges faced by labouring and birthing women who have experienced childhood sexual abuse. Their experiences impact on present day interactions with medical professionals during maternity care and Montgomery differentiates between their acquiescence to examination and meaningful and valid consent. This chapter exposes deep rifts between consent according to law and consent according to lived experience. In addition to exposing the gaps in the maternity care system, these rifts expose fault lines within the law itself. Montgomery problematises medical professionals' use of the law's construction of consent as an indication of true or valid consent and she reveals that this construction of legally valid consent tends to protect staff from claims in law but not women and their agency. There is here a tension for the law. The more formal approach to consent (requiring simply a manifestation of acceptance, a 'yes') protects the medical professional. Once they have received the formal manifestation of consent (the yes) they can proceed, confident they are acting lawfully. However, relying on a formal presentation of consent may mask the reality that the woman is not giving morally relevant consent (she is saying 'yes' outwardly, but that does not reflect her true wishes). Montgomery argues that, in its current construction, the law is a blunt tool in the context of securing respectful care, particularly for women with complex histories of violations.

Linked to issues of autonomy and agency, Neda Taghinejadi and Brenda Kelly trace in Chapter 4 the history of intimate examinations. They demonstrate that the very development of pioneering gynaecological tools, such as the speculum, is stained by a disregard for many women's lived experiences, particularly Black and minority women. According to today's standards, the history of gynaecology was brutal, racist and sexist[42] and even though women have pushed back in several ways, historical roots continue to shape present day experiences of autonomy and agency in this space. Chapter 5, by Stella Villarmea, 'When a Uterus Enters the Room, Reason Goes out the Window', makes this link very clear. According to Villarmea this is because patriarchal and sexist constructions of pregnant women's

---

[42] For more on this, see D Davis, 'Obstetric Racism: The Racial Politics of Pregnancy, Labor, and Birthing' (2018) *Medical Anthropology* 1; R Chadwick, *Bodies that Birth: Vitalizing Birth Politics* (Routledge, 2018); D Owens, *Medical Bondage: Race, Gender and the Origins of American Gynecology* (Athens, University Press of Georgia, 2017).

rationality are embedded in medical thought, so much so that these continue to form part of the conceptual furniture of obstetrics and midwifery. She offers a philosophical analysis of the medical profession's perception of pregnant women as 'obviously' lacking capacity and Villarmea reveals the roots of the 'obviousness' of women's lack of capacity. She demonstrates that, historically, medical professionals deemed that pregnant women lacked capacity and this was a consequence of the functioning of women's uteri. The 'influence of the uterus' on women's rationality during pregnancy continues to pervade contemporary approaches to maternity care services and this age-old position explains why healthcare professionals so easily ignore women's refusals in the maternity care context.

Collectively, these chapters reveal fundamental cracks in the maternity care system that are not mere surface cracks but ones that run deep into the very foundation of this area of health care. Cracks appear in the development of knowledge and these impact on the quality of training of healthcare professionals who make up the body of maternity care as it manifests today. Roberto Castro and Joaquina Erviti explain that incidences of abuse or disrespect towards women during childbirth 'are not isolated incidents of individual physicians who lack respect for their patients; rather, these tendencies reflect institutional norms that provide fertile ground for violations of women's reproductive rights'.[43] The cracks in the system do not merely reveal a quality of care issue; Castro and Erviti explain that violence and abuse during childbirth is a consequence of the formal organisation of gynaecology and obstetrics and its traditional ways of training professionals which, in part, draw from broader harmful social conceptions of women.[44]

The effects of socialisation during training and education are particularly obvious in the context of abuse towards birthing women by female healthcare providers. Ruth Zambrana et al conducted a study in the United States of the different attitudes that male and female obstetricians have towards the women they care for and their results demonstrate there was little marked difference.[45] Comparable studies have revealed similar findings.[46] Zambrana et al theorise that medical school socialisation 'may have a homogenizing effect on the attitudes of obstetricians in training' and that the 'power of this effect could erase differences

---

[43] Castro and Erviti (n 34) 95.

[44] ibid; R Castro and J Erviti, '25 Years of Research on Obstetric Violence in Mexico' (2014) 19 *Revisa CONAMED* 37.

[45] R Zambrana et al, 'Gender and Level of Training in Obstetricians' Attitudes towards Patients' in Childbirth' (1987) 12 *Women and Health* 5.

[46] S Mattila-Lindy et al, 'Physicians Gender and Clinical Options of Reproductive Health Matters' (1997) 26 *Women and Health* 15; M Klein et al, 'Attitudes of the New Generation of Canadian Obstetricians: How do They Differ from their Predecessors?' (2011) 38(2) *Birth* 129, although there are some studies that report some gender differences, see L Jefferson et al, 'Effect of Physicians' Gender on Communication and Consultation Length: A Systematic Review and Meta-analysis' (2013) 18 *Journal of Health Services Research & Policy* 242.

between females and males that have originally developed as a consequence of earlier sex-role socialization.[47] Rachel Jewkes et al record similar issues in the context of midwifery and nursing.[48]

Training and socialisation within the broader constitutive body of health-care goes beyond erasing differences in earlier sex-role socialisations; it also has the effect of changing values and attitudes more generally.[49] This is evident in the context of teaching vaginal examinations on anesthetised patients without their consent. Peter Ubel et al conducted a study to establish whether trainees' completion of an obstetrics/gynaecology clerkship (as part of overall professional training) impacted on trainees' position regarding the importance of obtaining informed consent from patients, particularly those upon whom they performed vaginal examinations while the patient was anesthetised. Their research findings are particularly telling:

> Students who have completed obstetrics/gynecology clerkships place significantly less importance on seeking permission from women who are to be anesthetized before performing pelvic examinations, even after data have been adjusted for the total number of clerkships that students have completed. It appears that something happens during obstetrics/gynecology clerkships that is associated with students placing less importance on consent for pelvic examinations after anesthetization.[50]

They theorise that this change in trainees' value systems stems from their observation and participation in harmful behaviour during training.[51]

Brione and Montgomery's contributions reveal that metaphorical 'deep cracks' manifest as real inflictions (whether intentional or not) of abuse and violence in maternity care wards and leave lasting imprints on the bodies and within the minds of women and their newborns. Unauthorised vaginal examinations during labour is just one resultant violation on the continuum of violations experienced during childbirth and throughout women's lives more generally. The cracks present in the maternity care system renders it a space that generates an unnecessary level of vulnerability and these conditions result in serious violations of women's human rights.

---

[47] Zambrana et al (n 45) 22. Klein et al (ibid) support this theory; their study finds that attitudes of obstetricians differ according to age and they suggest that we must give better attention to obstetricians' training to overcome problematic attitudes towards birthing women and their role in relation to birth.

[48] R Jewkes et al, 'Why do Nurses Abuse Patients? Reflections from South African Obstetric Services' (1998) 47 *Social Science & Medicine* 1781, 1793.

[49] P Ubel et al, 'Don't Ask, Don't Tell: A Change in Medical Student Attitudes after Obstetrics/ Gynecology Clerkships toward Seeking Consent for Pelvic Examinations on an Anesthetized Patient' (2003) 118 *American Journal of Obstetrics and Gynecology* 575.

[50] ibid.

[51] ibid.

II. Cracks in the Self: Vulnerability and Childbirth

Vulnerability is a theme which recurs throughout the book. The concept has been the subject of considerable academic interest. Traditionally, vulnerability comes with heavily negative connotations: the 'vulnerable' are not able to look after themselves and need protection. They have fallen short of the ideal of the self-sufficient, autonomous and competent citizen. This means that the normal rights of self-determination and bodily integrity which are respected for those who live up the ideal can be denied to them.

Pregnant and birthing women are, on this understanding, seen as classic examples of 'vulnerable people'. Their 'weakened' physical and mental capabilities means they need to be protected from foolish decisions. The healthcare professionals, basing decisions on science and knowledge, should have their views respected, rather than the 'emotional outbursts' of the pregnant women.[52] When we add into the picture the vulnerability of the soon to be born child, the case for prioritising the views of medical experts becomes overwhelming on this conception of vulnerability.

However, this understanding and presentation of vulnerability has been challenged. A universal and beneficial theory of vulnerability argues that being vulnerable is in the nature of all people and that there is nothing wrong in being vulnerable.[53] Martha Fineman has done more than anyone to develop the concept of universal vulnerability and she explains the theory in this way:

> The vulnerability approach recognizes that individuals are anchored at each end of their lives by dependency and the absence of capacity. Of course, between these ends, loss of capacity and dependence may also occur, temporarily for many and permanently for some as a result of disability or illness. Constant and variable throughout life, individual vulnerability encompasses not only damage that has been done in the past and speculative harms of the distant future, but also the possibility of immediate harm. We are beings who live with the ever-present possibility that our needs and circumstances will change. On an individual level, the concept of vulnerability (unlike that of liberal autonomy) captures this present potential for each of us to become dependent based upon our persistent susceptibility to misfortune and catastrophe.[54]

On this view, vulnerability is an inherent part of being human.[55] As Catriona Mackenzie et al explain: 'To be vulnerable is to be fragile, to be susceptible to

---

[52] For a detailed discussion see R Scott, *Rights, Duties and the Body: Law and Ethics of the Maternal-Fetal Conflict* (Oxford, Hart Publishing, 2002); E Jackson, *Regulating Reproduction: Law Technology and Autonomy* (Oxford, Hart Publishing, 2001).

[53] See J Herring, *Law and the Relational Self* (Cambridge, Cambridge University Press, 2019) Ch 2; M Fineman, 'The Vulnerable Subject: Anchoring Equality in the Human Condition' (2008) 20 *Yale Journal of Law & Feminism* 1.

[54] Fineman (n 53) 12.

[55] A Beckett, *Citizenship and Vulnerability: Disability and Issues of Social and Political Engagement* (Basingstoke, Palgrave Macmillan, 2006); M Shildrick, *Embodying the Monster: Encounters with the Vulnerable Self* (London, Sage, 2002).

wounding and to suffering; this susceptibility is an ontological conditional of our humanity'.[56] This is a profound challenge to the model of humanity which prides itself on capacity, independence, and autonomy. It claims we are all vulnerable because we are all profoundly dependent on others for our physical and psychological well-being.

There is clearly much more that can be said about this concept of vulnerability, but for now we will consider its application to unauthorised vaginal examinations. The insights from universal and beneficial vulnerability approach are not straight-forward. There is a debate among vulnerability theorists over how to respond to the fact that even though we may all be inherently vulnerable, this is experienced to a different extent by different people in different contexts. Fineman accepts that in a typical lifespan there will be times of different capacity and strengths. But the typical 'adult liberal subject' focuses on just one part of that life span (middle age) and essentialises this as the standard. That means the vulnerable nature can get overlooked. She argues:

> Throughout our lives we may be subject to external and internal negative, potentially devastating, events over which we have little control – disease, pandemics, environmen-tal and climate deterioration, terrorism and crime, crumbling infrastructure, failing institutions, recession, corruption, decay, and decline. We are situated beings who live with the ever-present possibility of changing needs and circumstances in our individual and collective lives. We are also accumulative beings and have different qualities and quantities of resources with which to meet these needs of circumstances, both over the course of our lifetime and as measured at the time of crisis or opportunity.[57]

Martha Fineman and Anna Grear argue: 'While vulnerability is universal, resil-ience is particular, found in the assets or resources an individual accumulates and dispenses over the course of a lifetime and through interaction with and access to society's instructions'.[58] Other writers have suggested that we are equally valuable throughout our lives and it is the provision of social resources which grant some people greater resilience to their vulnerability than others. Jonathan Herring has taken this line. He argues:

> It is true that at different times and in different circumstances we may be more overtly in use of societal resources should not disguise the fact that we are in need of communal and relational support for all our lives. We may be differently positioned within a web of economic and social relationships and this will impact on our experience of vulner-ability and the resources at our disposal.[59]

---

[56] W Rogers et al, 'Why Bioethics Needs a Theory of Vulnerability' (2012) 5 *International Journal of Feminist Approaches to Bioethics* 11, 12.

[57] M Fineman, 'Feminism and Masculinities: Questioning the Lure of Multiple Identities' in M Fineman and M Thomson (eds), *Exploring Masculinities: Feminist Legal Theory Reflections* (Abingdon, Routledge, 2016) 32.

[58] M Fineman and A Grear, 'Introduction' in M Fineman and A Grear (eds), *Vulnerability: Reflections on a New Ethical Foundation for Law and Politics* (Abingdon, Routledge, 2016) 2.

[59] J Herring, *Vulnerability, Childhood and the Law* (Cham, Springer, 2018) 65.

In some of her writings Fineman seems to take a similar view, observing that '[v]ulnerability ... is both universal and particular; it is experienced uniquely by each of us ... our individual experience of vulnerability varies according to the quality and quantity of resources we can command'.[60]

Applying this literature to unauthorised vaginal examinations, one argument might be used to challenge the view that birthing women are in their nature particularly vulnerable. It might be argued that some of the reasons why we see them as vulnerable – the pain, fear, bodily impacts of pregnancy – are not unique to birthing bodies. They are simply particularly vibrant manifestations of the fact that all of us have profoundly impaired mental capacity; limited autonomy; 'leaky bodies';[61] and are dependent on others.

However, using the school of thought that all people are in their nature vulnerable, and that the allocation of societal resources and general attitudes can thereby render people more or less vulnerable, some different messages approach. This approach would accept the particular vulnerability of the birthing woman, but argue the source of that comes not from the birth process as such, but the social context in which it takes place. It is the social expectations around motherhood, the privileged position of the medical profession, and patriarchal forces which generate the vulnerability, rather than the impact of pregnancy or labour itself. This means that rather than taking it for granted that labour is a time of vulnerability, we should note what it is about the social and medical response to labour that renders women in that context particularly vulnerable. And what it is about the legal regulation of, and social expectations around, pregnancy, which mean the wrongs of unauthorised vaginal examinations are invisible.[62]

The universal vulnerability model might also offer some insights into how to improve the position in respect of care. The legal conception of the self profoundly affects the kinds of legal rights we have. As adults we like to emphasise our independence, capacity for rational thought, and autonomy. Hence in our legal system autonomy and liberty are emphasised as key rights, and interference with them requires strong justification.[63] The law's role is, under that image of the self, to protect the individual from unwanted intrusions and to protect liberty to pursue one's goal for one's life. We are portrayed as independent, self-interested people. Hence, the natural response of the liberal-minded lawyer to unauthorised vaginal examinations might be to reinforce claims that explicit consent of the pregnant woman is required before any vaginal examination, and

---

[60] M Fineman, 'The Vulnerable Subject and the Responsive State' (2011) 60 *Emory Law Journal* 251, 269.

[61] M Shildrick, *Leaky Bodies and Boundaries: Feminism, Postmodernism and (Bio)Ethics* (London, Routledge, 1997).

[62] Charles Foster's chapter in this volume illustrates the invisible nature of the harms relevant here. His contribution is discussed in more detail below.

[63] C Foster, *Choosing Life, Choosing Death: The Tyranny of Autonomy in Medical Ethics* (Oxford, Hart Publishing, 2009).

strengthen the requirements for informed consent. If, however, we start with a norm of vulnerable, relational, interdependent, caring people then the nature of legal intervention becomes different. The importance of upholding and maintaining those caring relationships becomes key. The law does not emphasise independence, liberty, and autonomy, but rather seeks to uphold relationships of care. Susan Dodds argues:

> Attention to vulnerability ... changes citizens' ethical relations from those of independent actors carving out realms of rights against each other and the state, to those of mutually-dependent and vulnerability-exposed beings whose capacities to develop as subjects are directly and indirectly mediated by the conditions around them.[64]

Our mutual vulnerability requires us to reach out to others to offer and receive help from them. We have to be open to others, and our own and others' needs, in order to survive. A recognition of our mutual vulnerability leads to empathy and understanding.[65] It creates intimacy and trust. It compels us to focus on interactive, co-operative solutions to the issues we address. It encourages creativity in finding new ways of overcoming our human limitations and requires a desire to accept others as they are. As Amelia Case puts it: 'Our vulnerability is inextricably tied to our capacity to give of ourselves to others, to treasure and aspire, to commit to endeavors, to care about justice and about our own and other's dignity'.[66]

We move then to the language of care, of mutual support, of co-operative decision-making. It involves an acknowledgement too of the vulnerabilities of healthcare professionals: they too have fears and professional pressures and must maintain a 'professional distance'.[67] A legal system based on rigid rules requiring extensive disclosures of risks and careful recordings of consent processes may fail to acknowledge these.

Quite how an approach based on care would play out in practice will depend on the people involved and their individual characteristics. This makes it difficult to be subject to legal regulation, which traditionally has been based on abstract, universal principles. Chapters in this book explore how that may be worked out in practice. Elsa Montgomery, for example, emphasises the importance of 'compassionate care'; Stella Villarmea discusses shared decision making and person-centred care; Jonathan Herring draws on the literature on relational autonomy; and Claire Murray emphasises the importance of relationships of trust.

---

[64] S Dodds, 'Depending on Care: Recognition of Vulnerability and the Social Contribution of Care Provision' (2007) 21 *Bioethics* 500, 507.

[65] E Kittay, 'The Ethics of Care, Dependence, and Disability' (2011) 44 *Ratio Juris* 49.

[66] A Carse, 'Vulnerability, Agency and Human Flourishing' in C Taylor and R Dell'Oro (eds) *Health and Human Flourishing: Religion, Medicine and Moral Anthropology* (Washington, Georgetown University Press, 2006) 48.

[67] Soo Downe and Nancy Stone shed light on this tension in the context of midwifery, see S Downe and N Stone, 'Midwives and Midwifery: The Need for Courage to Reclaim Vocation for Respectful Care' in Pickles and Herring (n 10) 88.

III. Cracks in Regulation: Law, Power and Authority

In addition to exposing the cracks in the maternity care system and the self, this book seeks to expose some of the shortfalls present in the laws that would be relevant to various violations that women experience when they are subjected to violence and abuse during childbirth. The collection confronts widely-held assumptions that the laws relevant to unauthorised medical touch are adequately developed to tackle the specific issues around unauthorised medical touch of birthing women.

Before considering the details of the chapters that expose inadequacies (cracks) of the law and professional regulation, it is necessary to clarify why the law is deemed relevant here. This clarification is necessary because the law's value in this context is regularly challenged and its authoritative sway is brushed aside. Current collective responses to facility-based abuse and obstetric violence tend to be shaped by health system reform strategies. For instance, a health-systems approach to abuse and violence during facility-based care emphasises that this issue can be tackled through improved training of healthcare professionals and through the development and application of evidence-based guidelines and protocols.[68] While these measures hold the potential to make important changes for many women, they will not be enough on their own. Women continue to be harmed despite improvements in guidelines and protocols and they are left without redress. This response to the phenomenon of obstetric violence and abuse is far too limited and might constitute a serious failing on the part of governments if broader efforts are not employed. The Special Rapporteur on Violence against Women has certainly clarified the position of law in her thematic report on obstetric violence and mistreatment.

The Rapporteur has confirmed that facility-based abuse and obstetric violence is a form of gender-based violence, and as such it ignites states' international human rights obligations to actively address this issue, which must include law. The Rapporteur reiterates the approach required of states by the Committee on the Elimination of Discrimination against Women:[69]

> Under international law, acts or omissions by non-State actors attributable to the State include the 'acts or omissions of private actors empowered by the law [of that State] to exercise elements of governmental authority, including private bodies providing public services, such as healthcare or education, or operating places of detention, are considered as acts attributable to the State itself'. States parties also have an obligation under the Convention on the Elimination of All Forms of Discrimination against Women to pursue, by all appropriate means and without delay, a policy of eliminating

---

[68] See discussion in C Pickles, 'Eliminating Abusive "Care": A Criminal Law Response to Obstetric Violence in South Africa' (2015) 54 *South Africa Crime Quarterly* 5, 7–8.

[69] Committee on the Elimination of Discrimination Against Women, 'General Recommendation No 35 on Gender-Based Violence Against Women, Updating General Recommendation No 19', UN Doc CEDAW/C/GC/35 (2017) [24(a)].

discrimination and gender-based violence against women, including in the field of health. This is an obligation of an immediate nature and delays cannot be justified on any grounds, including economic, cultural or religious grounds.[70]

Article 2 of the Convention on the Elimination of All Forms of Discrimination against Women requires a state party to 'pursue all appropriate means' to ensure that women are not discriminated against, and it focuses on the law and the role of legislation in this context.[71] 'All appropriate means' or '[a]ll appropriate measures' offers flexibility in responses but 'all' underscores the obligation to adopt a comprehensive range of measures, which must include measures in law.[72] In line with this understanding of governments' obligations, the Special Rapporteur has made recommendations relevant to law which will help safeguard women against obstetric violence and facility-based abuse during childbirth.

The Special Rapporteur reiterates that governments have an obligation to adopt appropriate laws and policies to combat and prevent obstetric violence, to prosecute perpetrators and to provide reparations and compensation to women.[73] Adequate remedies include restitution, financial compensation, acknowledgement of wrongdoing, formal apology and guarantees of non-repetition.[74] All complaints and allegations of mistreatment must be investigated and the results and recommendations should be published.[75] In addition thereto, the results of investigations must be used to revise laws, policies and national plans to support women's reproductive rights.[76] States are required to adopt effective health laws and policies relevant to informed consent, and she frames informed consent as a key element needed to tackle this phenomenon.[77]

The Rapporteur stresses that governments must raise awareness among lawyers and judges about women's rights during childbirth so as to ensure effective use of remedies.[78] This recommendation places legal practitioners *at the centre* of the fight against obstetric violence and abuse during childbirth. Further, states must ensure professional accountability, sanctions by professional bodies, and access to justice in cases of human rights violations.[79] Importantly, the Rapporteur adds that states must ensure broader oversight of birth facilities by other regulatory bodies such as national human rights institutions, ethic commissions and equity bodies.[80] This oversight will ensure transparency, objective assessment of outcomes and exposure of inappropriate or incorrect application of the law in these

---

[70] United Nations General Assembly (n 8) [10].
[71] A Brynes, 'Article 2' in M Freeman et al (eds), *The UN Convention on the Elimination of all forms of Discrimination Against Women: A Commentary* (Oxford, Oxford University Press, 2013) 72.
[72] ibid 77.
[73] United Nations General Assembly (n 8) [75].
[74] ibid [81(i)] and [81(l)].
[75] ibid [77].
[76] ibid.
[77] ibid [81(b)].
[78] ibid [81(n)].
[79] ibid [81(j)].
[80] ibid [81(m)].

fora, and ultimately improve access to justice for women who lodge complaints with professional regulatory bodies. In addition to many other recommendations, the Rapporteur underscores states' obligations to review and strengthen laws that prohibit all forms of violence against women and specifically includes violence during pregnancy and childbirth within the scope of required reform efforts.[81]

Other UN Special Rapporteur's positions are relevant here too. For instance, writing in the context of domestic abuse the UN Special Rapporteur on Violence against Women, Yakin Ertürk has written of the importance of law in challenging violence against women:

> [P]rosecutors working on cases of domestic violence have the potential and the obliga-
> tion to change the prevailing balance of power [between men and women] by taking a
> strong stance to disempower patriarchal notions. Interventions at this level may have
> both consequential effects in that condemnations of patriarchy can lead to changes in
> socio-cultural norms, as well as intrinsic effects, in that prosecutors ... can be consid-
> ered to be the 'mouthpieces' of society, and strong statements condemning violence
> against women made on behalf of society through the ... prosecutorial services will
> make that society less patriarchal.[82]

It is not possible to offer comprehensive analysis of all the Rapporteur's recommendations in relation to obstetric violence in this introduction, but the law has a clearly defined role to play in the context of abuse and violence during childbirth. It needs to be used and developed where necessary to help prevent and address violence against women during facility-based childbirth and there needs to be adequate provision of remedies. Prosecution is presented as only one of many possibilities. This flexibility requires bringing together different stakeholders with different expertise to interrogate the appropriateness of existing avenues in law available to women who require a remedy, and explore the extent of law reform required in order for it to be suitably equipped to offer just remedies for women. The law chapters in this volume are relevant to this task. They link up with some of the key themes highlighted in earlier chapters of this volume and explore what is available to women who have been subjected to unauthorised vaginal examinations.

Christina Zampas, in Chapter 6, explores the landscape of gender stereotypes in the context of childbirth and the impact these have on the care that women receive. Her chapter can be linked back to Villarmea's contribution in this volume, which highlights underlying and prevalent sexist constructions of pregnant women's rationality. Zampas offers an analysis of the scope of state obligations to prevent obstetric violence and abuse during childbirth by drawing from regional and international human rights body standards. She does not narrow her focus to unauthorised vaginal examinations; instead she focuses on many different types

---

[81] ibid [81(o)].

[82] UN Commission on Human Rights, 'Report of the Special Rapporteur on Violence against Women, Its Causes and Consequences on the Due Diligence Standard as a Tool for the Elimination of Violence against Women' UN Doc E/CN.4/2006/61 (2006).

of violations that women experience around the world. Zampas offers a detailed analysis of select national level case law that help to explain how these violations amount to human rights violations and she uses these to clarify state obligations more generally.

Charles Foster, writing from the perspective of a barrister, returns the book to its narrow focus on unauthorised vaginal examinations in Chapter 7. He asks, 'how the law and various quasi-legal regulatory mechanisms should regulate the performance of periparturient vaginal examinations'? Foster notes that 'in the case of law and among practising lawyers, it is rare, if not unknown, to hear of case of unnecessary but non-sexually motivated vaginal examinations' and he assumes that even roughly performed vaginal examinations 'will often have been performed with the requisite consent', being consent in broad terms to an act of the relevant nature.[83] On the issue of using the law to regulate unauthorised vaginal examinations, Foster suggests that this issue would cause little legal controversy as most litigation concerns not performing vaginal examinations when these should have happened so as to detect the need for urgent medical interventions. Foster suggests that professional regula-tors are better placed than courts to tackle unauthorised vaginal examinations. He highlights several benefits of adopting this approach but also raises concerns that this regulatory mechanism favours the patient and tends to lack transparency and independence. Nevertheless, these are preferred because, according to Foster, crimi-nal and civil laws will have little meaningful impact on addressing this issue.

Foster's chapter exposes underlying tensions and schisms between the law and those who practise it and women's lived experiences as presented in Brione's and Montgomery's contributions. Working from precedent and other law texts, as lawyers do, Foster's position could be true *in the context of law* because there is no case law on the subject to say otherwise. This reveals a fundamental crack in the system. Brione and Montgomery (together with many other reports) reveal that unauthorised vaginal examinations do take place and that women experience these as highly traumatic, but redress remains out of reach. We have, therefore, harms to women which are invisible to the law.[84] This will continue if those in law maintain the position presented by Foster and cracks in the system will be glossed over and hidden. Furthermore, this schism presented here makes it clear why the Special Rapporteur requires states to raise awareness among lawyers and judges about women's rights during childbirth so as to ensure effective use of remedies. The rift that exists serves as a major barrier to the development of laws that give meaningful effect to women's human rights during childbirth.

Accepting that states have an obligation to develop the law into an empower-ing and responsive tool for women in the context of abuse during childbirth, the chapters that follow analyse and problematise the law identified as being relevant

---

[83] As required by *Chatterton v Gerson* [1981] QB 432, 444, in the context of civil battery.

[84] This is but one example of multiple circumstances in which the law, based around a male norm, fails to identify the harms to women. See, for example, N Naffine, *Criminal Law and the Man Problem* (Oxford, Hart Publishing, 2019).

to unauthorised vaginal examination: consent, sexual assault, criminal battery and civil battery and negligence.

Many women experience unauthorised vaginal examinations during labour as a form of sexual violation and Catarina Sjölin examines in Chapter 8 whether medical professionals commit common assault or sexual assault when they subject women to these procedures. In the context of common assault, Sjölin reveals that, theoretically, it might be possible to establish a case but, practically, the prosecution would struggle to prove that doctors did not hold a genuine belief that they had the required consent. She offers a detailed analysis of sexual assault laws and exposes serious shortcomings which require creative and tactical manoeuvring in order for sexual assault laws to be applicable to unauthorised vaginal examinations during labour. Camilla Pickles, in Chapter 9, considers the crime of battery as a possible charge against medical professionals who subject women to unauthorised vaginal examination. She focuses on this crime because it is well-established in law that unauthorised touch constitutes a criminal battery and there is a repeated assumption that it will be applicable to unauthorised vaginal examinations. Her chapter reveals that the mere existence of this crime does not guarantee its application to all instances of unauthorised touch, and Pickles exposes broader social structures that act as barriers when it comes to applying this crime to unauthorised vaginal examinations. Pickles goes further and demonstrates that battery is ill-suited to address gender-based violence of this kind and makes the case for a specific crime relevant to medical contexts and childbirth.

Clare Murray and Jonathan Herring explore consent in law and their chapters highlight further cracks in the system. In Chapter 10, Herring explains that in many cases, medical professionals act on implied consent and he problematises this approach to consent. He argues that vaginal examinations during labour are prima facie wrongs that require consent. Herring explores the reasons why consent is important during medical care; he defines implied consent and then explains why this form of consent is inappropriate. Implied consent is ambiguous in that a healthcare professional will not know for sure if the woman assessed whether the examination is in her best interests and as such, it cannot be deemed sufficient authority to perform the examination. According to Herring, only 'rich' consent is legally valid, which is consent that is free from undue pressure. The extent to which this approach is embodied and actively maintained through the application of the law regulating consent needs further consideration and this will undoubtedly vary from one jurisdiction to the next.

In Chapter 11, 'Troubling Consent: Pain and Pressure in Labour and Childbirth', Murray offers an analysis of case law on consent and treatment refusal involving pregnant women. Her chapter reveals that the current legal framework in the UK consists of an inflexible capacity/incapacity binary. She acknowledges that this binary might work well in some contexts but argues that it fails in complex situations like labour and childbirth where women experience pain which renders them vulnerable to broader pressures. According to the current framework, women in pain will be deemed to lack capacity and their consent will be invalid and a woman without pain will have capacity and her consent will be valid. Murray uses the 'prism of labour' to identify shortcomings in this binary. She explains that while the pain of labour is physically and emotionally demanding it does not completely incapacitate women. This feature of the natural process of labour means that women occupy spaces in between the capacity/incapacity binary, and this demands a new perspective on the framework of consent. Murray's chapter reveals that consent law as it has been developed to date is ill-equipped to include and respond to women's lived experiences.

Murray and Herring raise important issues around consent and while these chapters reveal shortcomings in the law, they also offer insights worthy of consideration for those jurisdictions that need to develop their informed consent laws in accordance with the Special Rapporteur's recommendations.

Andrea Mulligan considers redress through litigation in England, Wales and the Republic of Ireland in Chapter 12. Her contribution emphasises that women's desired remedies shape the litigation strategy, and this underscores the importance of the Rapporteur's recommendation to develop an adequate range of remedies for women in the context of obstetric violence and abuse during childbirth. Mulligan explores two actions in tort: battery and negligence, and she emphasises some important limitations within these branches of law. Mulligan builds on her analysis by comparing which of the two avenues in law might be better suited to addressing unauthorised vaginal examinations. It is her position that battery is best suited but Mulligan questions whether unauthorised vaginal examinations should be tackled as a human rights violation rather than a civil wrong. She investigates this litigation avenue, comparing the positions under the Human Rights Act 1998 and the Republic of Ireland's Constitution, the *Bunreacht na hÉireann*. Mulligan's contribution demonstrates the cost of having to use ill-equipped mechanisms in law to address the harms that women experience in the context of obstetric violence. There will always be a portion of their lived experience and harm discounted as irrelevant because it does not fit neatly within established causes of action in law. This is particularly evident in the context of medical negligence where access to this action is limited to harms of the 'relevant type' which do not include some of the harms that women experience.

The chapters exploring legal responses to vaginal examinations reveal limitations with the law. The law has deeply inbuilt assumptions about what constitutes a harm, which values underpin the rights that are protected, and the nature of the human self.[85] Feminist lawyers have long pointed out the harms to women which are not recognised by the law.[86] In particular, the law has struggled to recognise harms that are categorised as a physical injury, but are emotional, psychological or relational in nature.[87] In its understandings of wrong, the law is based on

---

[85] Herring (n 53).

[86] See, for example, the difficulties the law has faced in finding an appropriate response to domestic abuse: M Dempsey, *Prosecuting Domestic Violence: A Philosophical Analysis* (Oxford, Oxford University Press, 2009).

[87] Herring (n 53) Ch 6.

assumptions about what is normal for women. A good example is the response of the law to cases where as a result of negligence women's reproductive choices are not recognised. In *McFarlane v Tayside Health Board*[88] a woman who did not want to become pregnant sought a sterilisation, which was performed negligently. She could not recoup damages for raising the resulting child, with the court concluding that a child had to be seen as a 'blessing'. By contrast in *Whittington NHS Hospital v XX*[89] a woman who was negligently rendered unable to have a child was awarded damages to enable her to use surrogacy services. This contrast is one of many, which understands the production of children as core to women's identity but finds unfathomable a woman who is not complying with the image of the ideal baby producer. So too in this context it is almost unimaginable to the law that a woman would not want every examination possible during labour to protect the well-being of the child. Even where she does not consent, the law struggles to see as a wrong, something which enables a woman to perform her 'natural role'.

This discussion also reveals the abstracted nature of the law. Legal responses tend not to recognise the social context of behaviour and reduce issues to binary choices. Hence, in this context, the law's analysis reduces consent to either consent or non-consent, failing to recognise the complex nuances between these and the importance of the context within which any apparent consent is given.[90] Consent is similarly construed in the law typically in a non-contextualised way. The explicit and implicit pressures, the fear, the vulnerability – these are all invisible to the law if a 'yes' is given. Similarly, the act of vaginal examination is seen simply as medical procedure to facilitate childbirth, and not in the context of 'pornified'[91] culture, rife with violence against women. The Preamble to the Istanbul Convention[92] set out the background to their protections for Violence against Women

> Recognising that violence against women is a manifestation of historically unequal power relations between women and men, which have led to domination over, and discrimination against, women by men and to the prevention of the full advancement of women;
>
> Recognising the structural nature of violence against women as gender-based violence, and that violence against women is one of the crucial social mechanisms by which women are forced into a subordinate position compared with men.

It is in this context in which unwanted vaginal examinations must be considered.

---

[88] [2000] 2 AC 59.

[89] [2020] UKSC 14.

[90] V Munro, 'Constructing Consent: Legislating Freedom and Legitimating Constraint in the Expression of Sexual Autonomy' (2008) 41 *Akron Law Review* 899; J Herring, 'Relational Autonomy and Consent' in A Reed et al (eds), *Consent: Domestic and Comparative Perspectives* (London, Routledge, 2016).

[91] P Paul, *Pornified: How Pornography is Damaging our Lives, Our Relationships, and Our Families* (New York, Holt Paperback, 2007).

[92] Council of Europe Convention on Preventing and Combating Violence against Women and Domestic Violence (adopted 11 May 2011, entered into force 1 August 2014) CETS 210.

So, while the topic at the heart of this book might be thought of as somewhat narrow – focusing on one particular examination in a particular medical context – it reveals major issues with the law. It shows the gaping cracks between the lived experiences of women and what the law recognises as 'the facts'. It demonstrates the hidden values that permeate the law: assumptions about what it is to be 'a woman'; the expectations that are attached to pregnancy, which bear no comparison to expectations placed on men in any context; and the privilege given to 'medical expertise'. These are values which may not be recognised or accepted by birthing women. It is only in bringing these differences out into the open that an effective legal response can be found.

2

Non-Consented Vaginal Examinations: The Birthrights and AIMS Perspective

REBECCA BRIONE*

I. Introduction

This chapter outlines the experiences of non-consented vaginal examinations that women have shared with Birthrights and the Association for Improvements in the Maternity Services (AIMS). It gives a flavour of the issues that arise in cases brought to our attention, the impact on women who have to live with these experiences, and the lack of opportunity for proper redress faced by women. This chapter uses case studies to illustrate the experiences which lead women to seek support from AIMS and Birthrights. These are real case studies: real women. They are almost certainly the tip of the iceberg. As this chapter will show, one issue with vaginal examinations is that women often do not know that they can decline consent, and/or do not feel confident in doing so. There are no statistics held on the number of women who experience non-consented vaginal examinations but, with a system that includes vaginal examinations within standard maternity care, Birthrights and AIMS are certain that many more cases exist than those which have come to our attention.

Birthrights and AIMS speak as organisations who are trusted by women to provide information, advice and support to enable women to receive respectful care. Birthrights is the UK charity dedicated to improving women's experience of pregnancy and childbirth by promoting respect for human rights. Birthrights provides advice and legal information to women about their rights in maternity care, trains healthcare professionals to deliver rights-respecting care and campaigns to change maternity policy and systems. AIMS campaigns to improve maternity services, provides support and information to women through a volunteer-led helpline and shares evidence-based information online. The stories

* With many thanks to Maria Booker, Birthrights, and Emma Ashworth, AIMS, for their hugely helpful contributions to an earlier version of this chapter, presented as a paper at the seminar 'Without Consent: Vaginal Examinations during Labour and the Law' at the University of Oxford in February 2019, and for their comments on this chapter. Huge thanks also go to the women whose stories are shared here. Without them, this chapter would not be possible.

shared through this chapter are those of women who have come to Birthrights and AIMS for support and advice. They represent a range of experiences; as such they cannot be all-encompassing, but are aimed to act as a means of grounding theoretical discussion in this volume in the realities of women's experience.

II. Context: Vaginal Examinations within Standard Maternity Care

A vaginal examination is 'an intimate and intrusive action'.[1] In pregnancy and labour it involves a healthcare professional inserting their hand into a woman's vagina in order to carry out checks on the cervix, the foetal membranes and foetal presentation. Informed consent is always required (unless a woman has been assessed as lacking capacity to make the decision): 'An adult person of sound mind is entitled to decide which, if any, of the available forms of treatment to undergo, and her consent must be obtained before treatment interfering with her bodily integrity is undertaken'.[2]

Vaginal examinations form part of the standard care package offered to most women receiving maternity care in the UK. NICE Guideline CG62 (antenatal care for uncomplicated pregnancies) recommends that women are offered a vaginal examination for membrane sweeping ('a sweep') at 41 weeks' gestation, prior to induction of labour being offered.[3] NICE Guideline CG70 (inducing labour) makes the same recommendation and adds that first-time mothers should be offered vaginal examination for membrane sweeping at 40 weeks' gestation in addition.[4] The Guideline comments that 'When a vaginal examination is carried out to assess the cervix, the opportunity should be taken to offer the woman a membrane sweep'.[5] Additional sweeps may also be offered.[6]

NICE Guideline CG190 (intrapartum care for healthy women and babies) suggests a woman may be offered a vaginal examination if there is uncertainty about whether she is in labour and if she appears to be in established labour.[7] Examinations should be offered four-hourly during the first stage of labour, or

---

[1] M Scamell and M Stewart, 'Time, Risk and Midwife Practice: The Vaginal Examination' (2014) 16 *Health, Risk & Society* 84.

[2] *Montgomery v Lanarkshire Health Board* [2015] UKSC 11 at [87].

[3] National Institute for Health and Care Excellence (NICE), *Antenatal Care for Uncomplicated Pregnancies: Clinical Guideline 62* (London, NICE, 2008) (NICE Guideline CG62); 'Membrane sweeping involves the examining finger passing through the cervix to rotate against the wall of the uterus, to separate the chorionic membrane from the decidua. If the cervix will not admit a finger, massaging around the cervix in the vaginal fornices may achieve a similar effect'. NICE, *Inducing Labour: Clinical Guideline 70* (London, NICE, 2008) (NICE Guideline CG70).

[4] NICE Guideline CG70 (n 3) [1.3.1.2].

[5] ibid [1.3.1.4].

[6] ibid [1.3.1.5].

[7] National Institute for Health and Care Excellence, *Intrapartum Care: Care of Healthy Women and Their Babies during Childbirth: Clinical Guideline 190* (London, NICE, 2014) (NICE Guideline CG190) [1.4.2].

more often if there are concerns about progress or delay.[8] Women with intact membranes and suspected delay are advised to have an amniotomy, requiring a vaginal examination.[9] Other procedures carried out via a vaginal examination (digital foetal scalp stimulation and foetal blood sampling) may be offered if there are concerns about an electronical foetal monitoring trace.[10] For women who have previously had babies, a vaginal examination is recommended before any augmentation of labour is offered.[11] Augmentation then leads to a recommendation of four-hourly vaginal examinations.[12]

Once in the second stage of labour, a woman is advised to have an hourly vaginal examination.[13] Suspected delay again leads to recommendations of vaginal examination and amniotomy.[14] Vaginal examination is further recommended if there is a need to expedite the birth and if the placenta is retained.[15] The guideline recognises that a 'vaginal examination can be very distressing for a woman, especially if she is already in pain, highly anxious and in an unfamiliar environment'.[16] Nevertheless there are 18 separate recommendations to offer vaginal examinations given across these three guidelines.

It is clear that vaginal examinations are considered a normal part of late antenatal and labour care. Scamell and Stewart, in a paper on drawing on two ethnographic studies on vaginal examinations and midwives' understanding of risk, note that the vaginal examination forms part of an evidence-based practice generally accepted as necessary and complied with by midwives.[17] It can be uncomfortable for midwives and doctors if a woman does not wish to consent to routine practice. In their studies, Scamell and Stewart found there was distrust and criticism of midwives who chose to explicitly disregard this approach and rely instead on intuition and experience in assessing a woman's progress. At the same time, they found that midwives sometimes 'deliberately misrepresented' data gained from vaginal examinations (for example, the number of centimetres dilation) in order to buy a woman more time to labour when they judged it necessary.[18] Scamell and Stewart also documented a number of explicitly non-consented vaginal examinations, described by one study participant as 'a quick feel to see what you're doing'.[19] These non-consented examinations are described as being 'part of routine albeit covert practice'.[20]

---

[8] NICE Guideline CG190 (n 7) [1.12.7], [1.12.16].
[9] Artificial rupture of membranes, carried out via a vaginal examination; NICE Guideline CG190 (n 7) [1.12.17].
[10] Nice Guideline CG190 (n 7) [1.10.38], [1.10.44].
[11] ibid [1.12.19].
[12] ibid [1.12.23].
[13] ibid [1.13.2].
[14] ibid [1.13.5], [1.13.6].
[15] ibid [1.13.34], [1.14.25].
[16] ibid [1.4.5].
[17] Scamell and Stewart (n 1).
[18] ibid 96.
[19] ibid 93.
[20] ibid.

III. Consent and Coercion

Whilst the NICE guidelines almost universally talk about recommending vaginal examinations, in practice it can be very difficult for a woman to decline. When presented as part of standard practice, a woman may well not know that she *can* decline: Birthrights and AIMS regularly speak with women who come into contact with maternity services who are not aware that consent must always be sought for every intervention or treatment.

Even where women are aware that they can decline, doing so can be extremely difficult. Jenkinson et al, in an Australian study evaluating healthcare profession-als' and women's experience of declining recommended care, describe a variety of coercive and manipulative strategies (up to and including outright assault) used on women to induce them to comply where they were perceived as making a too-risky decision to decline care.[21] Birthrights and AIMS are aware of women feeling under pressure to 'consent' to vaginal examinations in order to access their preferred care. For example, we are aware of women feeling obliged to consent to membrane sweeps in order to delay a referral for induction of labour. One woman who accessed Birthrights' advice line was told she had to have a vaginal examina-tion to access the care she had chosen despite suffering from an intimate medical condition that would be reasonably expected to make an examination painful and unpleasant.

Declining recommended care is likely to be particularly difficult for women who are already dealing with other challenges during their maternity care, or who may feel that they lack power or legitimacy to challenge or decline healthcare providers' recommendations.[22] McLeish and Redshaw's study of women facing severe and multiple disadvantage describes a non-consented vaginal examination performed without any attempt at consent on a survivor of human trafficking who at that point did not know she could refuse.[23] McLeish and Redshaw note that 'It is inevitably difficult for more vulnerable mothers to have the confidence to disagree with professionals' recommendations or assertions', but that 'For women who often had little control over other aspects of their lives, it was of great signifi-cance to have some control over what was done to their bodies'.[24]

Recent research by Birthrights and Birth Companions on the rights issues experienced by women facing severe and multiple disadvantage during their maternity care cites one woman who had recently experienced trafficking and sexual exploitation who was unsure whether her waters had been broken during

---

[21] B Jenkinson et al, 'The Experiences of Women, Midwives and Obstetricians When Women Decline Recommended Maternity Care: A Feminist Thematic Analysis' (2017) 52 *Midwifery* 10.

[22] C McLeod and S Sherwin, 'Relational Autonomy, Self-Trust, and Health Care for Patients who Are Oppressed' in C Mackenzie and N Stoljar (eds), *Relational Autonomy: Feminist Perspectives on Autonomy, Agency, and the Social Self* (Oxford, Oxford University Press, 2000).

[23] J McLeish and M Redshaw, 'Maternity Experiences of Mothers with Multiple Disadvantages in England: A Qualitative Study' (2019) 32 *Women and Birth* 2.

[24] ibid.

a vaginal examination: 'I don't know what they're doing inside my body'.[25] It also describes a woman involved in sex work not being treated respectfully or sensitively, with healthcare professionals reportedly 'barely getting consent to do vaginal examinations' and other women with complex needs being denied care, worn down or ridiculed after having the confidence to decline or question the need for a vaginal examination.[26] Professionals with experience supporting women facing disadvantage considered that most women in this situation would neither know they could, nor feel confident, declining a vaginal examination, and that a woman who was ignored or ridiculed when she tried would be less likely to speak up for herself on another occasion.

Birthrights and AIMS are also aware of many cases of implicit coercion. NICE guideline CG190 suggests that a 'positive' vaginal examination is an important determinant for whether a woman is considered to be in established labour.[27] Many birth centres and hospitals will require a woman to be in established labour before she is admitted: an implicit requirement for the woman to agree to a vaginal examination in order to access her chosen care. AIMS have heard from many women who state they were explicitly told that they were required to reach a certain number of centimetres dilation to access a birth pool or other forms of pain relief. Both AIMS and Birthrights also describe encounters with healthcare practitioners who claim that access to the obstetric ward or birth centre is dependent on acceding to a vaginal examination, and even cases of women being told outright that examinations are an obligatory part of receiving any intrapartum care at all.

Birthrights and AIMS are also aware of cases where women report more direct coercion, such as in case study 1 below, in which the woman felt obliged – indeed understood she had been told – to acquiesce to healthcare providers' recommendations to avoid censure by social care. In this case, and similar cases seen by Birthrights, the woman cannot have given informed consent as she felt she had no option to decline, under threat or fear of having her children removed from her care. Similarly, during Birthrights' research with Birth Companions, maternity professionals reported concerns that women who are subject to social care interest, as well as younger women and women with mental health difficulties, may be more likely to face scrutiny of their decisions if they decline recommended care than women who are not under these pressures. They felt that women in these circumstances might 'feel cowed' into making decisions that are not right for them.[28]

---

[25] Birth Companions is the charity supporting women facing severe and multiple disadvantage during pregnancy, birth and early motherhood; Birthrights and Birth Companions, 'Holding it All Together: Understanding How Far the Human Rights of Woman Facing Disadvantage are Respected During Pregnancy, Birth and Postnatal Care' (London, Birthrights and Birth Companions, 2019) 30.

[26] ibid 35.

[27] NICE Guideline CG190 (n 7) [1.4.2].

[28] Birthrights and Birth Companions (n 25).

Case Study 1

C had wanted a home birth with her daughter. She had a history of trauma resulting in complex post-traumatic stress disorder (PTSD). When she started her maternity care, her community midwife made a 'mandatory' referral for mental health care that she did not want or need. She declined this because of experiences of being misdiagnosed in the past and because she felt sufficiently supported through her private and family networks and via her expertise from working in mental care.

C complained about the appointment with the community midwife and, as a result, was referred to social services with 'multiple inaccurate concerns'. C was not told about the referral until late in her pregnancy. The referral resulted in her daughter being placed on the child protection register and C being told to 'follow medical advice or risk losing her'. Under fear of losing her daughter, C 'agreed' to a consultant-led birth with a large number of interventions in birth including vaginal examinations, 'stretch and sweeps', continuous electronic foetal monitoring, and epidural analgesia. Her daughter also received interventions she would otherwise have declined, including vitamin K injections and immediate cord cutting. C's daughter developed an infection and was transferred to NICU, followed by a week in the high-dependency unit. C experienced this as highly traumatic.

During her experience, C also felt obliged to engage with mental health care and describes being 'forced to be assessed by multiple mental health providers to confirm [she] was correct' in her understanding that she had complex PTSD.

C received a first response to her complaint before her daughter was removed from the child protection register. In this, the Trust apologised for some aspects of her experience, but failed to address inaccuracies in the allegations made about C's mental health or recognise the harm caused to C. During C's treatment she felt abused, disempowered and afraid that she would lose her daughter. She now feels unable to access mental health services or risk another pregnancy. She cannot trust health services and has found the experience and child protection referral continue to follow her during engagement with other health services. She took her complaint to the Ombudsman who upheld a large part of her complaint but did not fully address C's complaints in relation to consent to interventions during birth. She has also investigated legal options for redress, without success.

Vaginal examinations are also sometimes carried out – or carried on – with the woman explicitly refusing consent. Case study 2 below sets out a clear, very shocking and distressing example of a woman and her birth partner both reinforcing her refusal of consent, and yet the healthcare practitioner carrying on regardless. This is not the only such case that Birthrights and AIMS have seen, with other women reporting being restrained and healthcare practitioners not responding to women imploring them to stop.

In law, treatment without consent would normally be considered negligent and to constitute both the crime of battery, and a civil wrong of trespass to the person.[29] Some women who have experienced non-consented vaginal examinations – that is, intimate examinations carried out explicitly against their wishes – describe them as more akin to sexual assault.[30] Healthcare and legal practitioners should recognise that the short- and long-term effects of non-consented vaginal examinations on women can be just as damaging as a sexual assault, especially since they take place in an arena where a woman might expect to feel safe and cared for.

Case Study 2

B has a chronic health condition causing pain, stiffness, inflammation and fatigue. She was admitted to hospital at 40+11 for an induction of labour. 36 hours after her arrival she was examined and found to be 3cm dilated. The midwife phoned the labour ward and was told there were no beds at that time. B was unable to sit or lie down because of the intense pain she was in and spent the next 12 hours contracting regularly and painfully whilst leaning on the bed. She had no one-to-one care or support during this time and describes feeling like 'just another pregnant woman', being ignored because she was silent.

Once on labour ward, 48 hours after her arrival in hospital, and after begging for an epidural for hours, B was examined by a midwife who said she thought she was 9cm dilated, but she had been unable to complete the examination because B had been so uncomfortable and had had a contraction during the examination. Her implicit advice appeared to be that B should do without an epidural because she was 'nearly there' and an epidural might 'slow things down'. B and her birth supporters believe this was because it was convenient for the busy labour ward rather than in B's interest.

B started pushing soon afterwards, and a senior midwife expressed concern about the foetal heart rate. She sought a doctor, who arrived and carried out a full examination with consent. B was advised that forceps would be likely to be needed, but that a kiwi cup would be tried first. This doctor, described as 'calm and comforting', was ready to start when a consultant arrived with a junior doctor, and announced he would take over.

The consultant told B he would need to examine her again. B consented to this but then the consultant instructed the junior doctor to examine her. B asked why, begged not to be examined again and explicitly refused consent for the

---

[29] Camilla Pickles and Andrea Mulligan consider these in their respective contributions to this volume: see Chapter 9, C Pickles, 'When "Battery" is not Enough: Exposing the Gaps in Unauthorised Vaginal Examination during Labour as a Crime of Battery' and Chapter 12, A Mulligan, 'Redressing Unauthorised Vaginal Examinations through Litigation'.

[30] Catarina Sjölin explores the application of sexual assault laws in this volume, see Chapter 8, C Sjölin, 'Including the Victim's Perspective: Can Vaginal Examinations ever be Sexual Assaults?'.

junior doctor to touch her. She was supported in this by her birth companions. Nonetheless the junior doctor examined her.

The junior's findings led to her being instructed to fetch an ultrasound, leaving B waiting for over ten minutes, exhausted and in extreme pain, having been told that her baby was in acute distress. On her return, B was scanned and the consultant, treating B as an educational opportunity, explained to the junior doctor that her examination findings had been incorrect. At this point the doctors prepared for an assisted birth.

B asked for pain relief and was laughed at. The consultant clarified that lidocaine was available, prepared it and handed it to the junior doctor. B again refused consent for the junior doctor to treat her and again, the junior doctor started regardless. The consultant took over when she made an error, treating B so roughly and impersonally that she screamed in agony.

The junior doctor was then instructed to place the kiwi cup. B again refused consent, saying 'not her'. The junior doctor placed the cup incorrectly, the consultant corrected her, then detached it and asked the junior doctor to try again. She was then given three unsuccessful attempts to assist the birth using the cup, leaving B and her companions splattered with blood from where it had snapped off mid-pull and B – ignored – saying 'not her, not her, not her'.

The junior doctor was then given the forceps to insert. B's birth companion repeatedly said 'not her' but was ignored. The junior doctor was unable to place the forceps and left one in whilst B had a contraction. She was again allowed three unsuccessful attempts to place the forceps. At this point B's birth companion screamed 'Not her! She cannot touch her again! Stop this!' Only at this point did the consultant take over. B's baby was delivered, grey, floppy and covered with meconium, after an episiotomy described by her birth companion as being 'hacked at with scissors'. B describes her memory of the birth as one of excruciating pain and abject terror.

After the birth, B was left with the placenta inside her (the cord had snapped in the force of the birth), legs in the air, bleeding onto the floor whilst the paediatrician resuscitated the baby. The consultant prepared to leave the room. After prompting by the junior doctor, he instructed her to pack some dressing into B, who was then taken to theatre and given an epidural for the removal of the placenta. Neither doctor spoke to B or her birth companions. B finally saw her baby 12 hours later after he was returned from intensive care. B has been left with life changing pelvic floor injuries including faecal incontinence. B's birth companion describes the experience, saying that B and her family granted the doctors respect and deference in their space and in return they treated B with utter disrespect and an absolute lack of care or dignity.

This case – as with the others presented in this chapter – is difficult to read for everyone, including clinicians who strive every day to provide kind and respectful care. It describes disrespectful and harmful 'care' that includes, but undoubtedly goes beyond, non-consented vaginal examinations. It is clear that women who experience broader severely disrespectful care will be harmed – in some cases very seriously – by these experiences, with long-term impacts on women's mental and physical health, lives and ability to access healthcare for themselves and their families.[31]

This analysis, however, focuses on non-consented vaginal examinations as the core subject of this volume. Such non-consented examinations can be associated with both psychological and physical long-term injury for the women who experience them, as demonstrated by the cases presented in this chapter. Non-consented vaginal examinations fail to respect an individual's bodily autonomy and integrity, and their rights to make decisions about their care and their bodies. High quality care, choice and control are strongly associated with positive experiences, birth outcomes and mother-baby relations – a vaginal examination that is unconsented denies this to women.[32] As demonstrated by many of the cases described in this chapter, poor quality and disrespectful care are associated with trauma and post-traumatic stress disorder.[33] This can be particularly acute for women with a history of maltreatment, who may already feel less able to advocate for their rights.[34]

Women who have experienced sexual trauma in their past may be even more at risk. Montgomery et al, in a study exploring maternity care for women with a history of childhood sexual abuse (around 20% of women, although only a small proportion disclose their experiences during maternity care), noted that vaginal examinations were not 'universally difficult': 'They could cope if they trusted those performing them and if they retained control over the conduct of the examinations'.[35] In contrast, '"Re-enactment of abuse" occurred both as a result of events that involved the crossing of a woman's body boundaries and more subjective internal factors that related to her sense of agency'.[36] Birthrights and AIMS can

---

[31] R Harris and S Ayers, 'What Makes Labour and Birth Traumatic? A Survey of Intrapartum "Hotspots"' (2012) 27 *Psychology & Health* 1166; Birthrights, *Dignity in Childbirth: The Dignity Survey 2013: Women's and Midwives' Experiences of UK Maternity Care* (London, Birthrights, 2013); M Greenfield et al, '"It Can't be Like Last Time" – Choices Made in Early Pregnancy by Women who have Previously Experienced a Traumatic Birth' (2019) 10 *Frontiers in Psychology* 56. Further in-depth information and a research directory on birth trauma and post-traumatic stress can be found on the Birth Trauma Association website at www.birthtraumaassociation.org.uk.

[32] Birthrights (n 31); K Cook and C Loomis, 'The Impact of Choice and Control on Women's Childbirth Experiences' (2012) 21 *The Journal of Perinatal Education* 158; National Maternity Review, *Better Births: Improving Outcomes of Maternity Services in England* (NHS England, 2016); Birthrights and Birth Companions (n 25).

[33] R Reed et al, 'Women's Descriptions of Childbirth Trauma Relating to Care Provider Actions and Interactions' (2017) 17 *BMC Pregnancy and Childbirth* 21; Harris and Ayers (n 31); MH Hollander et al, 'Preventing Traumatic Childbirth Experiences: 2192 Women's Perceptions and Views' (2017) 20 *Archive of Women's Mental Health* 515; Birthrights and Birth Companions (n 25).

[34] J Seng, 'How Does Traumatic Stress Affect Pregnancy and Birth?' in J Seng and J Taylor (eds), *Trauma Informed Care in the Perinatal Period* (Edinburgh, Dunedin Academic Press, 2010); Birthrights and Birth Companions (n 25).

[35] E Montgomery et al, 'The Re-Enactment of Childhood Sexual Abuse in Maternity Care: A Qualitative Study' (2015) 15 *BMC Pregnancy and Childbirth* 194, 200.

[36] ibid 194.

attest to this from the experiences of women who have sought advice and support. One woman, a rape survivor supported by Birthrights, described experiencing panic attacks during non-consented vaginal examinations, leading to flashbacks during and after labour of the rape she had experienced, ongoing re-living of the violation that occurred during her maternity care and post-traumatic stress.

IV. Complaints and Redress

Despite the impact on women, Birthrights and AIMS find that complaints about non-consented vaginal examinations are not always taken seriously by healthcare Trusts. As already set out, vaginal examinations generally take place within a broader set of clinical guidelines aimed at ensuring a safe birth for the woman and her infant. Birthrights and AIMS believe it is likely that many non-consented vaginal examinations go unreported, in some cases because women are not confident or supported by those around them in their understanding that what happened to them is a wrong. In other cases, women may not consider complaining because of other pressures in their lives (for example the not inconsiderable task of looking after a newborn) or because they do not have confidence that a complaint will effect change. This may again be more pronounced for women who are facing disadvantage or other challenges in their lives: as one participant in Birthrights' and Birth Companions' research noted: 'The women who come forward saying "this wasn't okay for me" are the women who've been taught in their lives to expect better'.[37]

When women do complain, Birthrights finds that non-consented vaginal examinations are often not treated with the seriousness they deserve. Birthrights does not have sufficient data to comment with certainty on the reasons for this. In some cases, it appears that the psychological harm and trauma suffered by a woman following a non-consented vaginal examination has been discounted for being 'hidden', and considered less important than an overall outcome of a healthy mother and baby. Even where psychological harm is recognised – either within or outside of the complaints process – treatment and support is not always accessible. One woman supported by Birthrights was offered counselling, but was unable to access it because it was offered at the same hospital where the original violation occurred.

Case Study 3

> J was in induced labour with her third child. She was attended by a doctor, who sat opposite her and played with his phone through her contractions, which made her feel very uncomfortable. She had an agreed approach for managing vaginal examinations based on her experiences in other births.

---

[37] Birthrights and Birth Companions (n 25).

J uses gas and air for vaginal examinations. She signals for the health-care practitioner to begin the examination, and signals or says 'stop' when a contraction is coming. She signals again when the practitioner can continue the examination. This was respected by her midwife, who explained it to the doctor when he insisted on doing a vaginal examination just after the midwife had done one. The doctor began the examination on J's signal but failed to stop when asked. J, her husband and the midwife all shouted for the doctor to stop. He did not. J was in agony and tried to 'kick him out'; he continued to insert his hand inside her. The midwife eventually managed to push the doctor away, who then said she wasn't even 'that far gone' and walked out. J was immensely shocked and distraught.

The midwife put in a complaint about the doctor to the General Medical Council, and J complained to the Trust via the Patient Advice and Liaison Service. This process required J to fill in a lot of paperwork, retraumatising J at a time when she was already experiencing flashbacks and anxiety as a result of her treatment. J was referred to rape counselling by her GP.

Sometime later, a senior midwife from the hospital visited J. J describes this person as completely dismissing her account, telling her she needed counsel-ling and to 'move on'; J was so upset that her husband had to stop the meeting. J sought reassurance that the doctor has been appropriately sanctioned but has received no such reassurance. She was told that the doctor would not work in the local area again; however, she has received no reassurance that this will impact on his practice elsewhere in the country.[38]

In this case, J was supported in her initial complaint by the midwife who witnessed her experience. This is not always so, as will be discussed below.

In other cases where complaints are not taken seriously, the reasons may be more nuanced and result from, for example, communication failures and/or a misapprehension by staff that the woman in question had given fully informed consent including the opportunity to decline: something that clearly requires more than a woman simply being told 'I'm just going to do a vaginal examination'.

Regardless of reason, many complaints that reach Birthrights appear to have been inadequately investigated, with the woman perceiving that the investigation had been focused more on protecting the healthcare practitioners involved than providing resolution or redress. In some cases, basic elements of investigation have been missed: for example, eyewitness accounts being sought from only a subset of those present, or accounts from birth partners being discounted as 'unreliable' as the individuals were deemed to be there as 'guests' of the woman. In other cases, maternity notes have been lost or located only shortly before meetings to discuss

---

[38] J has also shared her story in the national press: C O'Reilly, '"I Felt Violated": How "Birth Rape" Affects Millions of Mums – But Why Do Doctors Perform Invasive Procedures Without Our Consent?' *The Sun, Fabulous Magazine* (London, 22 May 2019) at www.thesun.co.uk/fabulous/8778305/birth-rape-obstetric-violence-mums-doctors-childbirth.

the complaint, leaving little time for women to prepare. In cases where they are available, maternity notes may not match the woman's understanding of what happened to her: it is highly unlikely that any non-consented examination would be explicitly documented as such. This can lead to situations where the evidence of healthcare providers sits at odds with women's experiences, and a 'he said, she said' situation with no clear lines of accountability, compounded by little regard being paid to the woman's testimony when compared with the official notes.

These experiences are not dissimilar to Scamell and Stewart's findings that note-taking was managed to show compliance with the expected care protocols, and did not necessarily reflect actual findings or, in the case of non-consented and undocumented vaginal examinations, practice.[39] If representative, this approach to investigations implies a lost opportunity both to provide appropriate redress to a woman who has suffered a non-consented examination being performed on her, and – in cases where genuine misunderstandings may have occurred – to make certain that staff are appropriately trained and empowered to ensure that the women they care for in future for are always supported to give, or decline, informed consent.

Case Study 4

T is a midwife and was planning a homebirth with her second baby. However, after experiencing some blood loss after a (consented) vaginal examination, she and her midwives decided that she would transfer to hospital. Combining her professional expertise with the excruciating pain she was in, led T to suspect a serious problem. T had not said she was a midwife.

On arrival at the hospital, T was hyper-stimulating and getting very little rest between contractions. The hyper-stimulation was not appropriately picked up by her midwives. The doctors arrived on the ward round but did not introduce themselves or speak to T. She was lying flat, heard a packet of gloves open and suddenly felt a hand inside her. She said 'not until after the contraction', but the doctor ignored her and continued. She heard the doctor speaking to colleagues over – but not to – her about her dilation.

Several minutes later T was asked whether she had passed urine and then felt a catheter be inserted. No-one had sought her consent. At this point, she then felt a hand inside her carrying out a second vaginal examination. At this point she pulled herself upright, waved her finger across the doctor's face and said 'no consent' as loudly as possible. The doctor looked her in the eye but failed to stop.

The doctor then withdrew her hand and saw blood which confirmed T's suspicion about what was happening in her body. T was rushed for an emergency (immediate threat to life of woman or baby) Caesarean section.

---

[39] Scamell and Stewart (n 1).

After the birth, a midwife arranged for T to speak to the consultant who was present during the unauthorised vaginal examinations and catheter insertion. The consultant was defensive and adamant that only one vaginal examination had been done. T was told that 'sometimes we perform Caesarean sections in an emergency without consent, if we need to' and 'you should be happy you are alive'. T then disclosed that she was a midwife and pointed out the second vaginal examination documented on the CTG trace.[40] At this point, T describes the consultant 'backing down' and becoming patronising, saying T would need a debrief in six weeks' time. After she was discharged, T's notes went missing; when they returned the vaginal examinations had disappeared.

T reported her experience to the General Medical Council. They found that there was no case to answer and that the situation was a one-off. T appealed, including witness statements from her birth companions, and from a midwife who was present and remembered her being reluctant to have the vaginal examination. The appeal was not successful.

For a woman who is unhappy with the Trust investigation, the usual next step would be for the woman to apply to the Parliamentary and Health Service Ombudsman, or in cases where a particular healthcare professional's conduct was concerned, to the professional regulatory body. However, Birthrights' and AIMS' experience of the Ombudsman to date is that decision-making is usually based on the documentary evidence provided. If the notes do not support the woman's point of view, there are few new routes for the Ombudsman to investigate under current practice. Where complaints are taken to professional bodies and regulators – for example where a woman brings a misconduct claim – one case may be considered insufficient to support sanctions being taken, with the General Medical Council (GMC) in particular seeking evidence on a recurring pattern of behaviour. If many women who experience non-consented vaginal examinations do not complain then this may be very hard to demonstrate. In some cases that Birthrights and AIMS have seen, a regulator or the Ombudsman seem to have received erroneous advice from their own experts which suggested that a woman is not required to give explicit consent to each and every intervention, particularly in labour.

In a number of cases seen by Birthrights and AIMS there seems to be uncertainty between different state actors as to how a non-consented vaginal examination should be dealt with, by whom, and the respective roles and interactions of different potential redress routes. AIMS have supported one of the women who has shared her story in this chapter to go to the police following a non-consented vaginal examination but were told that the police would not investigate until the GMC had investigated the woman's complaint. By the time the GMC had investigated and responded, the woman was told that the case was 'out of time' as the charge

---

[40] Continuous cardiotocography, otherwise known as electronic foetal monitoring, used to monitor the baby's heartbeat and the labour contractions and recommended when certain risk factors are present during labour (set out in NICE Guideline CG190 (n 7) [1.10.4]).

involved had to be prosecuted within six months. Another woman asked the police whether her experience could be investigated as a sexual assault but was told this was not possible without proof of intent.

Some of the women who have shared their experiences in this chapter have also attempted to seek redress directly through the legal system. However, none have been successful. The women who have attempted to bring cases describe difficulties proving psychiatric (rather than physical) harm, such that damages may be payable and a civil case taken on. They also describe difficulties – even after a diagnosis of post-traumatic stress disorder – in proving that psychiatric harm resulted from the non-consented vaginal examination rather than from a complex birth experience. Women also describe difficulties securing support they need to bring a case within time limits whilst also negotiating complaints processes.

V. Seeking Solutions

This situation leaves many women who have experienced non-consented care with nowhere to seek redress. This is a completely unacceptable position to be in following such a gross breach of autonomy, dignity and bodily integrity: something which many women who have experienced it describe as rape. Birthrights and AIMS recognise that the women's stories shared in this chapter have unconsented vaginal examinations in common but differ in other ways and a spectrum of effective solutions need to be available. These may include legal and regulatory options for women to seek redress, as well as routes to address practice through training and professional development. However, it is clearly not acceptable for unconsented vaginal examinations to be normalised and left unchallenged.

Birthrights and AIMS are delighted to contribute to this volume as a means of starting a more in-depth process to develop concrete actions to reduce the incidence of non-consented vaginal examinations, to ensure that they are taken seriously, and to ensure that women who experience them have appropriate and thorough avenues for redress available to them. Throughout these processes, and for the readers of this book, it is vital to grapple with the realities of healthcare practice and the intricacies of why neither regulatory nor legal processes yet seem to be offering women resolution and redress. Above all, however, it is vital to root these discussions in the lived reality of women's experience. This chapter opened by saying that the stories and cases within were real stories, from real women; that they probably reflect the tip of the iceberg. As we start to develop a more appropriate, compassionate response to non-consented vaginal examinations and to stop them from happening in the first place, we must always remember that solutions need to address issues as experienced by women. Only by grounding this work in women's experiences can we start to build systems which can truly ensure dignified and respectful care for all women.

3

Silence, Acquiescence or Consent: Interpreting Women's Responses to Intimate Examinations

ELSA MONTGOMERY*

I. Introduction

Vaginal examinations have become an accepted part of maternity care in obstetric units in the UK and elsewhere. They are frequently used to confirm the onset of labour and assess its progress. National Guidelines on intrapartum care for healthy women and babies in the UK advise that women are offered four-hourly vaginal examinations once they are in established labour or, where there is concern about possible delay, more frequent examinations.[1] These procedures become routine for clinicians who are performing them every day, and in busy clinical areas it is easy to overlook the needs of the individual women involved. However, for the woman, a vaginal examination is not an everyday occurrence. These are intimate examinations that can leave her feeling exposed and vulnerable. Indeed, if such actions were to take place outside a clinical situation without consent, they would be classified a sexual assault.[2] While this is potentially of concern to any woman, for the 1 in 5 women (20%) worldwide who have experienced childhood sexual abuse it is likely to be particularly distressing.[3] Women with a history of childhood sexual abuse know what it is like to lack control and feel powerless.[4] A sense of autonomy

---

* I am grateful to Jonathan Montgomery for his comments on my draft and for his insights to help make this chapter meaningful for a legal audience.

[1] National Institute for Health and Care Excellence (NICE), *Intrapartum Care: Care of Healthy Women and Their Babies during Childbirth: Clinical Guideline 190* (London, NICE, 2014) (NICE Guideline CG190) at www.nice.org.uk/guidance/cg190.

[2] Sexual Offences Act 2003, s 2.

[3] N Pereda et al, 'The Prevalence of Child Sexual Abuse in Community and Student Samples: A Meta-Analysis' (2009) 29 *Clinical Psychology Review* 328.

[4] E Montgomery, 'Feeling Safe: A Metasynthesis of the Maternity Care Needs of Women Who Were Sexually Abused in Childhood' (2013) 40 *Birth* 88.

is not likely to be part of their experience as they become adults, and this can make their experience of maternity care very difficult.

This chapter will explore issues in the context of challenges faced by women who have experienced childhood sexual abuse, specifically focusing on consent for intimate examinations during maternity care. It will also consider the challenges often faced by those who offer care to these women. Much of the content of this chapter is based on a program of research investigating the maternity care experiences of women who have experienced childhood sexual abuse that began with a doctoral study.[5] It uses the participants' powerful words to provide examples and where names are mentioned, these are pseudonyms chosen by the women themselves.

II. Ethical and Legal Context

The right to autonomy is a fundamental ethical principle. It has been argued in the context of healthcare that respect for autonomy requires consent to be obtained for any intervention.[6] This is enshrined in the General Medical Council's (GMC) ethical guidance for doctors (currently under review) and the Nursing and Midwifery Council's (NMC) Code.[7] However, linking consent to the concept of autonomy is not straightforward and is potentially limiting.[8] Respect for autonomy requires more than the right to veto physical interventions. Individual agency is important and requires both an appropriate range of choices available to women and sufficient information about risks and reasonable alternatives. The GMC recognises the importance of working in partnership with those to whom doctors are providing care. This is in keeping with the woman-centred, personalised care envisaged in the National Maternity Review but is not yet the experience of many women giving birth in the UK.[9] The NMC requires that practitioners get 'properly informed consent'.[10] Although the NMC Code does not elaborate on what that

---

[5] E Montgomery, *Voicing the Silence: The Maternity Care Experiences of Women Who Were Sexually Abused in Childhood* (PhD thesis, University of Southampton, 2012). Unless otherwise stated, quotations are taken from the interview transcripts from this study.

[6] T Beauchamp and J Childress, *Principles of Biomedical Ethics*, 8th edn (Oxford, Oxford University Press, 2019).

[7] General Medical Council, *Consent: Patients and Doctors Making Decisions Together* (London, GMC, 2008); Nursing and Midwifery Council, *The Code: Professional Standards of Practice and Behaviour for Nurses, Midwives and Nursing Associates* (London, NMC, 2018).

[8] N Manson and O O'Neill, *Rethinking Informed Consent in Bioethics* (Cambridge, Cambridge University Press, 2007).

[9] National Maternity Review, *Better Births: Improving Outcomes of Maternity Services in England* (2015) at www.england.nhs.uk/ourwork/futurenhs/mat-review.

[10] Nursing and Midwifery Council (n 7) [4.2].

means, the GMC guidance indicates that patients should be given the information they want or need in a balanced way with consideration of how well they understand the details and implications of what is proposed. It also requires respect for a person's decision to withhold consent, even if that seems irrational.[11]

Although the GMC's preference is for written consent in cases that involve 'higher risk', it recognises that in some situations oral or implied consent are acceptable alternatives, particularly in the case of routine procedures.[12] However, as mentioned above, although intimate examinations may well be routine for clinicians, they are less likely be so for the woman. The concept of 'risk' is also complicated. Effective discussion about risk needs identification of the 'adverse outcomes that may result from the proposed options'.[13] The clinician may not have insight into risks for the individual woman nor indeed, as will be seen later, may the woman herself at the start of a procedure. This means there are particular complexities related to risk for those with a history of childhood sexual abuse.

The assessment of risk is also crucial to health professionals meeting their legal obligations, as material risks should be disclosed when consent is sought for clinical interventions. In law, since the judgment in *Montgomery v Lanarkshire Health Board*, the assessment of whether risk is 'material' is to be judged from the perspective of patients not professionals, ie whether 'a reasonable person in the patient's position would be likely to attach significance to the risk'.[14] The same case also established that where a clinician is, or should be, aware that a particular woman would attach significance to a risk then this will make it 'material' and therefore something that should be discussed.[15] This is worthy of further exploration in relation to intimate examinations for all women but especially for those who have suffered sexual abuse.

The law also addresses the need for women to be offered an appropriate range of choices. The question of what care options are appropriate is regarded by the law as a matter for clinical judgement, but women are entitled to know about more than the preferred care plans.[16] Under *Montgomery*, all reasonable alternatives should be disclosed to women. In the case itself, the Supreme Court found that a Caesarean section should have been discussed with the claimant and the doctor was found liable in negligence for failing to do so. This raises issues about whether and when there are reasonable alternatives to the intimate examinations that have become part of routine care.

---

[11] General Medical Council (n 7) [43].

[12] ibid [46]–[47].

[13] ibid [29].

[14] *Montgomery v Lanarkshire Health Board* [2015] UKSC 11 at [87].

[15] ibid.

[16] *Aintree University Hospitals NHS Foundation Trust v James* [2013] UKSC 67. For discussion, see E Cave, 'Selecting Treatment Options and Choosing Between Them: Delineating Patient and Professional Autonomy in Shared Decision-Making' (2020) 28 *Health Care Analysis* 4.

III. Childhood Sexual Abuse: Prevalence and Impact

Childhood sexual abuse has been described as one of the most serious public health issues facing society and it 'casts a long shadow'.[17] As the resulting physical and psychological morbidity can last a lifetime, survivors are frequent users of health services. However, the shame, guilt and secrecy that accompany childhood sexual abuse mean that disclosure to healthcare professionals is infrequent.[18] The term 'survivor' is used here as an accepted shorthand but it is important to recognise that some women who have lived experience of childhood sexual abuse do not find this a helpful term.[19] This is particularly so for women who are still in abusive relationships.

Survivors of childhood sexual abuse are a silent, hidden population.[20] Appearing 'normal' and fitting in is often an important goal for survivors when accessing health services, not least because they perceive themselves to be very different from other people and want to hide that from them. These women spent their childhoods trying to fade into the background and they have described taking a similar approach as adults within health services. This involves a lot of pretending and 'playing the game'. Those caring for women may not know or even suspect that they are encountering a survivor. In a busy clinical setting, especially if they have not had an opportunity to meet the woman before, they will not necessarily anticipate any difficulties as they seek consent for a 'routine' procedure.

IV. Conflicting Perspectives

In the context of labour and birth, appropriate sharing of information in a balanced way is not easy for any woman and evidence suggests that staff are not always explicit about what a vaginal examination involves. Stewart has described the 'verbal asepsis' of language used in connection with vaginal examinations.[21] She suggests that abbreviations (VE) or euphemisms ('internal') reflect discomfort and embarrassment on behalf of staff who are involved in a procedure that is outside usual day-to-day interactions other than in a professional encounter.

---

[17] N Pereda et al, 'The International Epidemiology of Child Sexual Abuse: A Continuation of Finkelhor (1994)' (2009) 33 *Child Abuse and Neglect* 331; Children's Commissioner for England, *Protecting Children from Harm: A Critical Assessment of Child Sexual Abuse in the Family Network in England and Priorities for Action* (Children's Commissioner for England, 2015) 5.

[18] J LoGiudice and C Beck, 'The Lived Experience of Childbearing from Survivors of Sexual Abuse: "It Was the Best of Times, It Was the Worst of Times"' (2016) 61 *Journal of Midwifery and Women's Health* 474.

[19] See further www.survivorsvoices.org.

[20] E Montgomery et al, 'A Feminist Narrative Study of the Maternity Care Experiences of Women Who Were Sexually Abused in Childhood' (2015) 31 *Midwifery* 54.

[21] M Stewart, '"I'm Just Going to Wash You Down": Sanitizing the Vaginal Examination' (2005) 51 *Journal of Advanced Nursing* 587, 592.

Stewart describes observing a birth as part of her research in which the midwife, responding to cues from the woman that labour was progressing rapidly, stated: 'I'd just like to examine you to see what's happening'.[22] There was no detail in the encounter as to what the examination would actually involve and an assumption that the woman would know. Although most women realise that vaginal examinations are part of expected care during labour, not everyone will realise what that means. During a focus group as part of my doctoral study, a midwife recounted talking to a woman about a vaginal examination and being asked how she would 'get the ruler in there'.[23] The midwife acknowledged the need to take more care with the explanations she provides about what will be involved in examinations and how dilation is measured. This is a salutary reminder of the need for careful consideration of what appropriate sharing of information might entail for the individual receiving care.

The potential difference in the woman's perception of a situation and that of the healthcare professionals involved is powerfully illustrated by Elizabeth's experience.[24] At the time of her first pregnancy, Elizabeth had embarked on a pathway leading to a professional career. She was fully aware of her history of abuse, but believed it was in the past and that she had moved on. She did not disclose her abuse to those providing her maternity care for fear of being judged a bad mother. During pregnancy Elizabeth had worried about how she would deal with the vaginal examinations she knew she would need but decided that she would manage if people respected her and asked permission. Unfortunately, this was not her experience: 'I felt they thought they had a right to do it … and I found that very difficult and I remember just being very, very angry with them and just wanting to run away'.[25]

Elizabeth's baby was born following induction of labour at 41 weeks' gestation for decreased foetal movements. Her medical records suggest that about twelve and a half hours elapsed between the start of her induction and end of the first stage of labour. During that time, ten vaginal examinations are documented, four of which were performed in a ninety-minute period in which it was acknowledged that she was very distressed. The notes give no suggestion that there was concern about delay, which may have been an indication for more frequent vaginal examinations, rather there appear to have been signs that might indicate good progress (strong, regular contractions, urges to push, blood-stained 'show').[26] However, the notes record that determining dilation of the cervix was very difficult and Elizabeth was not tolerating the examinations. Some discussion about the way forward is recorded, as is consent for the examinations.

---

[22] ibid.
[23] Montgomery (n 5) 198.
[24] Montgomery (n 5).
[25] ibid.
[26] NICE Guideline CG190 (n 1).

Elizabeth's account differed from the clinicians' as follows:

> I felt like I wasn't involved in any of it. I felt like everyone was doing things around me and to me without even asking. Umm and one of the things I found really difficult was the internal examinations and I, I felt, I mean maybe I wasn't with it and maybe they did ask, but I don't ever remember anyone saying 'we've got to do an internal examination, is that OK?' They just kept on doing it and d … and it felt like it was happening really, really regularly. And every time it really, really hurt and the last time they did it I li … I, I fe … I mean, I might, my memory might not be perfect, but I remember trying to kick the midwife and saying 'just get out of me, I've had enough, I've just had enough of it'.[27]

Elizabeth had found the vaginal examinations very painful and intrusive but remembers being told: 'It shouldn't be painful; we don't know why you're saying it's painful'.[28] After the birth, Elizabeth accessed the 'Birth Afterthoughts' service in which she was able to go through her record with a midwife and discuss her labour experience. She was angry to discover that consent had been recorded, as neither she nor her husband recall permission being obtained and this was further evidence for Elizabeth of her own experience being invalidated. Whether or not permission had been obtained, Elizabeth's distress had been recognised and at the very least an ethical approach from staff might have been to double check that she had not revoked her consent, particularly given that no rationale for the examinations was recorded. A cross-sectional study by Swahnberg et al indicates that women who experience unexpected strong discomfort during vaginal examinations were more likely than others to have experienced some form of abuse.[29] The authors also recognise that there is a risk of feelings of re-traumatisation during health care. This was true for Elizabeth and most of the other women in my study both during intimate examinations and other much less obviously intrusive aspects of care.

V. Lack of Control

Elizabeth was determined to breastfeed her baby but was confused by the conflicting advice she received. Staff were concerned that the baby had not fed properly. Elizabeth reports returning from taking a bath to discover that one of the midwives had given the baby a bottle of formula milk:

> My whole life is – my whole childhood was about everyone doing stuff to me. Never asking, just doing stuff to me and now someone's taken my baby and they've not even asked me and I'm supposed to be responsible and they've not even asked me. They've not give … asked me to give permission.[30]

---

[27] Montgomery (n 5).

[28] ibid.

[29] K Swahnberg et al, 'Strong Discomfort during Vaginal Examination: Why Consider a History of Abuse?' (2011) 15 *European Journal of Obstetrics & Gynecology and Reproductive Biology* 200.

[30] Montgomery (n 5).

This experience, which undermined Elizabeth's position as a parent, also replicated the lack of agency she experienced as a child.

Sue was transported back to her childhood one night when she was an inpatient on the antenatal ward. As she was afraid of the dark, she had drawn the curtains round her bed in a four-bedded bay and left her bedside light on. A midwife had approached during the night and turned the light off:

> I, I'm completely scared of the dark and to lie there with someone walking into your little curtain bit and turn the light off was horrible because you can hear the footsteps coming … and, and you know, footsteps have a real big meaning when you've been treated not well as a child. And those footsteps – you just don't know who they are until they come round the curtain and um and then switch the light off and you're so scared.[31]

Unlike Elizabeth, Sue's history of abuse was recorded in her notes. Whether or not staff are aware of the history of women in their care, triggers are very individual and they cannot be expected to know what women will find difficult. However, the common theme in both these examples is the lack of respect for autonomy – a fundamental ethical principle for healthcare.

VI.   Acquiescence is not Choosing

Sue, who was also induced in her first pregnancy, found vaginal examinations very painful too. Her experience was dismissed by staff, like Elizabeth's was: 'they were really, really painful and I – the midwives on the ward just kept telling me to stop being so silly – everybody goes through it, everybody has it done'.[32]

There is no suggestion in Sue's narrative that she was offered any options but even if she had been, she would not have spoken out. In a subsequent pregnancy she was talking to a midwife she trusted:

> she said 'you should have asked for gas and air when you had the in … you know, when they had to do the internals', but you just can't ask for anything, you feel so – you just wanna curl up and be part of the wallpaper. You just don't want to make a fuss or anything.[33]

Such lack of protest could be interpreted as implied consent but Sue's language, 'when they *had to* do the internals' suggests she did not realise she had any choice. For healthcare professionals, gaining consent should be part of the process of discussion to facilitate decision-making and needs to include consideration of options. The midwives' language as reported by Sue, 'everybody has it done', suggests that no other possibilities were considered, and no choice was offered.

---

[31] ibid.
[32] ibid.
[33] ibid.

According to NICE a vaginal examination is one aspect of assessing the woman's progress in labour and the guideline development group is clear that it is important to be led by what the woman wants when deciding whether or not to perform a vaginal examination.[34] None of the women in my studies have reported such a process.

Compliance may be the way women try to avoid attention, as it was with Sue, but can also be the result of a dissociative state that is very common in women who have experienced previous trauma. The following quote is from a participant in an online survey conducted to inform the development of a resource for survivors contemplating pregnancy and birth:

> The only thing I remember is having to have loads and loads of internal examinations and being so numb to people violating me that I just didn't really show any anxiety or embarrassment at all. People probably thought it was confidence or comfort with the professional but it wasn't, it's a numb, dissociative state.[35]

Again, it is worth reflecting on the language used; 'having to have loads and loads of internal examinations'; 'being so numb to people violating me'. What was almost certainly interpreted as consent by the staff providing care, was an experience of disempowerment and trauma for the woman.

VII. Care Causing Harm

Traditional health care ethics has long held that its first principle is to avoid harming patients (*primum non nocere*). However, the familiarity of vaginal examinations to staff can mean they overlook the possibility that the procedures may be harmful to women. Intimate examinations can be triggering and lead to flashbacks, a situation that is often unexpected.[36] This was Sally's experience. She had an epidural for her first birth, so the pain she felt as her second baby was born took her by surprise:

> because obviously with the first one I didn't feel it so much but with the second one, it's that pain, brings back memories, if that makes sense, ... because of what happened when I was, you know, um cos I was sexually abused basically and I was only five ... and ... it's that pain. I'll never forget that. It's, it's ... it's horrible. You don't forget it. And that's the same as when you're having your baby.[37]

Sally's birth experience was complicated by the fact that she was attended by a male medical student when she had particularly asked for female staff and had refused consent for the student's presence. Mia on the other hand, was receiving

---

[34] NICE Guideline CG190 (n 1).

[35] Montgomery (n 5).

[36] LoGiudice and Beck (n 18); C Roller, 'Moving Beyond the Pain: Women's Responses to the Perinatal Period after Childhood Sexual Abuse' (2011) 56 *Journal of Midwifery and Women's Health* 488.

[37] Montgomery (n 5).

compassionate care from a midwife she trusted and to whom she had disclosed. Nevertheless, her experience of a vaginal examination was triggering. The midwife caring for Mia, taking a gentle approach, had inserted one finger and then another at the start of the examination and in so doing had unwittingly replicated what her abuser had done.

These examples are evidence of the trauma that women can face whether or not they have given consent and the challenges that can arise for those seeking it. Beauchamp and Childress recognise complexity in respecting autonomy. Although the 'basic paradigm' is explicit informed consent, implied, tacit or presumed consent may also be valid.[38] Healthcare professionals are expected to provide clear, accurate information about the risks of any proposed procedures to help those in their care make informed decisions.[39] They also need to check that this information has been understood.[40] As demonstrated by Mia's experience, the risks for people who have experienced previous trauma may be unexpected for both those giving and receiving care. These women had capacity and were given information that they understood. With the exception of Sally, whose refusal of consent was apparently ignored, in law these situations would not be seen as examination without consent. However, from the women's perspective, they were disempowering and unwelcome. Even when they have given consent, in the context of intimate examinations and other potentially triggering situations the women may not be able to exert autonomy. Healthcare professionals are also advised that they must make it clear that people can change their mind about a decision. As discussed above, such agency is not usually available to survivors of childhood sexual abuse.

An additional challenge is created by the fact that memories of childhood abuse may be buried very deep and the women themselves may not remember their abuse during maternity care. Although for some survivors birth is the trigger that brings memories to the surface, for others memories remain subconscious but a physical connection is made. Jane gave birth to three children without remembering her abuse.[41] Her memories surfaced after she left her violent husband. With hindsight she realised that physical responses she found perplexing during birth were reactions to her abuse:

> I had this tendency to sort of breath out and stop, under extreme stress, or, or pain, and so there was this, you know, sort of like – and I, and I, and I could feel myself disappearing because I couldn't, I couldn't breathe in, even though she [the midwife] was asking me to … it's almost like when things are so similar, even if you don't know that there's a connection, it's almost like your body makes it anyway and you and and it takes over.[42]

Responses like this are confusing for both the women and the clinicians caring for them. Interpreting their implications for consent is complicated. In common with

---

[38] Beauchamp and Childress (n 6) 108.
[39] General Medical Council (n 7).
[40] *Montgomery v Lanarkshire* (n 14).
[41] P Simkin and P Klaus, *When Survivors Give Birth* (Classic Day Publishing, 2004).
[42] Montgomery (n 5).

several of the other women whose experiences have been shared in this chapter, there is no way when Jane gave consent that she could have had any understanding of the adverse reaction she would experience in response to care given.

I have described situations in which staff believe they have consent for vaginal examinations but the lived experience of women is violation or confusion. The consent is likely to be legally valid: staff presented the requisite information in a way that was understood, to a person with capacity who appeared to comply. What they were proposing has been recommended by NICE. Especially if documented, such consent would almost certainly protect staff from accusations of assault. However, as these examples show, although consent may protect staff, it does not necessarily protect women. Rather than reinforcing autonomy for women and facilitating agency and partnership in care provided, the women lacked control and felt disempowered. Control is of paramount importance to women who have experienced childhood sexual abuse and is essential in enabling them to feel safe.[43] Staff should be able to facilitate choices for women so that they can feel safe as they begin the transition to parenthood.

VIII. Compassionate Care

Caring for women who have experienced childhood sexual abuse is complex. Survivors are often a silent, hidden population and many aspects of care can be experienced as a re-enactment of abuse. Some of these will be predicted by the women concerned; others will take them by surprise and be very traumatic, even when they happen in the context of sensitive maternity care. Whether there can be meaningful ways forward in law to address these issues is an interesting area for debate. Focus on autonomy in relation to consent, diverts attention away from other fundamental ethical principles such as beneficence and non-maleficence. Law is a blunt instrument when it comes to delivering respectful care to individual women. This is not to say that the legal principles on which our healthcare system is founded are not important, but to recognise the need for a nuanced response. Above all, women who have experienced previous sexual abuse need insightful and compassionate care. Returning to the issue of vaginal examinations, Swahnberg et al suggest that the interpersonal relationship between examiner and woman is the most important aspect of the vaginal examination experience.[44] This is borne out by women in my study too. The fact that Helen trusted the midwife she had got to know during pregnancy, meant she was happy to agree to a vaginal examination, even though she had indicated that she did not want 'too many internals'. On arrival at the maternity unit the midwife had asked Helen how she was before broaching the issue of examinations and made it clear that the choice as to whether

---

[43] Montgomery (n 4).
[44] Swahnberg et al (n 29).

to have one was Helen's. Respect for women as people rather than objects in need of processing is key, as demonstrated by another of the women who participated in the study to inform the development of a resource mentioned earlier:

> it just didn't feel like a procedure that I wasn't part of, it felt like my body was part of me and that she was paying attention to me as opposed to just doing something to my body and that was in the way she was questioning me and explaining and kind of keeping eye contact with me … there was something about the way that she created time and space and thought and care and, kind of, yeah, having someone look at you and really see you and talk to you while they're doing something was really, yeah, made a massive difference.[45]

Such respectful care provides an excellent example of beneficence. However, many of the examples considered so far in this chapter indicate less concern for the individual's wellbeing.

The behaviour of women who are experiencing flashbacks can be difficult to interpret, may seem unreasonable or even be inexplicable to health professionals.[46] When a flashback is triggered, the woman is likely to surrender to the memories invoked and any emotional connection between clinician and woman will be disturbed. Loss of control and power differential between the two may well be the catalyst for such a situation.[47] Often, as was the case for Elizabeth, the woman's distress will be obvious, even if the cause is not. The principle of non-maleficence should require healthcare professionals to stop the examination and consider what responses are appropriate. Even if a woman has consented to vaginal examination, an acknowledgement that she has control over the timing, pace and especially when the examination should end is important.[48] The following, in which a workshop participant describes an experience of cervical screening, provides an eloquent example:

> I thought why am I feeling so anxious when I've met this nurse before? The thing that just really switched it right around for me, she said 'you're in control, just tell me to stop if you want me to' and instantly I was like 'OK, yeah'.[49]

At the very least, recognition of the woman's distress is important and that should prompt the clinician to ask themselves whether a vaginal examination is really necessary. Guidelines advise those providing care to consider what information the examination would add to the decision-making process and to take the woman's emotional and psychological needs into account.[50] The guideline group

---

[45] Montgomery (n 5).
[46] G Güneş and Z Karaçam, 'The Feeling of Discomfort during Vaginal Examination, History of Abuse and Sexual Abuse and Post-Traumatic Stress Disorder in Women' (2017) 26 *Journal of Clinical Nursing* 2362; Swahnberg et al (n 29).
[47] Swahnberg et al (n 29).
[48] L Sobel et al, 'Pregnancy and Childbirth after Sexual Trauma: Patient Perspectives and Care Preferences' (2018) 132 *Obstetrics and Gynecology* 1461.
[49] www.thesurvivorstrust.org/pbpaftercsa.
[50] NICE Guideline CG190 (n 1).

has acknowledged that no relevant study was identified that provided evidence that outcomes are affected by any of the aspects of assessment recommended following admission and throughout labour, which includes four-hourly vaginal examinations. This practice is, therefore, a conventional routine rather than evidence-based requirement for good care.

IX. Conclusion

In considering women's birthing bodies and the law, the focus of this chapter has been vaginal examination, the most intimate of procedures. The importance of autonomy and agency has been explored, particularly in relation to women who have experienced childhood sexual abuse. The potential for retraumatisation of women undergoing these examinations is commonly recognised. However, I have also shown how women are retraumatised through aspects of care that are neither intimate nor necessarily predictably problematic to either the woman or those providing care. Agency remains crucial to the wellbeing of these women, but, as I have argued, consent is not necessarily the mechanism by which that is achieved. In the preceding discussion I have made the case that consent is too blunt an instrument to meet the changing and complex needs of women during labour. The principles underlying legal requirements for consent are important: information, understanding, choice and control, but I have provided examples when consent obtained by staff was not reflected in an experience of autonomy or agency for the women concerned. What is needed is a more personalised approach in the moment that reflects the principles of beneficence and non-maleficence. Respectful, trauma-informed care enables staff to respond to spoken and unspoken messages from women, whether or not a history of abuse has been disclosed. Appropriate responses help women to have control and feel safe. Interdisciplinary education is needed so that staff are able to work with women and recognise the difference between silence, acquiescence or consent in the care they offer.

4

Female Genital Examination and Autonomy in Medicine

NEDA TAGHINEJADI AND BRENDA KELLY

I. Introduction

The practice of female genital examination is undoubtedly a central part of modern gynaecology. Performed in a variety of forms (including external inspection, internal inspection with the aid of a speculum, and digital assessment), genital examination may serve as an invaluable diagnostic tool or as a necessary prerequisite for a number of common procedures. Historically, however, the practice of female genital examination has extended far beyond its scope as a simple clinical tool. It is unsurprising that representations of this act carry with them, perhaps more than any other medical examination, so much cultural weight. At their worst, illustrations of the vaginal examination (legs dangling in stirrups, toes wiggling undeniably in anticipation of the cold metal speculum) are used frequently and emotively to signify the vulnerability of women's bodies. Conversely, tales of self-examining feminists, rejecting male hegemony with hand-mirrors and torches in hand, have formed equally powerful and iconic images within feminism.

In this chapter we present and discuss the uniquely complex relationship between female genital examination and bodily autonomy. The principle of autonomy is defined very simply as 'the ability to make your own decisions without being controlled by anyone else'.[1] It is a key principle of medical ethics; in this context it is central to a patient's ability to make informed choices which are free from coercion. As described by the British Medical Association:

> In medical practice autonomy is usually expressed as the right of competent adults to make informed decisions about their own medical care. The principle underlies the requirement to seek the consent or informed agreement of the patient before any investigation or treatment takes place.[2]

---

[1] *Cambridge Dictionary* (Cambridge University Press, 2019) at dictionary.cambridge.org/dictionary/english/autonomy.

[2] British Medical Association, 'Autonomy or Self-Determination' (BMA, 2018) at www.bma.org.uk/advice/employment/ethics/medical-students-ethics-toolkit/2-autonomy-or-self-determination.

Presented here is an introduction to the historical tensions between the practice of female genital examinations and the autonomy of the women undergoing them. The development and practice of this clinical act have a dark past, having played a key enabling role in the degradation of women's bodily autonomy. Even more concerning still are the parallels identifiable between historical examples and current practice in contemporary medicine. The act of female genital examination need not, however, become synonymous with oppression; examples of its use by women as a method of liberation and reclamation of bodily autonomy offer hope for the future. The following discussion is limited primarily to cases within the modern history of Western medicine and the experiences of cisgender women, but we acknowledge that there is a much wider history and range of experiences, the discussion of which is beyond the scope of the present chapter.

II. Medicine's Discovery of the Cervix

'I saw everything, as no man had seen before' remarked the mid-nineteenth century physician, James Marion Sims, after developing his eponymously named speculum.[3] Its invention was heralded as a medical innovation; as described by one fellow nineteenth century physician, the speculum 'has been to diseases of the womb what the printing press is to civilisation, what the compass is to the mariner, what steam is to navigation, what the telescope is to astronomy'.[4]

Indeed, Sims' speculum remains an essential tool in clinical gynaecology today, and its creator is lauded as one of the fathers of modern gynaecology. What many clinicians using this tool today are not aware of, however, is the story of its development. The evolution of Sims' speculum from its first rudimentary prototype (which was fashioned from a pewter spoon) was the result of years of experimentation on African-American slaves without anaesthesia.[5] Harrowing descriptions can be found of the suffering of these women, who were subjected to examinations and procedures, often under physical restraint and the spectatorship of groups of students or medical professionals. A handful of debates around the legacy of James Marion Sims can be found in the medical literature. One such paper poses the question: should he be labelled 'a hero or a villain'?[6]

---

[3] J Sims cited in D McGregor, *From Midwives to Medicine: The Birth of American Gynecology* (New Bunswick, New Rutgers University Press, 1998) 49.

[4] W Baldwin cited in J Sims, *The Story of My Life* (New York, Appleton, 1884) 434.

[5] D Axelson, 'Women as Victims of Medical Experimentation: J Marion Sims's Surgery on Slave-Women (1845–1850)' (1985) *Women's Bodies: Health and Childbirth* 2, 2.

[6] J Sartin, 'J Marion Sims, the Father of Gynecology: Hero or Villain?' (2004) 97 *Southern Medical Journal* 500.

Those who seek to justify his actions and the suffering of those he experimented on often evoke utilitarian sentiments. One historian writes:

> Montgomery has not forgotten the heroic roles of three slaves, Anarcha, Luca and Betsy, who suffered, not only that themselves might be cured, but that women injured in childbirth in future generations might be saved from lives of misery and invalidism. A movement has been begun, sponsored by leading women in Montgomery to establish a memorial to the three slave heroines.[7]

Other defenders have emphasised the importance of historical context when passing judgement and questioned the validity of comparing the practice of a 'man of his time' to modern standards.[8]

Perhaps it is precisely the fact that he was a man of his time that is the point. The history of the Sims' speculum serves as an explicit example of the nature in which the practice of vaginal examination is inextricably entangled within its social context. The Sims' speculum acted as both mirror to and enabler of the gender politics and racial imperialism of mid-nineteenth century America, in which the bodily autonomy of Black women was openly utterly disregarded. It is unsurprising that Sims' reaction upon 'discovering' the cervix is dripping with the sentiment of a colonialist conqueror.[9]

There is much to be learnt from the stories of Black women who made any attempt to protect their bodily autonomy by refusing unwanted genital examinations. The story of Saartjie Baartman is perhaps one of the most widely-discussed examples.

Baartman was one of several Khoikhoi women who were taken from their homes in South Africa in the early nineteenth century and put on display as public exhibits in the UK. She was renamed the 'Hottentot Venus' and advertised as an attraction in part due to rumoured abnormalities of her genitals (her purportedly long labia were referred to as the 'Hottentot Apron').[10] There were multiple and prolonged attempts to submit Baartman to a genital examination by scientists who 'were seeking a classificatory wedge that would distinguish the Hottentot from the European on the level of species'.[11] She refused to comply. In her premature death, however, they were granted this unobstructed opportunity. A plaster cast

---

[7] S Harris, *Woman's Surgeon* (New York, Macmillan, 1950) 375–76.

[8] Sartin (n 6).

[9] In recent years there has been an increasing acknowledgement of the ways in which gynaecology and reproductive health have been, and continue to be, colonised. See for example, A Sowemimo, '#DecolonisingContraception – The Importance of Preventing Unethical Practice in SRH and Learning from History' (2018) *BMJ Sexual and Reproductive Health* at blogs.bmj.com/bmjsrh/2018/09/20/decolonisingcontraception-the-importance-of-preventing-unethical-practice-in-srh-and-learning-from-history.

[10] Z Maseko, *The Life and Times of Sara Baartman, 'The Hottentot Venus'* (Dominant 7, Mail and Guardian Television, France 3, and SABC2 1998).

[11] S Davis, 'Loose Lips Sink Ships' (2002) 28 *Feminist Studies* 7.

was made of her body, and her genitals preserved in a jar.[12] In the conflict between her wishes and the doctors' 'scientific' endeavour, it was ultimately the latter which triumphed.

When analysing the contemporary practice of female genital examination, it is essential to understand its enabling role in discriminatory processes including racism, colonialism and eugenics.

III. The Utilitarian Exception

'It's still my vagina, even if I am naked and unconscious. I didn't lend it to anyone to practice technique.'[13]

In an era in which women enjoy considerably more freedom than their predecessors, it is dismaying to identify multiple contemporary cases of patients' autonomy being disregarded when performing vaginal examination. The tradition of teaching vaginal examination to medical students on anaesthetised patients without their consent is one example, which is not only recognised amongst but until very recently was sanctioned by the medical profession. As pointed out by Dr Susan Bewley in the 1990s 'as students most doctors will have performed examinations on anaesthetised patients who have not given explicit consent'.[14] This would sometimes mean a patient being subjected to repeated speculum and/or digital examinations by a queue of medical students, without ever having any knowledge of the event.

As standards for gaining consent within medicine have evolved, the tradition of using non-consenting women's bodies as guinea pigs within medical education was exposed: at best as a threat to the doctor-patient relationship, and at worst as assault. This was not, however, without considerable resistance from clinicians who supported the practice. Consider, for example, the following quote from Dr Linda Cardozo in 1992:

As a teacher I could take no sense of pride in watching fumbling medical students desperately trying to impress on an examiner that they knew what they were doing when clearly they had rarely, if ever, inserted a vaginal speculum during their training … Personally, I would prefer to see a new generation of well-trained doctors who are able to relate appropriately to women who require gynaecological examination rather than a notion of women whose vaginas are protected from battery by medical students.[15]

---

[12] Maseko (n 10).

[13] PregnantAt51, *Pelvic Exam During General Anesthesia??* (The Student Doctor Network, 2007) at forums.studentdoctor.net/threads/pelvic-exam-during-general-anesthesia.412814, also cited by P Friesen, 'Educational Pelvic Exams on Anesthetized Women: Why Consent Matters' (2018) 32 *Bioethics* 298.

[14] S Bewley, 'The Law, Medical Students, and Assault' (1992) 304 *British Medical Journal* 1551.

[15] L Cardozo, 'Teaching Vaginal Examination' (1992) *British Medical Journal* 305, 113.

Or the following quote taken from an online forum for medical students in 2007:

> If you get into this habit of being deathly afraid of the patient's feelings about an internal exam you will never learn how. I'm not saying that you should be a jerk about it, but you owe it to your future patients to get some idea of what stuff feels like.[16]

The message here is clear: that a future doctor's right to training is superior to a woman's right to autonomy. The justifications of the 'utilitarian exception' are eerily reminiscent in sentiment to those used to support Sims' experimentation on Black female slaves.[17]

Whilst almost every medical school in the UK today has protocols in place to ensure that consent is gained by medical students before examinations, there is evidence that the practice has not been completely eradicated. Coldicott et al published findings from a medical school in the UK in which they identified that around a quarter of examinations on anaesthetised or sedated patients occurred without adequate consent.[18]

IV. Disapproval and Degradation

> 'A significant amount of women would gladly swap their real vaginas for something less troublesome – an unexploded warhead in their back garden, say.'[19]

The concept of autonomy extends far beyond the freedom to make informed choices about one's medical care; it refers to our ability to make decisions in all aspects of our life. It is essential, therefore, to include in this discussion the many tensions that have existed between the practice of female genital examination and women's ability to express autonomy over their body outside of a strictly medical context. Writers have pointed out that certain genital features have, in the Western world, been linked to sexually deviant behaviour and 'conditions' from masturbation, to hypersexuality, to homosexuality.[20] These views have been taken on and legitimated by the medical profession. As recently as the 1930s, a study was conducted on a group of lesbians to identify and characterise their specific genital characteristics.[21] The research identified ten characteristics which differentiated

---

[16] AmoryBlaine in *The Pelvic Exam During General Anesthesia??* (The Student Doctor Network, 2007) at forums.studentdoctor.net/threads/pelvic-exam-during-general- anesthesia.412814, also cited by Friesen (n 13).

[17] Friesen (n 13).

[18] Y Coldicott et al, 'The Ethics of Intimate Examinations – Teaching Tomorrow's Doctors' 2003 (326) *British Medical Journal* 97.

[19] B Ellen, 'The Brazilian Wax ... have the Americans gone a Pluck too Far?' *The Guardian* (London, 6 June 1999).

[20] F Green, 'From Clitoridectomies to "Designer Vaginas": The Medical Construction of Heteronormative Female Bodies and Sexuality through Female Genital Cutting' (2005) 7 *Sexualities, Evolution & Gender* 153.

[21] J Terry, 'Lesbians under the Medical Gaze: Scientists Search for Remarkable Differences' (1990) 27 *Journal of Sex Research* 317.

a lesbian from a 'normal' woman, including labia minora that were longer than normal, protruded or were wrinkly. Their belief was that a strong homosexual or hypersexual desire could actually reconstruct the vulva, making it a 'site of transformation'.[22] In extension of such views, examining or even altering the female genitalia has long been seen as a means of identifying and controlling those women who made decisions about their bodies within the private sphere which fell short of societal norms and standards. Many clitoridectomies (where the glans clitoris is fully or partially removed) have been performed upon 'women and girls of whose behaviour middle-class men disapproved'.[23]

It must be noted that whilst healthcare professionals may knowingly or unknowingly contribute to the marginalisation of groups of patients, they also play a key role in speaking out against unethical and degrading practices within medicine. A recent example of this took place in the American State of Missouri, after the State health department issued a requirement for all women undergoing termination of pregnancy to have an additional pelvic examination three days prior to their abortion. The practice faced significant criticism, both nationally and internationally, from healthcare professionals concerned that it would serve as a barrier to women accessing termination services. One clinician working within termination care services in Missouri described it as 'dehumanizing' to patients.[24] Another doctor described it as a 'violation': 'What I realized was I effectively have become an instrument of state abuse of power … as a licensed physician, I am compelled by the state of Missouri to put my fingers in a woman's vagina when it's not medically necessary'.[25]

Following a significant backlash from groups including the American College of Obstetricians and Gynecologists the requirement has been lifted; the case serves as a sobering reminder of the powerful role that medical professionals can play in serving as advocates for their patients, by recognising dehumanising and degrading practice and speaking out against it.

V. Taking Back Control

'A mirror. A flashlight. A twenty-five-cent speculum. That's all you need to meet your cervix'.[26]

As one examines the history of female genital examination, it is perhaps unsurprising to identify the trend of its use as an oppressive tool. The act of

---

[22] See Davis (n 11) 16.

[23] A Dally, *Women under the Knife: A History of Surgery* (London, Routledge, 1992) 64.

[24] Anonymous quoted in M McArdle, 'St Louise Abortion Clinic will Flout State Pelvic Exam Requirement' (2019) *National Review* at www.nationalreview.com/news/st-louis-abortion-clinic-will-flout-state-pelvic-exam-requirement.

[25] C McNicholas quoted in McArdle (n 24).

[26] J Edelson cited in G Corea, *The Hidden Malpractice: How American Medicine Mistreats Women* (New York, Jove, 1977) 292.

vaginal examination has in many circumstances acted to diminish and degrade the autonomy of women. But where there is repression there is resistance, and this discussion would not be complete without mention of its use as an act of liberation and reclaiming bodily autonomy. In this section of our chapter we focus on such examples.

> Carol said she had something really exciting to show us ... she pushed everything off the desk and took her pants off and climbed up on the desk and showed us the speculum and immediately demonstrated how she could, herself, insert this plastic vaginal speculum into her own vagina, and with the use of a flashlight, a simple flashlight, and a handmirror, she was able to see that portion of her body that had been inaccessible.[27]

This image of Carol Downer, pioneer of the vaginal self-examination, is still considered a revolutionary moment in the history of feminism.[28] First promoted by the Los Angeles Feminist Women's Health Centre in 1971, this self-examination provided women with the means to take control and reject male hegemony of the female body, be it through the system of patriarchy or the institution of medicine.[29] The speculum (in a woman's own hands, as opposed to in her doctor's) became in itself a tool for self-governance. Central to this act was the mantra that knowledge is power; only through knowledge of her own body could a woman take control of her genitals, sexuality, reproductive health and – by extension – take charge of her life.

Although not routine, the practice of self-insertion of the speculum during medical examination does exist. Reports can be found in the literature of individual clinicians encouraging self-insertion of the speculum by the patient, particularly in cases where patients expressed anxiety about the procedure or disclosed a prior negative experience. Dr Susan Bewley describes her surprise following an encounter with one such clinician: 'I was shocked by the strangeness of what I was seeing and the topsy-turvy relationship between doctor and patient'.[30] She goes on to question why this method is used in practice so rarely. Could the answer lie in an understanding of power dynamics and, as she posits, in the fact that 'doctors find it hard to give up control'?

One area in which the baton of power is increasingly being handed back to the patient is within the field of medical education. The use of expert 'patient tutors' has been encouraged amongst all specialties, and the field of obstetrics and gynaecology has been no exception. Gynaecology teaching associates are specially trained to instruct medical students how to discuss and perform vaginal

---

[27] L Rotham quoted in N Baehr, *Abortion without Apology: A Radical History for the 1990s* (Boston, South End Press, 1990) 22.

[28] S Morgan, *Into Our Own Hands: The Women's Health Movement in the United States, 1969–1990* (New Brunswick, Rutgers University Press, 2002).

[29] M Murphy, 'Immodest Witnessing: The Epistemology of the Vaginal Self-Examination in the US Feminist Self-Help Movement' (2004) 30 *Feminist Studies* 115.

[30] S Bewley, 'A Doctor who Changed my Practice: Putting Women in Control' (2000) 321(7274) *BMJ Clinical Research* 1454.

examination in a number of countries including the UK, Canada, the USA, Sweden and Australia.[31] Their introduction in medical education programmes was in part fuelled by controversies around conventional teaching methods for female genital examination and have been demonstrated to improve clinical performance of students.[32] Few studies have, however, sought to explore the women's experience of using their own bodes in teaching. What motivates them to volunteer in such programmes? And how, if at all, are they affected? These questions were posed to a small group of professional patients as part of a qualitative interview study in 2006.[33] Amongst their answers, the concept of 'redrawing private boundaries' emerged as a strong theme. One participant commented: 'it was a kind of a new situation, undergoing a gynaecological examination but not as a patient and not standing beside'. The transformative act of engaging in vaginal examination as an active partner, as opposed to passive bystander, contrasts starkly with historical methods of teaching.

VI. The Rise of 'Genital Liberation'

'Yes, ladies, David Matlock, aka Dr Sex, can "fix" you. Didn't know you needed to be fixed?'[34]

Does the key to protecting and respecting the bodily autonomy of women during vaginal examination then lie in enabling their role as active agent as opposed to passive subject? The contemporary example of female genital cosmetic surgery (FGCS) may aid in addressing this question. The term FGCS denotes any surgery to alter either the aesthetic or functional features of the female vulva but which is not medically indicated.[35] This includes a growing array of procedures, from vaginal tightening, to labial reduction, to G-spot amplification.

The field of FGCS has recently become a booming business in the Western world.[36] Although data on frequency is limited, a steep rise in demand amongst both private and public sectors has been noted.[37] It is likely that the popularity

---

[31] P Smith et al, 'The Effectiveness of Gynaecological Teaching Associates in Teaching Pelvic Examination: A Systematic Review and Meta-Analysis' (2015) 49 *Medical Education* 1197.

[32] V Jha et al, 'Patient Involvement in Teaching and Assessing Intimate Examination Skills: A Systematic Review' (2010) 44 *Medical Education* 347.

[33] K Siwe et al, '"A Stronger and Clearer Perception of Self": Women's Experience of being Professional Patients in Teaching the Pelvic Examination: A Qualitative Study' (2006) 113 *BJOG: An International Journal of Obstetrics and Gynaecology* 890.

[34] J Brinton, 'Dr Sex: The Plastic Surgeon Changing the Shape of "Down There"' (2008) *Style Magazine* issue 36–7.

[35] V Braun, 'Female Genital Cosmetic Surgery: A Critical Review of Current Knowledge and Contemporary Debates' (2010) 19 *Journal of Women's Health* 1393.

[36] V Braun and C Kitzinger, 'The Perfectible Vagina: Size Matters' (2001) 3 *Culture, Health & Sexuality* 263.

[37] See Braun (n 35). See also L Liao and S Creighton, 'Requests for Cosmetic Genitoplasty: How should Healthcare Providers Respond?' (2007) 334 *British Medical Journal* 1090.

will continue to increase, with predictions that FGCS will embark upon a similar upward trajectory to that taken by breast surgery.[38]

The theme of autonomy is evident in much of the language used by both FGCS providers and popular women's magazines to discuss a woman's desire for FGCS.[39] The rise of FGCS is often framed within a climate in which women are finally able to address their concerns and be open about their problems. The modern woman is able to consider the way she experiences her vulva and is allowed to have her own desires, standards, and expectations.

FGCS providers argue that they are responding to the needs of this new, modern woman, for whom a request for assistance from a gynaecologist is only natural if her experiences fall short of these self-imposed expectations. They set themselves apart from a traditional, paternalistic medical profession which has neglected the needs of women: 'Physicians have neglected aesthetic surgery of the female external genitalia … Because very few physicians are concerned with the appearance of the female external genitalia, many women seeking help are frustrated'.[40]

The autonomy of the woman is emphasised through stressing the absence of male influence or coercion in her decision making. The surgeons themselves insist that their patients are free from the pressure of their doctor's values and preferences. Dr Matlock of the Laser Vaginal Institute claims that 'the woman is the designer … the doctor is just the instrument'.[41] Similarly evident is the denial that patients undergoing FGCS may be doing so to please a partner.[42] A multi-centre study of FGCS asserted that:

> The male partner's role in FGCS decision making appears to be limited, or at least indirect … 'It does not bother him; he says he loves me as I am' is a typical comment. Requests for FGCS procedures appear not to be generated by male partners.[43]

Cases where women may be altering their vulvas to please a partner are met with disapproval or even cited as an exclusion criterion.[44]

Within this narrative, the experience of a woman presenting herself for vaginal examination and assessment by a gynaecologist could be viewed as the ultimate expression of 'genital liberation'.[45] It is reflective of a modern climate in which women can 'get out your hand mirrors', not only to get to know themselves, but to address any concerns they may have about their bodies.[46] Examination is a means

---

[38] V Braun, 'In Search of (Better) Sexual Pleasure: Female Genital "Cosmetic" Surgery' (2005) 8 *Sexualities* 407.

[39] V Braun, '"The Women are Doing it for Themselves": The Rhetoric of Choice and Agency Around Female Genital Cosmetic Surgery' (2009) 24(60) *Australian Feminist Studies* 233.

[40] G Alter, 'Female Genital Surgery' (2004) cited in E Krivenko, 'Rethinking Human Rights and Culture Through Female Genital Surgeries' (2015) 35 *Human Rights Quarterly* 107, 111.

[41] Quoted in Davis (n 11) 7.

[42] See Braun (n 35).

[43] M Goodman et al, 'A Large Multicenter Outcome Study of Female Genital Plastic Surgery' (2009) 7 *Journal of Sexual Medicine* 1565, 1574.

[44] See Davis (n 11).

[45] See Braun (n 35).

[46] L Kamps, 'Labia Envy' *Salon* (San Francisco, 17 March 1998).

of expressing these concerns and offers hope that their vulva can be constructed into a form that meets their own expectations. In all of these processes the narrative of the woman in control is emphasised; her actions are not shaped by her partner or her doctor, but are autonomous.

What such an account fails to consider, however, are the diffuse forces at play when a woman self-examines or presents for vaginal examination. Many commentators have argued that whilst the focus on aesthetics is new, FGCS is a re-emergence of medical perceptions of the vulva as problematic. Descriptions of pre-operative labia minora often invoke images of not only abnormal, but pathological anatomy. In their study of labiaplasty, Liao et al found that terms such as 'protruding', 'grossly enlarged', 'looks like spaniels' ears' and 'deformed' are often used to describe the labia minora of women seeking surgery.[47] Increasingly, the somewhat more proprietary medical term of 'labial hypertrophy' is applied to labia minora that extend beyond a certain length. One website explains:

> Labial hypertrophy, or protuberant overgrowth of labia minor tissue beyond the labia majora, is a common concern for many women of all ages … a patient with concerns about her anatomy can rest assured that there is a simple surgical solution. Labiaplasty using the V-wedge technique can be done safely in an outpatient setting.[48]

Where there may have been any room for doubt about the normality or abnormality of a woman's labia minora, the use of the medical term 'labial hypertrophy' legitimates concerns about the length of a woman's labia minora, providing an apparent medical warrant for surgery.[49]

What length is too long? Even amongst FGCS providers there is no clear consensus.[50] The cut-off is to some extent, in itself, irrelevant. Regardless of the numerical value, within this context vaginal examination is required as a tool to classify normality versus pathology. It is important to note that examination by a medical professional is not necessary for the concept of illness and dysfunction to be introduced. Self-examination has its own role to play. Consider the following quote from the Vagina Institute, which positions itself as an online 'encyclopaedia' of vulvas:

> We have properly catalogued photographs with sub information of what makes a certain vagina look good or bad. What is normal and what is abnormal? What is perfect and what is a deformity? Within this section of the site you can visually compare yourself and determine your level of femininity with that of other women. Please note this section of the website is highly graphic, containing all sorts of varieties of female genital variations, from pretty vulvas to ugly vulvas.[51]

---

[47] L Liao et al, 'Labial Surgery for Well Women: A Review of the Literature' (2011) 117 *An International Journal of Obstetrics and Gynaecology* 20.

[48] R Karamanoukian et al, 'Outpatient Labiaplasty for Correction of Labia Minora Hypertrophy' at www.the-dermatologist.com/content/outpatient-labiaplasty-correction-labia-minora-hypertrophy.

[49] V Braun and L Tiefer, 'The "Designer Vagina" and the Pathologisation of Female Genital Diversity: Interventions for Change' (2010) 8 *Radical Psychology*.

[50] See Braun (n 35).

[51] Vagina Institute, *The Visual Vagina* (2010) at www.vaginainstitute.com/Photos/photos.html.

The above quote invites women not just to examine themselves, but to judge oneself with a critical eye.[52] This is performed within a social context of normality versus abnormality, beauty versus disgust, and wellness versus pathology.

For women who are unsure where they fit within this dichotomy, genital inspection by a medical professional may be the next step. Encounters between women and their doctors have the potential to reinforce or challenge their self-image, regardless of its origin. As discussed previously, FGCS providers purport to exclude themselves entirely from the decision-making process, emphasising the woman's control. However, medical professionals do not work within a vacuum; they develop their perceptions of vulvas in the same social and cultural contexts as others. When Davis received a free consultation for labiaplasty, her doctor explained that 'the ideal look for labia minora was not only minimal and unextended but also symmetrical, "homogenously pink" and "not wavy"'.[53] Dr Matlock described the Playboy model as 'the ideal woman per se' noting that 'you don't see women in there with excessively long labia minora'.[54] Several videos can be found on YouTube of surgeons ending their procedures with the comment: 'She is like a 16-year-old now'.[55] This reiteration of the pre-pubescent look is concerning, as it is not based on medical parameters but reinforces a societal ideal. Bringing their own values to the vaginal examination can in fact play a role in a woman's decision-making process, aptly highlighted by one magazine's description of Dr Matlock as the 'Picasso of vaginas'.[56] Liao and Creighton note that lack of immediate reassurance from doctors following vaginal examination may be interpreted by women as proof of the abnormality.[57] Actively reinforcing perceptions of what is the 'ideal' vulva and what is not, is likely to have an even more significant effect. Women who already perceive their vulvas to be abnormal may be further swayed by authoritative opinion following examination.

Contrasting current day FGCS with the Western history of gynaecological examinations and procedures on women provides some interesting parallels. In the past, these were practised upon women (often without their consent or even knowledge) when men disapproved of their actions.[58] These acts served far beyond their role as simple clinical tools, but instead were a form of social control, of enforcing patriarchy upon woman, and rendering 'women more docile'.[59] Today, many writers argue that FGCS continues to be a form of social control, of power exerted upon women to create 'docile bodies'.[60] This form of disciplinary power is peculiarly modern; no one physically forces a woman to self-present for

---

[52] See Davis (n 11).

[53] ibid 15.

[54] Quoted in Davis (n 11) 7.

[55] T Spivak, 'In the Pink' *Houston Press* (Houston, 11 May 2006) at www.houstonpress.com/2006-05-11/news/in-the-pink.

[56] S Breslin, 'Designer Vaginas', *Harper's Bazaar* (New York, November 1998) issue 130.

[57] See Liao and Creighton (n 37).

[58] See Green (n 20).

[59] H Lightfoot-Klein, *Secret Wounds* (Bloomington, First Books, 2002) 28.

[60] See Green (n 20).

examination or surgery, and perhaps with the exception of hymenoplasty, it does not rely upon real violent and public sanctions.[61] Those exerting the control are diffuse and anonymous, enforcing the standard of the imagined Other. Because of this diffusion and anonymity, FGCS – like all cosmetic surgery – is immersed in a language of choice, liberation and self-expression. However, many believe that it is a woman's obligation to conform to standards of beauty and to a femininity defined as submissive. A woman's desire to surgically alter her vulva then becomes a form of obedience to the requirements of society. Braun and Kitzinger describe FGCS as evidence that disciplinary power now extends to hidden aspects of the body.[62] Whilst the acknowledgment of a patient's concerns may be liberating for the individual, the very act of requesting genital examination and assessment for aesthetic concerns marks, to some, the 'degrading depths of women's oppression' – a modern form of internalised oppression.[63]

VII. Conclusion

Although the speculum, in its evolving forms, has existed as a medical device since ancient times, it was not until the mid-nineteenth century that its use became more routine amongst Western physicians. Its increase in popularity was met with a strong backlash within the medical profession, who raised concerns about 'this most dangerous instrument' and its potential in 'the dulling of the edge of the virgin modesty, and the degradation of the pure minds of [our] daughters.'[64] As predicted the speculum, alongside all forms of genital examination, has indeed posed a threat to women's bodies, although not for the reasons they anticipated. The genitals are cultural terrain upon which the personal meets the political, social battles are fought and lost, and the boundaries of power are drawn and reclaimed. The practice of female genital examination has played a central part in this story, acting as a key method by which autonomy has been both eroded and restored. More research into the contemporary lived experiences of women, and in particular Black women, undergoing genital examination is essential. An awareness of these narratives past and present is critical to understanding the persistence of threats to patient autonomy, and to tip the balance of power in women's favour.

---

[61] SL Bartky, 'Foucault, Femininity, and the Modernization of Patriarchal Power' in R Weitz (ed) *The Politics of Women's Bodies* (Oxford, Oxford University Press, 2003) 43.

[62] See Braun and Kitzinger (n 36).

[63] See Davis (n 11) 22.

[64] R Lee, 'On the Use of the Speculum in the Diagnosis and Treatment of Uterine Diseases' (with discussion) (1850) 2 *The Lancet* 701; M Hall, 'On a New and Lamentable Form of Hysteria' (1850) 1 *The Lancet* 660.

5

When a Uterus Enters the Room, Reason Goes out the Window

STELLA VILLARMEA*

'Gender-politics don't undo the formal appeal of the fairy tale, though they do mean you have to take a longer detour through cultural history to arrive at lightness'.[1]

I. Introduction

In this chapter I address three questions. First, why is it important to talk about vaginal examinations without consent during labour? Second, what are the barriers to asking and giving consent to vaginal examinations during labour? Third, what can we do to stop vaginal examinations without consent during labour?

The philosophical analysis of the history that precedes us adds an illuminating dimension that explains why it is important to deal with unauthorised vaginal examinations during labour: because pregnant women should not so *obviously* be deprived of their full capacity; because pregnant subjects are still fully entitled subjects; and because women ought not to lose their citizenship just because they enter the maternity ward. My conceptual discussion on the barriers that hinder consent looks at the hidden patriarchal premises which, aloof to all real changes in paradigms and praxes, still permeate certain aspects of contemporary obstetrics and midwifery. It takes as its subject matter the philosophical reconstruction of one component of the thesis of the naturalisation of female rationality being that which associates the working of the brain in women to the working of the

* This contribution was generously supported by the following projects: *Controversies in Childbirth: from Epistemology to Practices (VOICEs)*, EC Marie Skłodowska-Curie Individual Fellowship Research Project, University of Oxford, EC-H2020-MSCA-IF-2017 (SEP-210456162), and *Philosophy of Birth: Rethinking the Origin from Medical Humanities (PHILBIRTH)*, Program for Research, Development and Innovation Oriented to Societal Challenges, Ministry of Economy in Spain/AEI/FEDER/UE, University of Alcalá (FFI2016-77755-R). I would like to thank Camilla Pickles, Claire Murray, Rosana Triviño, Francisca Fernández Guillén and Ibone Olza for their valuable comments on earlier drafts.

[1] L Sage, *Moments of Truth* (London, Fourth State, 2001) 227.

uterus or womb. The discussion also considers the persistence of a series of age-old commonplaces that still beset contemporary obstetrics and midwifery.

This chapter explores some of the associations between the use of the brain and the functioning of the uterus that have been in place over the centuries. This association has become so deeply engrained that it seems to be part of our contemporary conceptual furniture. In the face of emerging new medical practice, it remains a desire to hold onto old ways and ideas. However, it is critical that we talk more about what needs to change in relation to our understanding of consent in order to make consent meaningful for pregnant women in labour. At risk here is nothing less than our view on woman's rationality and citizenship.

II. Why is it Important to Talk about Vaginal Examinations without Consent During Labour?

The first and direct answer is, because those interventions are harmful and unlawful. The second and invisible answer is, because unauthorised vaginal examinations tell us something important about women's citizenship, ie women are not *listened to* by others in general, and especially during labour. Both answers are related. After all, the reason why the law even says these types of examinations are worthy of regulation – why the law is there in the first place – is because it is widely accepted in law and practice that women cannot be subjected to medical procedures without their consent. Women are autonomous human beings, and human beings have the right to have their autonomy protected.

A. Unauthorised Interventions Contravene the Law and Other Systems of Regulation

The first reason why we should concentrate on vaginal examinations without consent during labour is because it is against the law to do to a patient/user what she does not allow to be done to herself. This is a core principle of medical law: an adult with capacity has an absolute right to consent to or to refuse medical treatment. This position stands even if the decision will lead to the death of the patient/user of health services.

Respect for autonomy and the central role of women during childbirth as the decision-makers are the rights enjoyed by all users of health services in general. The UNESCO Universal Declaration on Bioethics and Human Rights protects the principle of autonomy.[2] The European Convention on Human Rights and

---

[2] Universal Declaration on Bioethics and Human Rights (adopted 19 October 2005, General Conference of UNESCO) SHS/EST/BIO/06/1.

Biomedicine: Convention for the Protection of Human Rights and Dignity of the Human Being with regard to the Application of Biology and Medicine recognises basic rights of health service users.[3] The following rights are recognised in it: the right to receive truthful information about the nature, indications, risks, consequences and alternatives to proposed diagnostic or therapeutic procedures; the right to respect for dignity and privacy; the right to choose freely between the various existing alternatives and to have those decisions respected; the right to be asked for consent before undertaking any operation; and the right not to be included in teaching or research projects without consent.

Users' autonomy in the context of midwifery and obstetrics is also promoted by the World Health Organization (WHO). In 1985, a meeting of the WHO European region, the regional office of the Americas, together with the Pan American Health Organization in Fortaleza, Brazil, made a number of recommendations, recorded in The Fortaleza Declaration.[4] As its first premise it declares:

> Every woman has a fundamental right to receive proper prenatal care; that every woman has a central role to play in all aspects of this care, including participation in the planning, carrying out, and evaluation of the care; and that social, emotional, and psychological factors are decisive in the understanding and implementation of proper prenatal care.

Although most of the Fortaleza Declaration recommendations are of a medical-clinical nature, its general framework is of a moral, psychological, social, and legal nature.[5] The basis of this framework is that, for the WHO, respect for the woman's autonomy and central role is a key indicator when evaluating the standard of childbirth care. The Fortaleza Declaration's claim that a woman has 'a central role to play in all aspects' of perinatal care is much more than a simple request for courteous and kind treatment by health professionals. It also implies that she must be given information, that she should be able to choose between the different options available, make decisions and exercise her right to have those decisions respected. Asserting the woman's claim to 'a central role' means, in short, that the only motive for any medical intervention should be the protection of the health of a woman and her baby.[6]

The position taken at an international level is not controversial and many countries' laws are aligned thereto. For instance, in the UK there are classic cases

---

[3] Convention on Human Rights and Biomedicine: Convention for the Protection of Human Rights and Dignity of the Human Being with regard to the Application of Biology and Medicine (adopted 4 April 1997, entered into force 1 December 1999, Council of Europe).

[4] The Fortaleza Declaration published in World Health Organization, 'Appropriate Technology for Birth' (1985) 2 *The Lancet* 436.

[5] For instance, it focuses on avoiding the routine use of oxytocin or the routine performance of episiotomies.

[6] Of course, the interpretation and use of 'health' is part of the debated issue, in the sense that 'health' tends to be defined by healthcare professionals, thus leaving little room for women to play a role. What should we do in the case when a woman refuses but the intervention is framed as needed for her or the baby's health? Whether or not a woman can define or interpret what she means by 'health' is at the core of the controversies in childbirth.

that support the position that no one can be forced to undergo medical interventions. For instance, *Re MB* reiterates that pregnancy does not affect a woman's capacity to make decisions.[7] A woman could 'for religious reasons, other reasons, for rational or irrational reasons or for no reason at all, choose not to have medical intervention, even though ... the consequence may be the death or serious handicap of the child she bears, or her own death.[8] Also, *St George's Healthcare NHS Trust v S* confirmed

> that, although pregnancy increased the personal responsibilities of a woman, it did not diminish her entitlement to decide whether to undergo medical treatment; that [foetal] need for medical assistance did not prevail over her right not to be forced to submit to an invasion of her body against her will, whether her own life or that of her unborn child depend on it, and that right was not reduced or diminished merely because her decision to exercise it might appear morally repugnant.[9]

To acknowledge mothers' autonomy is to assume the rights of women to life, health, bodily integrity and freedom from discrimination, ie to respect their dignity, equal status and human rights.

The importance of autonomy, consent and good communication in maternal healthcare decision-making has been confirmed by *Montgomery v Lanarkshire Health Board*.[10] *Montgomery* has become the leading case about women's right to make decisions regarding their care during childbirth. Particularly significant are Lady Hale's words: '[g]one are the days when it was thought that, on becoming pregnant, a woman lost, not only her capacity, but also her right to act as a genuinely autonomous human being.[11] *Montgomery* has normalised the pregnant subject as a fully entitled subject.

The UK legal landscape is more complex than I can convey here, but, as Claire Murray develops in Chapter 11,

> it is well-established that informed consent is the principal mechanism through which autonomy is protected in the healthcare context and this legal principle is reflected in professional and clinical guidance, including those related to the provision of maternity care.[12]

This same framework is reflected in the NICE Clinical Guideline on 'Intrapartum Care for Healthy Women and Babies'.[13] It states the conditions under vaginal examinations are to be offered and it confirms that women's consent must be obtained.

---

[7] *Re MB (Caesarean Section)* [1997] EWCA Civ 1361.

[8] ibid [30].

[9] *St George's Healthcare NHS Trust v S* [1998] 3 WLR 936 (CA) 937.

[10] *Montgomery v Lanarkshire Health Board* [2015] UKSC 11.

[11] ibid [116].

[12] See Chapter 11, Claire Murray, 'Troubling Consent: Pain and Pressure in Labour and Childbirth', text at note 2. Murray also cites Royal College of Obstetricians and Gynaecologists, *Obtaining Valid Consent: Clinical Governance Advice No 6* (2015) and Royal College of Midwives, *Evidence Based Guidelines for Midwifery-Led Care in Labour: Assessing Progress in Labour* (2012).

[13] National Institute for Health and Care Excellence (NICE), *Intrapartum Care: Care of Healthy Women and Their Babies during Childbirth: Clinical Guideline 190* (London, NICE, 2014) [1.4.5].

Montgomery, the European Convention on Human Rights and Biomedicine, the Fortaleza Declaration, and the UNESCO Universal Declaration on Bioethics and Human Rights are just some examples of the regulatory landscape that warrants the protection and promotion of patient autonomy and they make no distinction based upon gender or the particularities of childbirth. If, according to the laws discussed above, the user's consent is needed, then a pregnant woman's refusal to submit to a vaginal examination during labour should also be included. No intervention should be performed upon her body without her consent. To ignore her refusal is to act contrary to the law.

Despite this very clear landscape, many labouring women are unable to say 'no' to a vaginal examination and the law does not seem to have a place in practice. Some women experience unwanted vaginal examinations during labour and many more are not even asked for their consent.[14] Although formally protected in law and clinical guidance, women's voices are still too often not listened to in the maternity ward, and their autonomy during labour is frequently not respected. Their condition of citizenship counts formally, but not materially. It is acknowledged in this chapter that respect for autonomy is not considered a central principle in the lived context of birth-rooms. With an astonishing frequency, a woman's refusal to be subjected to an intervention such as a vaginal examination is not taken seriously there. Too often in those situations her words do not count, they are not listened to, or her input is not even asked for. To understand why this happens requires unveiling a first layer of meaning: mothers' autonomy is closely linked to women's rights.[15]

B. Unauthorised Interventions Tell Us Something Important about Women's Citizenship

Let us ask again, why (and how) is it so easy for a woman who enters the delivery room to speak without being heard? Why does it take so much for healthcare professionals to behave appropriately to a pregnant woman's 'no'? Here, I contend, a second layer of meaning is uncovered.

True, it is difficult to recognise women's voices in many dimensions of their citizenship and this phenomenon has been exposed and analysed in a never-ending stream of feminist essays. Examples of places and times of women being ignored can be found, without much effort, as much in history as today. For a direct, powerful and recent approach, one can read Mary Beard's '*Women & Power: A Manifesto*'.[16] Her book covers the fluidity of women's social status since the times

---

[14] See the case studies in Chapter 2, by R Brione, 'Non-Consented Vaginal Examinations: The Birthrights and AIMS Perspective'.

[15] For more on implied consent see Chapter 10, by Jonathan Herring, 'Implied Consent and Vaginal Examination in Pregnancy'.

[16] M Beard, *Women & Power: A Manifesto* (London, Profile Books, 2017).

when Penelope was silenced by her son in Homer's 'Odyssey' to the present day, when harassment on social media platforms targets mainly women's participation. As the #*MeToo* movement against sexual harassment and assault has demonstrated to everyone, saying 'no' is particularly difficult in sexual contexts. One representation of the romantic courtship ritual is where the woman hides her sexual desire or appears to say 'no' when she actually means yes, and this representation is still widely and deeply influential in our environment.[17] The slippery slope between courtship and rape can depend on whether or not one follows (and can or wants to follow or can and wants not to follow) such pattern of behaviour and interpretation of behaviour. Beyond the sphere of sexuality, the fact that women have more difficulties than men in expressing their 'no' in all kinds of social interactions – eg the workplace – or in uttering their 'no' without receiving extra punishment in return, is a pressing contemporary topic, still to be dealt with on many levels.

Yes, it is an historical fact that women have spoken without being heard, that women's words did not count, and that women's wishes or utterances about their wishes would not count. Yes, these issues have been repeated through history. The vote is just one example of how long it took for women to speak and be heard, and there are countless more examples. However, we are here to analyse the issue of vaginal examinations without consent during labour, a particular civil instance where women's voices are still not readily heard. On the face of it, one could argue that women's birth room experiences of not being taken seriously when speaking are just more instances of a general cultural pattern – a pattern that is visible in so many other dimensions of their citizenship. And yet, in the particular scenario of childbirth, it seems even more difficult for women to say 'no', to exercise their autonomy and claim their citizenship.[18]

In this chapter, I will explore this deeper issue, specifically focusing on why we so frequently fail to listen to women who say 'no' *in the birth room*. In my account, the core aspect about this 'why' is better revealed if we bear in mind how *easy* it is for the medical institution to not listen to what women are saying, when the women who are saying 'no' are *in labour*. Thus, to better understand unauthorised vaginal examinations during labour, we need to expose a third layer of covered meaning, one that displays the conceptual meaning remaining underneath the constraints of law and historical or cultural patterns.

---

[17] For a discussion of this, see for example J Elvin, 'Rape: A History from 1860 to the Present' (2009) 21 *Current Issues in Criminal Justice* 337.

[18] On my conception of autonomy and citizenship, see S Villarmea, 'Razón y Útero: El Debate Ilustrado y la Obstetricia Contemporánea' [Reason and Uterus: The Enlightenment Debate and Contemporary Obstetrics] in J Borrego and C Barroso (eds), *Mujer, cerebro y salud* (Madrid, Síntesis, 2018); S Villarmea, 'Rethinking the Origin: Birth and Human Value' in J Yan and D Schrader (eds), *Creating a Global Dialogue on Value Inquiry* (Lewiston, Edwin Mellen Press, 2009); S Villarmea and F Fernández Guillén, 'Sujetos de Pleno Derecho: El Nacimiento como Tema Filosófico' [Fully Entitled Subjects: Birth as a Philosophical Topic] in E Pérez Sedeño and R Ibáñez (eds), *Cuerpos y Diferencias* (Madrid, Plaza y Valdés, 2012).

C. Unauthorised Vaginal Examinations Challenge Women's Capacity During Labour

In what follows, I would like to explore a hypothesis of interpretation that could help reveal the third layer of meaning mentioned above. The hypothesis states that even if we don't say it out loud and clearly, we do not listen to women's statements during labour because we take them to obviously lack 'full capacity'. And why do they *obviously* lack full capacity? Well, here the answer is also not openly provided but it points to the following: women's lack of capacity during labour is presented as a de facto consequence of the pain and fear associated with contractions. Women are deemed to be in an altered state of body and consciousness and this altered state is taken to affect their capacity too deeply to retain and recall information and balance it when taking a decision. Hence, what women say is taken to not necessarily convey what they mean, or what they need, or what is good for them and their babies. In short, women who are subject to the 'uterine influence' during labour *do not* reason well.

Since we take it as *obvious* that they are not fully capacitated, we normalise such judgement, and this normalisation encourages us to ignore what women say, and works to deny women the space and time to say what they need to say. The philosophical analysis I would like to conduct here focuses on this key aspect: that they *obviously* lack capacity. I think there is much to be gained from noting, and then challenging, the apparent lack of capacity of women in labour, due to their being subject to the uterine influence.[19]

To analyse this issue, I reflect on the conceptual relationship between the notions of reason and uterus in the history of Western thought, from a philosophical perspective. To understand how certain obstetric and midwifery procedures have survived and how these are directly related to the endurance of a particular view of pregnant women, I aim to untie a critical conceptual knot in the history of patriarchy with a particular focus on the link between the uterus and reason at the dawn of obstetrics, during the Enlightenment.

I argue that it is necessary to reconstruct the history of the naturalisation of female rationality in order to understand what is going on in the context of unauthorised vaginal examinations during labour and in other abusive and violent perinatal practices. The philosophical analysis of the conceptual history that precedes us helps to explain what happens in the maternity ward, and why.[20]

---

[19] I have examined this conceptual knot in Stella Villarmea, 'Reasoning from the Uterus: Casanova, Women's Agency and Philosophy of Birth' *Hypatia, A Journal of Feminist Philosophy*, forthcoming.

[20] Although my philosophical analysis is based on a conceptual revision of the history of ideas – hence it does not need nor use the methodology of meta-analysis or systematic reviews, not even the methods that lead empirical or case studies – it might be worth citing two poignant and paradigmatic examples of this normalisation. The first is a case that came from the Namibian Supreme Court concerning the involuntary sterilisation of HIV positive women during their Caesarean section childbirths, *Government of the Republic of Namibia* v LM [2014] NASC 19. The Supreme Court approaches women's decision-making during childbirth in extremely problematic ways and the expert witness, an obstetrician, offers evidence that is sexist and which appears to lack any meaningful understanding of women in general. See C Pickles, 'Sounding the Alarm: Government of The Republic of Namibia v LM

III. A Hypothesis: 'It is the Uterine Influence, Stupid!'

The Enlightenment was a key moment in the construction of the relationship between the 'female' body and reason, for it set in motion the chain of associations which would be crucial to later conceptual developments which are, I contend, still in place today.[21]

Under the paradigm of the New Science, eighteenth-century medicine was particularly interested in the relationship between the body's constitution and human capacities. According to Cinta Canterla, the empirical approach to physiology of the new enlightened medicine gave new strength to old theories about sexual difference.[22] These theories were old, but they were given the new gloss of scientific discoveries related to health. The sexism of this new science and medicine lay hidden beneath the welter of data, procedures and studies leading to conclusions which, though in many respects undoubtedly new, were also hamstrung by fixed, preconceived ideas and prejudices regarding everything that had anything to do with a comparison between the sexes. It became common once again to believe that natural bodily differences had irrevocable consequences on behaviour and capacities, which not only could not be changed but should actually be preserved. In short, the medicine of the period became a powerful source of legitimacy for sexual inequality.

This approach meant that misogynistic theories relating the female sexual configuration and procreative function to the supposedly inferior mental capacities of women were given a new lease of life. Time and again, enlightened medical treatises regard the uterus as the organ responsible for female bodily decadence and the female tendency towards nymphomania and 'uterine frenzy'. These views, which enjoyed the credibility and authority conferred by medical science, would be accepted by enlightened thinkers to add respectability to their proposals that women should be educated in modesty and subjected to external supervision (from the father in the first instance, and then the husband).[23] And this in turn fed back into the prejudices and practices of the physicians.[24]

and Women's Rights during Childbirth in South Africa' (2018) 21 *Potchefstroom Electronic Law Journal* 1. The second example is Mariam's story. Her story emerges from the 2015 Greek refugee crisis and it exposes extreme forms of obstetric violence perpetrated against refugee women in Greece. Included in her ordeal is a forced Caesarean section procedure, a post-partum episiotomy, and general denial of care. The procedures she was subjected to were all performed without medical indication or informed consent. For more, see I Olza et al, 'Mariam's Birth Story: Obstetric Violence against Refugee Women in Greece' (10 May 2016) at www.elpartoesnuestro.es/blog/2016/05/10/mariams-birth-story-obstetric-violence-against-refugee-women-greece. The disparity of these two scenarios is intended to emphasise common standpoints as to the interpretation of women's capacity during labour.

[21] Villarmea (2018) (n 18).

[22] C Canterla, *Mala Noche: el Cuerpo, la Política y la Irracionalidad en el Siglo XVIII* [Bad Night: Body, Politics and Irrationality in the XVIIIth Century] (Seville, Fundación José Manuel Lara, 2009). I draw from her work in this section.

[23] A most paradigmatic and influential example of the ideological connection between the uterine constitution, rational disability and education towards submission can be found in J-J Rousseau, *Emile or Treatise on Education* (Mineola, Dover Publications, 2013). Chapter 5 is devoted to the education of Sophie, Emile's future wife.

[24] G Casanova, *Lana Caprina, Une Controverse Médicale sur 'L'utérus Pensant'* à *l'Université de Bologne en 1771–1772*, P Mengal (ed), R Poma (trans) (Paris, Honoré Champion, 1999).

The defence of the pernicious influence of the womb on the rational capacities of women had one consequence that was even more blatant: their uteruses made women sink into chaos and nervous breakdowns. Irrationality, sensitivity, emotionality, volubility, or imaginative disorder, peculiar to and extreme in women, were the result of, and could be explained by, the fact that only they had a womb. This buttressed the relationship between uterus and madness which is present in the etymology of 'hysteria' and has been so exploited in the history of medicine and psychology.[25] Once again, we see how in the case of women, *and only in their case*, sexuality and reproductive function are what account for cognitive capacity and mental state or health.

This insistence that women are chronically ill and in thrall to their reproductive function goes hand in hand with the emphasis on the female body as source of irrationality. Thanks to their ability to become pregnant and therefore to submit themselves to organic processes, women were soon classified as bodies incapable of complete self-control, which was the paradigm of rationality. It would be of no use to argue that a woman in labour could well be interpreted as a supreme paradigm of self-control – not so much in the sense in which 'self-control' is identified with being able to display a modest or contained behaviour but in the sense in which it is related to enduring pain and going through the pushes, for example. But this kind of interpretation of self-control was far beyond the usual approach. As a result, the processes of pregnancy and childbirth were associated with the inability to control the body and became another pillar supporting arguments for their irrationality.

On the spectrum from animal to human, the pregnant or labouring woman was especially positioned near the former and well away from the latter. The truth is that the relationship between women and full capacity has been tainted since the eighteenth century by discourses of disparagement and incapacity which go far beyond empirical data. Patriarchal prejudices pervaded the study of pregnancy, childbirth and breastfeeding to such an extent that these states and experiences were made akin to irrationality or mental disorders.

With the increase during the eighteenth century in the number of medical men interested in midwifery, the suitability for reproduction of the female body was cast into doubt. The 'new methods of scientific investigation into the human body (and the scientific "proof" of female inferiority) brought new insights that seemed to root the woman more firmly in ... maternity, and her body was best understood and managed by the male authorities around her'.[26] The attitudes towards childbirth displayed in the male-authored medical texts differed from earlier midwifery texts. The female body came to be seen as something to be examined and penetrated

---

[25] H Meek, 'Motherhood, Hysteria and the Eighteenth-Century Woman Writer' in R Stephanson and D Wagner (eds), *The Secrets of Generation, Reproduction in the Long Eighteenth Century* (Toronto, University of Toronto, 2015).

[26] J Peakman and S Watkins, 'Making Babies: Eighteenth-Century Attitudes towards Conception, Reproduction and Childbirth' in Stephanson and Wagner (n 24) 459. I follow their work closely in this section.

by male midwives. An example of this scrutiny is the discussion about problems caused by obstructions in the vagina or the existence of a hymen. This can be seen in William Smellie's detailed explanation of an examination of a young married woman. The oft-called 'father of British midwifery and obstetrics' describes his giving access to a female body:

> I then directed her to lean forwards on the back of a chair, and seating myself behind, attempted to examine the uterus by the vagina, when I found the entrance obstructed. Through the persuasion of her mother she consented to have the parts inspected; and being laid supine upon a coach, I separated the labia, when I perceived the hymen ... effectually obstructing the introduction of the penis. Having snipped this attachment asunder, I introduced my finger into the vagina.[27]

The professional struggle between male and female midwives reflected different attitudes towards what constituted appropriate insertions or pain. Midwifery texts written by women counter-argued the nature of what constituted appropriate insertions. In Margaret Stephen's estimation, 'manually stretching the vagina, inserting the hand and putting the fingers into the cervix were all painful procedures, and only those who had gone through childbirth could say, what it would be to have this practised upon themselves'.[28] Her judgment makes the pivotal shift that is needed to address the topic of vaginal examination during labour with sense, ie the move from the observer's to the subject's standpoint.

The thesis of the clash between nature and culture enjoyed the support of enlightenment medicine and philosophy when arguing that the female condition was deficient, weak and sick because it was controlled by its reproductive function. We should pause to ponder whether this idea – that the female condition is deficient, weak and sick because it is controlled by its reproductive function – is still current in obstetrics today. We should investigate carefully whether it is one of the reasons why pregnant women are still not *listened to* when they reject being vaginally examined during labour. The recent reports on disrespect and abuse by international health institutions have put onto the agenda how practitioners and childbirth facilities infringe basic legal parameters and health-care guidelines:[29]

> Many women experience disrespectful and abusive treatment during childbirth in facilities worldwide. Such treatment not only violates the rights of women to respectful care, but can also threaten their rights to life, health, bodily integrity, and freedom from discrimination. This statement calls for greater action, dialogue, research and advocacy on this important public health and human rights issue.[30]

---

[27] W Smellie, *A Treatise on the Theory and Practice of Midwifery*, vol 3 (London, Alexander Cleugh and M Watson, 1790) 173, cited in Watkins and Peakman (n 25) 462.

[28] M Stephen, *Domestic Midwife: Or, the Best Means of Preventing Danger in Child-Birth Considered* (London, S W Fores, 1795) 37, cited in Watkins and Peakman (n 25) 465.

[29] M Bohren et al, 'The Mistreatment of Women during Childbirth in Health Facilities Globally: A Mixed-Methods Systematic Review' (2015) 12(6) *PLoS Medicine* p.e1001847.

[30] World Health Organization, *The Prevention and Elimination of Disrespect and Abuse During Facility-based Childbirth: WHO Statement* (Geneva, World Health Organization, 2014).

The data have been addressed by specific laws on obstetric violence in some countries, as well as by the recent UN report and Council of Europe resolution.[31] For those who are familiar with women's history and the feminist ideas that help illuminate it, there are too many covertly active associations to be revealed in the discourses and practices one hears of – or experiences – today around childbirth.

IV. A Counterhypothesis: 'It is the Content, Stupid!'

One might not be convinced at all by my posing such a hypothesis as an effective way to tackle vaginal examinations without consent during labour. One could insist instead upon a different and frequent explanation: the reason why such interventions are performed is connected to the image of a pregnant woman as a container and the baby as its content. Here, what is valuable is the content, the baby. Hence, the baby matters; the mother does not. From this perspective, saying that the reason why the mother does not count is because she is (considered to be) affected (or alienated) by her uterus would miss the point. The point would be that women in labour do not matter; a healthy baby is what matters. The baby needs to come out of a container and the container (the mother's body) is perceived to be an eventual danger to the baby. From this perspective, the focus on the content would be the direct reason to treat the mother's body as a container.

My answer to this criticism has three elements: First, I agree that the use of the 'container-content' metaphor to describe the relationship between the pregnant woman and her baby is influential and permeates much of childbirth practice. Second, I agree that it is an inappropriate metaphor because it does not properly describe what the relationship is.[32] Third, however, I think that the use of such metaphor is precisely what needs to be examined. For we usually stop there: we say that the metaphor fails, that it does not properly describe what is going on. And, we do not move beyond its use and establish where the metaphor comes from.

---

[31] Venezuela, Argentina and Puerto Rico have recognised 'obstetric violence' as a legal term. Venezuelan law defines obstetric violence as: 'the appropriation of the body and reproductive processes of women by health personnel, which is expressed as dehumanized treatment, an abuse of medication, and to convert the natural processes into pathological ones, bringing with it loss of autonomy and the ability to decide freely about their bodies and sexuality, negatively impacting the quality of life of women', *Ley Orgánica sobre el Derecho de las Mujeres a una Vida Libre de Violencia* [Organic Law on the Right of Women to a Life Free of Violence] 2007 15. See further, R D'Gregorio, 'Obstetric Violence: A New Legal Term Introduced in Venezuela' (2010) 111 *International Journal of Gynaecology and Obstetrics* 201; M Sadler et al, 'Moving Beyond Disrespect and Abuse: Addressing the Structural Dimensions of Obstetric Violence' (2016) 24(47) *Reproductive Health Matters* 47; United Nations General Assembly, 'Report of the Special Rapporteur on Violence Against Women, its Causes and Consequences on a Human Rights-Based Approach to Mistreatment and Violence Against Women in Reproductive Health Services with a Focus on Childbirth and Obstetric Violence', UN Doc A/74/137 (2019); Council of Europe Parliamentary Assembly, 'Obstetrical and Gynaecological Violence' Resolution 2306 (2019).

[32] I cannot engage in a metaphysics of pregnancy in detail here. For more on the metaphysical relationship between the foetus/embryo and the pregnant organism, see E Kingma, 'Lady Parts: The Metaphysics of Pregnancy' (2018) 82 *Journal of the Royal Institute of Philosophy Supplement* 165.

But how did we get here? How did we end up with a 'container and its content' when we start with a subject? The genealogy of such metaphor is what needs to be explored.

And here is my *intuition* – a word that does not appear frequently in philosophical or academic essays but that I would want to justifiably use here – the move from a subject to a container concerns the deletion/removal/vanishing of that constitutive part of subjectivity that is reason. For, once we deprive a subject of her rationality (full capacity), it is easy to slide into treating it as an object – in this case, as a container.

I argue that the process of objectification occurs in the following order: we first deprive women of their rationality (full capacity), and then we are left with a container. If this is correct, the genealogy of the container-content metaphor takes us, once again, back to the basic issue of the relationship between a woman's use of her uterus and the use of reason. Concerning the foetal-container argument, my counter-argument is, in brief, that being treated as a foetal container is a consequence or result of not being considered worthy of being listened to.

Given the above, the metaphor of the container and its content in itself does not explain anything. We must ask a much deeper question: we must ask 'why'.[33]

V. A Second Counterhypothesis: 'It's the Pain, Stupid!'

When addressing vaginal examinations without consent during labour, one is confronted with another key issue: the vulnerability of the woman. Ultimately, what is really unique about obstetrics and midwifery is that the woman is conscious, sentient, yet in pain or experiencing high levels of anxiety. Does this vulnerability affect the consent process? And if so, how?

In simple and logical terms, there are three possible answers: (1) vulnerability should not affect consent, ie consent has to be asked for and has to be given; (2) vulnerability affects consent, ie consent cannot be properly asked for, nor given; and (3) vulnerability can affect consent, ie consent has to be asked for but it can or cannot be given – in the sense that a woman is in a position to give or refuse.

Given these three logical possibilities, the counterhypothesis that I explore in this section is in line with either (2) or (3). Its supporters would say something akin to the following: when a labouring woman is in so much pain or when she is experiencing an increased level of anxiety, she lacks full capacity and is therefore unable to consider whether or not to give her consent.

One could think that it is realistic/sensible for healthcare professionals to avoid engaging the shared-decision processes when a woman does not seem to have full

---

[33] Incidentally, this approach would also help to explain part of the reasons why women can sometimes be treated badly in other medical contexts, such as when they receive abortion care or care during or after a miscarriage. In those instances, they are not foetal containers (the foetus is dead or will soon be dead) but they face very similar 'bad treatment'.

capacity, or where she has capacity but finds that she is unable to focus, listen or be quiet. However, there are shared decision-making situations in medicine that allow time for consideration, reflection and exchange that would precede the action. Nevertheless, in other situations (ie in transplantation clinical practice), it is difficult to discuss the ideal treatment before it is decided and applied. Similarly, in the context of labour and childbirth, defenders of the counterhypothesis would say that it is not always possible to engage in shared decision-making given the circumstances inherent in the childbirth process. This view is so deeply entrenched that, whatever a pregnant woman said before labour (ie in a birth plan) might not be respected at the given moment when the decision is taken. In other words, there is a discussion before the onset of labour regarding what the woman wants next, but when it comes to acting on those decisions during labour, the previous discussions appear to vanish and seem to be ignored during the decision-making process.

True, for many women labour is a peculiar physiological process that can be exhausting, stressful and painful; this significant context must be taken into account when reflecting on their autonomy and consent. But it is also true that there are different phases in labour, and many of the decisions that are frequently not shared could have been shared and taken at a time when the woman could have participated in the decision-making process. After all, the pain during labour is singular in that as soon as the contraction finishes, the woman is not in pain anymore and enjoys full capacity in all senses. It might be that, at certain stages during labour, the woman could be in a tricky position to decide. Now, does that mean that during the whole labour a pregnant woman is, in general, not entitled to engage the decision-making process *because* she is in pain and distressed? Of course, if we accept that being in pain or experiencing high levels of anxiety impedes/limits women's ability/capacity to give their consent – or behave like we are accepting it – we are confronted with a problem because such a statement/practice is not aligned with the laws that protect patients' autonomy.

Given the above, it seems to me that the key question we must ask is what is the nature of the consent of a woman in the special situation that labour is, namely, a situation of vulnerability where the woman is conscious and yet in pain. On the one hand, and as Claire Murray states in Chapter 11, 'the courts have acknowledged that pain (unrelated to labour) can have an impact on the capacity of the person, and therefore on the validity of consent'.[34] Murray cites *Re T (Adult: Refusal of Medical Treatment)*[35] and the decision of the Irish Supreme Court in *Fitzpatrick v White* as recognising that pain or stress can have an impact on the ability of a person to fully comprehend and make an informed decision on a proposed medical intervention.[36] On the other hand, the need to normalise the pregnant

---

[34] Murray (n 12), text after note 9.
[35] *Re T (Adult: Refusal of Medical Treatment)* [1992] EWCA Civ 18.
[36] *Fitzpatrick v White* [2008] 3 IR 551.

subject has also been acknowledged, as also emphasised in Murray's chapter: 'the significance of *Montgomery* ... is that it reaffirmed the importance of autonomy and consent in healthcare decision-making in a case centred on a pregnant woman'.[37] In conclusion, acknowledging the impact of pain, stress or anxiety during labour has to be compatible with ensuring that the pregnant subject, merely by virtue of being pregnant, is no less a subject.[38]

The altered state of consciousness that women describe as characteristic of physiological childbirth is an understudied phenomenon, but one that is deeply relevant to our topic. Ibone Olza et al's pioneering research emphasises: 'the experience of spontaneous altered states of consciousness may well be a hallmark of physiological childbirth in humans and therefore its research may offer a unique opportunity to understand consciousness and transcendental growth'.[39] The fact that physiological labour implies/includes transient alteration of consciousness does not support performing interventions without consent. On the contrary, this information ought to be considered when investigating how to meaningfully inform the woman in labour and ask for her consent.

Beyond these needed considerations, however, let me emphasise that the basic point that I am tracking in this paper is slightly different: not so much whether the woman *is* or *is not* fully capacitated, as whether or not we *take* her to *obviously* be or not be such *by default*. The fact that many practitioners do not ask for consent, as if it were not needed, together with the fact that they never openly discuss or state whether the woman is or is not fully capacitated, supports the interpretation that the lack of capacity is portrayed directly and by default. On the one hand, the law maintains that she is fully entitled to engage in the informed consent process. On the other hand, the practice does not seem to be influenced by the law. For me it is the *obviously* that is very concerning. Such *obviously* comes from the historical construction of the uterine influence. That is why I have used the expression, 'it is the uterine influence, stupid!'

Reconstructing the history of the naturalisation of female rationality requires what is going on in birth to be addressed. Female rationality has always been interrupted by her nature and by naturalising (in excess) her subjectivity.[40] The perfect situation in which to perform such naturalisation is labour, because there have not only a female body but a female body working through contractions. The working of the uterus becomes the paradigmatic example of reasoning not working. A woman using her uterus is thus taken to obviously not be able to reason. This suggests that when a uterus enters the door, reason *must* go out the window.

[37] Murray (n 12), text at note 21.

[38] S Villarmea and F Fernández Guillén, 'Fully Entitled Subjects: Birth as a Philosophical Topic' (2011) 11 *Ontology Studies/Cuadernos de Ontología* 211; Villarmea and Fernández Guillén (n 18).

[39] I Olza et al, 'Birth as a Neuro-Psycho-Social Event: An Integrative Understanding of Maternal Experiences and their Relation to Neurohormonal Events during Childbirth' *PloS Medicine* (forthcoming).

[40] L Schiebinger, *The Mind has No Sex? Women in the Origins of Modern Science* (Cambridge, Harvard University Press, 1991).

VI. What Can We Do to Stop Vaginal Examinations without Consent During Labour?

So, what can we do to stop unauthorised vaginal examinations during labour? The change can be influenced by several specific but interrelated trends. First, ask for consent, of course. Realise that intended, implied, or ambiguous consent is not effective in the labour room; only full, rich, and express consent can be accepted.[41] Second, improve our communication skills. Let us all learn and develop better communication skills that prevent misunderstandings about express, implicit and implied consent. Third, engage in shared decision-making, person-centred care and the values agenda. As the UK National Health System (NHS) policy documents note, shared decision-making involves health professionals, patients and users working together with the goal of putting people at the centre of decisions about their own treatment and care.[42] This approach has been reinforced by the Supreme Court in *Montgomery*, which makes shared decision-making based on values and evidence the basis of consent to medical treatment, with wide-ranging implications for healthcare practices, law and policy.[43] Fourth, assume that the spontaneous and transient altered state of consciousness that women experience in physiological labour requires a reconsideration of how consent is understood and obtained. Fifth, respect decisions. After all, it is a core principle of medical law that an adult with capacity has absolute right to consent to or to refuse medical treatment, and a pregnant woman is *no less* such an adult.[44] Sixth, listen to the women. The design and provision of good quality maternity care should incorporate what matters to childbearing women.[45]

Are those six measures – consent, communication, shared decision-making, attention to state of consciousness, respect, listening to women – enough to produce a real innovation in health practices? These elements need to be implemented, I suggest, together with two more interlinked aspects: gender and philosophical awareness. Understanding the cultural construction of the vagina and the layers of conceptual meanings that still influence women's bodies and agency today is part of the needed solution.[46] Ultimately, and as Camilla Pickles emphasises, 'unauthorised vaginal examinations are gendered experiences of highly traumatic

---

[41] Jonathan Herring's definitions of each category can be found in Chapter 10 below, 'Implied Consent and Vaginal Examination in Pregnancy'.

[42] National Maternity Review, *Better Births. Improving Maternity Outcomes in England* (London, NHS, 2016); National Health Service, *Universal Personalised Car:. Implementing the Comprehensive Model* (London, NHS, 2019).

[43] J Herring et al, 'Elbow Room for Best Practice? Montgomery, Patients' Values, and Balanced Decision-Making in Person-Centred Clinical Care' (2017) 25 *Medical Law Review* 582.

[44] Discussing the situation of pregnant women who are under 18 years old, and thus not legally adults, is not the focus of this contribution.

[45] S Downe et al, 'What Matters to Women During Childbirth: A Systematic Qualitative Review' (2018) 13(4) *PloS one*; World Health Organization, *WHO Recommendations: Intrapartum Care for a Positive Childbirth Experience* (Geneva, World Health Organization, 2018).

[46] E Rees, *The Vagina: A Literary and Cultural History* (New York, Bloomsbury, 2015).

interactions that take place within a system that sometimes facilitates these types of abuses'.[47] Philosophical mindfulness becomes, in my approach, a cornerstone in unveiling the symbolic or 'cultural violence' – defined as any aspect of a culture that can be used to legitimise violence in its direct or structural form – around childbirth.[48]

A developed understanding of the role of rationality explains why harmful behaviour continues to occur and it help us to develop better responses to unauthorised vaginal examinations. We need to know the answer to the question 'why does this happen' before we can say 'how to fix it' effectively. For instance, if we accept the above arguments, then we need to consider training to address the underlying discriminatory tendencies. Understanding stereotypical approaches to female rationality will not in itself prevent unconsented interventions. But the long shadow of the naturalisation of female rationality is increasingly foreshortened and this, at least, is a step in the right direction to diminish disrespectful, abusive, or violent practices in childbirth.

VII. Conclusion

Philosophers, lawyers and health personnel must still walk a long path to achieve a conception of the pregnant subject that is truly a human subject (not just a human body).[49] To start with, they need to question the concept of pregnancy, labour, and birth as a non-rational process that is more comfortably placed in the field of nature than in the field of subjectivity and humanity. That is why it is important to talk about vaginal examinations without consent during labour: because what is at risk matters too, namely women's rationality and citizenship.

[47] See Chapter 9 below, by C Pickles, 'When "Battery" is Not Enough: Exposing the Gaps in Unauthorised Vaginal Examinations During Labour as a Crime of Battery'. For further discussions of obstetric violence as gender-based violence see S Cohen Shabot, 'Making Loud Bodies "Feminine": A Feminist-Phenomenological Analysis of Obstetric Violence' (2016) 39 *Human Studies* 231; D Ruiz Berdún and I Olza, 'The Past and Present of Obstetric Violence in Spain' in A Pereira and J Pita (eds), *VI Jornadas Internacionais de História da Psiquiatria e Saúde Mental* (Coimbra, Universidad de Coimbra, 2016); J Goberna and M Boladeras (eds), *El Concepto 'Violencia Obstétrica' y el Debate Actual sobre la Atención al Nacimiento* [The Term 'Obstetric Violence' and the Present Debate on Childbirth Care] (Madrid, Tecnos, 2018).

[48] On the theory of cultural violence and the relations between direct, structural and cultural violence, see J Galtung, 'Cultural Violence' (1990) 27 *Journal of Peace Research* 291.

[49] Villarmea (2009) (n 18).

6

Human Rights and Gender Stereotypes in Childbirth

CHRISTINA ZAMPAS

I. Introduction

The right to sexual and reproductive health is grounded in a constellation of human rights, including in the rights to life; health; freedom from torture and cruel, inhuman or degrading treatment; information; and non-discrimination and equality, among others. It entails,

> a set of freedoms and entitlements. The freedoms include the right to make free and responsible decisions and choices, free of violence, coercion and discrimination, over matters concerning one's body and sexual and reproductive health. The entitlements include unhindered access to a whole range of health facilities, goods, services and information, which ensure all people full enjoyment of the right to sexual and reproductive health.[1]

Bodily autonomy and decision-making are imbedded in the realisation of these human rights, including in the health care context and in childbirth. Worldwide, about 140 million women give birth every year.[2] For health care facilities, in addition to providing the clinical care specific to labour and childbirth, this also means making sure that women are treated with dignity and respect. Continuum of care, regular monitoring and documentation of events as well as clear communication between health care providers and clients are essential, as is ensuring that a referral plan is in place should more advanced medical care become necessary. These are all essential elements of good quality labour and childbirth care that every woman should receive.[3]

---

[1] Committee on Economic, Social and Cultural Rights, 'General Comment No 22: On the Rights to Sexual and Reproductive Health (Article 12)', UN Doc E/C.12/GC/22 (2016) [5].

[2] World Health Organization, *WHO Recommendations: Intrapartum Care for a Positive Childbirth Experience* (Geneva, World Health Organization, 2018) at www.who.int/reproductivehealth/publications/intrapartum-care-guidelines/en.

[3] ibid.

However, studies show that the abuses against pregnant women during facility-based childbirth are occurring *across the globe*.[4] As noted by the World Health Organization's (WHO) Assistant Director-General for Family, Women, Children and Adolescents, 'This can totally overshadow one of the most pivotal moments in a woman's life – the day she welcomes her baby into the world'.[5] A 2015 systematic review synthesised the existing global qualitative and quantitative evidence on the mistreatment of women during childbirth in health facilities, and identified 65 studies containing research findings from 34 countries.[6] In 2015, the WHO issued a statement condemning abuses during childbirth, recognising such abuses as a threat to women's health and life and a violation of their human rights.[7]

Human rights bodies and non-governmental organisations have also published reports documenting the abuses women and girls experience during childbirth in health care facilities around the world.[8] In 2019, the United Nations

---

[4] This chapter refers to 'women' and 'girls' in discussing mistreatment and violence during facility-based childbirth. Although the majority of personal experiences with these abuses relate to cisgender women and girls, who were born female and identify as female, transgender men and people who identify as neither men nor women may have the reproductive capacity to become pregnant and so may be subject to mistreatment and violence in the context of childbirth. This research did not find studies that included individuals with these gender identities, and as a result this chapter does not reflect any experience they may have had with facility-based childbirth. There is an increase in skilled birth attendance globally that requires efforts to improve both the coverage and quality of care provided to women at health facilities, including women's rights to dignified and respectful care. Mistreatment can occur at the level of interaction between the woman and provider, as well as through systemic failures at the health facility and health system levels. See G Sen et al, 'Beyond Measurement: The Drivers of Disrespect and Abuse in Obstetric Care' (2018) 26(53) *Reproductive Health Matters* 6; World Health Organization, *The Prevention and Elimination of Disrespect and Abuse during Facility-Based Childbirth: WHO Statement* (Geneva, World Health Organization, 2015) WHO/RHR/14.23.

[5] P Simelela, 'A "Good Birth" Goes Beyond Having a Healthy Baby, Commentary' (World Health Organization, 15 February 2018) at www.who.int/mediacentre/commentaries/2018/having-a-healthy-baby/en.

[6] M Bohren et al, 'The Mistreatment of Women During Childbirth in Health Facilities Globally: A Mixed-Methods Systematic Review' (2015) 12(6) *PLOS Medicine*. This work built on earlier work by researchers in this area. See D Bowser and K Hill, *Exploring Evidence for Disrespect and Abuse in Facility-Based Childbirth: Report of a Landscape Analysis* (Washington DC, United States Agency for International Development, 2010); L Freedman and M Kruk, 'Disrespect and Abuse of Women in Childbirth: Challenging the Global Quality and Accountability Agendas' (2014) 384 *The Lancet* 42. See also S Silal et al, 'Exploring Inequalities in Access to and Use of Maternal Health Services in South Africa' (2011) 12 *BMC Health Services Research* 120; R Small et al, 'Immigrant Women's Views About Care During Labor and Birth: An Australian Study of Vietnamese, Turkish, and Filipino Women' (2002) 29 *Birth* 266; A d'Oliveira et al, 'Violence Against Women in Health-Care Institutions: An Emerging Problem' (2002) 359 *The Lancet* 1681.

[7] World Health Organization 2015 (n 4).

[8] See, for example, Center for Reproductive Rights and Federation of Women Lawyers Kenya, *Failure to Deliver: Violations of Women's Human Rights in Kenyan Health Facilities* (New York and Nairobi, Center for Reproductive Rights and Federation of Women Lawyers Kenya, 2007); Amnesty International, *Deadly Delivery: The Maternal Health Care Crisis in the USA* (London, Amnesty International Secretariat, 2010); A Odhiambo, '"Stop Making Excuses": Accountability for Maternal Health Care in South Africa' (*Human Rights Watch*, 8 August 2011) at www.hrw.org/report/2011/08/08/stop-making-excuses/accountability-maternal-health-care-south-africa; J Debrecéniová, *Women – Mothers – Bodies: Women's Human Rights in Obstetric Care in Healthcare Facilities in Slovakia* (Bratislava, Občan, Demokracia a Zodpovednosť [Citizen, Democracy and Accountability], 2015); Center for Reproductive Rights, *Vakeras Zorales – Speaking Out: Roma Women's Experiences in Reproductive Health Care in Slovakia* (Geneva, Center for Reproductive Rights, 2017).

(UN) Special Rapporteur on Violence against Women issued a report to the UN General Assembly, the first ever UN report on abuses and violence during childbirth, recognising this as an issue that needs a comprehensive and multi sectoral response. She noted that these practices are often justified in the name of tradition, culture and religion – grounds that human rights bodies have expressly stated may 'not [be] used to justify violations of women's right to equality before the law and to equal enjoyment of all … rights'.[9]

The ground-breaking report recognises that underpinning these laws and practices that seek to limit women's autonomy and agency are harmful gender stereotypes and forms of intersecting discrimination against women and non-conforming individuals, and recommends that states take measures to eliminate both in law and in practice the stereotypes that drive such abuses.[10] The UN Office of the High Commissioner for Human Rights (OHCHR) has also issued a paper addressing the need for the judiciary to tackle the underlying stereotypes driving human rights violations in the context of sexual and reproductive health and rights, including during childbirth.[11]

These stereotypes arise from strong religious, social and cultural beliefs and ideas about sexuality, pregnancy and motherhood.[12] They negate autonomy during pregnancy and during childbirth; and they are often compounded by other characteristics, such as age, HIV status, ethnicity, race, sexual orientation and gender identity, and disability, which make people particularly vulnerable to abuses in this context. States are required under international human rights law to respect, protect and fulfil human rights, including the obligation to combat stereotypes and stereotyping.[13]

This chapter begins by introducing stereotypes in the context of reproduction generally and is followed by stereotypes during childbirth focusing on abuses during childbirth and denying choices during childbirth. In the context of pregnancy and childbirth, persistent gender stereotypes that depict women as vessels for reproduction and demean them as incompetent decision-makers have fuelled policies and practices that deprioritise the health needs and desires of persons who

---

[9] United Nations General Assembly, 'Report of the Special Rapporteur on Violence Against Women, its Causes and Consequences on a Human Rights-Based Approach to Mistreatment and Violence Against Women in Reproductive Health Services with a Focus on Childbirth and Obstetric Violence', UN Doc A/74/137 (2019); see also UN Human Rights Committee, 'General Comment No 28: Article 3 (Equality of Rights Between Men and Women)', UN Doc CCPR/C/21/Rev.1/Add.10 (2000) [5]; Committee on the Elimination of Discrimination Against Women, 'General Recommendation No 35 on Gender-Based Violence Against Women, Updating General Recommendation No 19', UN Doc CEDAW/C/GC/35 (2017) [7], [31].

[10] United Nations General Assembly 2019 (n 9).

[11] Office of the High Commissioner for Human Rights, *Background Paper on the Role of the Judiciary in Addressing the Harmful Gender Stereotypes Related to Sexual and Reproductive Health and Rights* (Geneva, OHCHR, 2018).

[12] R Cook and S Cusack, *Gender Stereotyping: Transnational Legal Perspectives* (Philadelphia, University of Pennsylvania Press, 2010) 34.

[13] Convention on the Elimination of All Forms of Discrimination Against Women (adopted 18 December 1979, entered into force 3 September 1981) 1249 UNTS 13 (CEDAW), Art 5(a); Convention on the Rights of Persons with Disabilities (adopted 13 December 2006, entered into force 3 May 2008) 2515 UNTS 3 (CRPD), Art 8(1)(b).

are pregnant, subject them to ill-treatment during pregnancy, delivery and in the post-natal period, and deprive them of their ability to make informed choices in connection with childbirth and control over their bodies.

This chapter provides an analysis of how these and other stereotypes remove autonomous decision making, violating human rights, as well as state obligations to prevent such violations and to ensure redress when violations have occurred. It focuses on international and regional human rights body standards on these topics and looks at select national level case law. It concludes by recognising that while the WHO, and UN and regional human rights experts are beginning to call attention to the mistreatment of, and violence against, women during childbirth and are pushing for states to take steps to ensure that women receive dignified, respectful health care during labour and childbirth, gaps in standards persist, but existing law and standards provide a strong basis for ensuring autonomous decision-making during childbirth.

II. Informed Consent and Autonomy

Informed consent to medical care is fundamental both in law (including human rights law) and in ethics. Patients have the right to receive information and ask questions about recommended treatments so that they can make informed and well-considered decisions about care. As noted by the UN Committee on the Elimination of All Forms of Discrimination against Women (CEDAW) in a case regarding forced sterilisation, informed consent is a process of ongoing communication and interaction between patient and provider, and a signature alone is not an indication of informed consent.[14] The provider should be *proactive* in their provision of information. For consent to be valid, it must be voluntary and informed. Consent of the patient is needed regardless of the procedure, whether it is a physical examination or surgery or something else, and consent can be withdrawn at any time. Obtaining and providing consent should always be a patient-centred approach.

The information provided should emphasise the advantages and disadvantages, the health benefits, risks and side-effects, and it should enable comparison of various options of treatment. Information should be provided in a manner and language that is understandable, accessible and appropriate to the needs of the individual making the decision. Educational level, physical or intellectual impairments and the age of the individual should be considered in

---

[14] Committee on the Elimination of Discrimination Against Women, 'Views Communication No 4/2004', UN Doc CEDAW/C/36/D/4/2004 (2006); Federation of Gynecology and Obstetrics Committee for the Study of Ethical Aspects of Human Reproduction and Women's Health, *Ethical Issues in Obstetrics and Gynecology* (London, FIGO, 2012).

determining the manner in which counselling and information is provided; individual needs and preferences should be respected. Persons with disabilities should be provided with all the necessary support for making their decisions. Extreme caution must be exercised, especially in the case of individuals who have limited ways of being understood by others, to ensure that decisions that should be made using the process of supported decision-making are not de facto substituted decisions.[15]

The International Federation of Gynecology and Obstetrics (FIGO) recognises that implementation of informed consent is an obligation, even though it can be challenging and time consuming, for example:

> where women have little education, or where very unequal power relationships in a society mitigate against women's self-determination. Nevertheless, these difficulties do not absolve physicians caring for women from pursuing fulfilment of these criteria for informed consent. Only the woman patient can decide if the benefits to her of a proce-dure are worth the risks and discomfort she may undergo. Even if, for example, other family members feel they should make the decision, it is the ethical obligation of the physician to ensure that the woman's human right of self-determination is met by the process of communication that precedes any informed consent.[16]

Violations of the right to informed consent occur in a number of contexts related to labour and childbirth, including forced sterilisation immediately following child-birth, over-medicalised and unconsented to procedures during and immediately after childbirth, and breaches of privacy during a person's stay in the facility. Lack of informed consent has been reported for various procedures, including vagi-nal examinations, and forced contraception, including immediate post-partum intrauterine contraceptive devices, as well as injectables. Women are either not consulted at all, and therefore never given the opportunity to make an informed choice, given insufficient information to make an informed decision, or their pref-erences are disregarded by health care providers in the provision of care.

The UN Committee on Economic, Social and Cultural Rights decided, in the context of fertility treatments, that the transfer of an embryo to a woman's uterus without her informed consent constitutes a violation of her right to the highest attainable standard of health and her right to gender equality in the enjoyment of her right to health 'as it can lead to forced medical interventions or even forced pregnancies'.[17] The European Court of Human Rights has also found that

---

[15] Federation of Gynecology and Obstetrics Committee Report, 'Guidelines Regarding Informed Consent: FIGO Committee for the Ethical Aspects of Human Reproduction and Women's Health' (2008) 101 *International Journal of Gynecology and Obstetrics* 219; see also *Ethical Issues in Obstetrics and Gyne-cology* (n 14); CRDP (n 13); World Health Organization et al, *Eliminating Forced, Coercive and Otherwise Involuntary Sterilization: An Interagency Statement* (Geneva, World Health Organization, 2014).

[16] Federation of Gynecology and Obstetrics 2008 (n 15).

[17] UN Committee on Economic, Social and Cultural Rights, 'Views Adopted by the Committee Under the Optional Protocol to the International Covenant on Economic, Social and Cultural Rights, Concerning Communication No 22/2017', UN Doc E/C.12/65/D/22/2017 (2019) (*SC and GP v Italy*) [10.3], [11.2].

vaginal examinations without informed consent impinge on a woman's physical integrity and are thus a violation of the right to private life.[18]

One pervasive and false stereotype driving denial of informed consent is that women are vulnerable and emotionally volatile and therefore incapable of making rational decisions about their reproductive capacity and decisions concerning the medical care that they need. Women are thus perceived as individuals in need of being controlled and incapable of exercising their agency, and should therefore 'be denied access to health care services of their choice'.[19] Accordingly, this stereotype maintains that men and people in positions of authority, such as doctors who perform medical procedures, male family members, or society at large, are better positioned to make decisions for women.[20] This stereotype operates to deny women information to make informed decisions about their reproductive health, substitutes the decisions of others for their own, and deprives them of control over their own bodies.

As the UN Working Group on discrimination against women has recognised, this 'Patriarchal negation of women's autonomy in decision-making leads to violations of women's rights to health, privacy, reproductive and sexual self-determination, physical integrity and even to life'.[21] Moreover, stereotypes that depict individuals who deviate from traditional gender roles as abnormal and pathologise them, work to deprive these persons of autonomy in decision-making in the health care context as well.

Another stereotype is that women's natural role in society is primarily as a mother and caregiver. This stereotypes ascribes 'motherhood' as an essential attribute of being a woman.[22] As a case before the UN Human Rights Committee has argued, this gender stereotype holds that 'women should continue their pregnancies regardless of the circumstances, their needs and wishes, because their primary role is to be mothers and self-sacrificing caregivers'.[23] In the Inter-American Court case of *Artavia Murillo et al v Costa Rica*, further discussed below, an expert witness on this issue explained,

> The ideal for women … is embodied in sacrifice and dedication, and the culmination of these values is represented by motherhood and the ability to give birth … A woman's fertility is still considered by much of society to be something natural that admits no

---

[18] *YF v Turkey*, App no 24209/94 (European Court of Human Rights 22 July 2003).

[19] R Cook, 'Modern Day Inquisitions' (2011) 65 *University of Miami Law Review* 792.

[20] ibid.

[21] United Nations General Assembly, 'Report of the UN Working Group on the Issue of Discrimination Against Women in Law and in Practice, Note by the Secretariat', UN Doc A/HRC/32/44 (2016) [63].

[22] L Oja and A Yamin, '"Woman" in the European Human Rights System: How Is the Reproductive Rights Jurisprudence of the European Court of Human Rights Constructing Narratives of Women's Citizenship?' (2016) 32 *Columbia Journal of Gender and Law* 62, 73.

[23] UN International Covenant on Civil and Political Rights, 'Views Adopted by the Committee under Article 5(4) of the Optional Protocol, Concerning Communication No 2324/2013' UN Doc CCPR/C/116/D/2324/2013 (2016) (*Mellet v Ireland*) [3.19], individual opinion of committee member Sarah Cleveland.

doubts ... Motherhood has been assigned to women as an essential part of their gender identity, transformed into their destiny.[24]

Similarly, the CEDAW Committee in the case of *LC v Peru*, has affirmed that this stereotype, 'understands the exercise of a woman's reproductive capacity as a duty rather than a right'.[25] As such, the Committee has noted that this stereotype suggests that the protection of a foetus is paramount to a pregnant woman's or girl's personal interests and needs. Furthermore, it leads to the subordination of women and girls since they are seen only as reproductive instruments and not as full human beings and members of society.[26]

In the health care context, health care providers may engage in wrongful stereotyping of women that can ultimately lead to human rights violations as recognised by quasi-judicial bodies in the cases above. These bodies and courts have recognised directly and indirectly that they may seek to advance sex-specific norms based on their personal, religious or cultural beliefs in the context of providing care.[27] They may view and treat all women as mothers or potential mothers, and exploit their authority to deny patients access to services or subject them to certain medical treatments.[28]

The UN Special Rapporteur on Health has recognised this power dynamic, noting that states must protect the right to autonomy over medical decisions as a counterweight to 'the imbalance of power, experience and trust inherently present in the doctor-patient relationship'.[29] Additionally, the CEDAW Committee, in an inquiry regarding a contraceptive ban in Manila, the Philippines, has recognised that 'gender stereotypes may impact women's capacity to make free and informed decisions and choices about their health care, sexuality and reproduction and, in turn, also impact on their autonomy to determine their own roles in society'.[30]

Courts and quasi-judicial bodies have recognised these stereotypes in the laws, regulations and practices related to consent to abortion and contraception, including the practice of sterilising certain groups of women or transgender people without their free and informed consent. They have recognised directly or indirectly that these stereotypes are fundamental causes of abuse and non-consensual medical treatment during childbirth.

---

[24] *Case of Artavia Murillo et al ('In Vitro Fertilization') v Costa Rica*, Series C No 257 (Inter-American Court of Human Rights, 28 November 2012) [298].

[25] Committee on the Elimination of Discrimination Against Women, Views Communication No 22/2009, UN Doc CEDAW/C/50/D/22/2009 (2011) *(LC v Peru)* [7.7].

[26] Oja and Yamin (n 22) 74.

[27] See, eg, *Case of RR v Poland*, App no 27617/04 (European Court of Human Rights 28 November 2011) [20].

[28] ibid [132], [139].

[29] United Nations General Assembly, 'Right of Everyone to the Enjoyment of the Highest Attainable Standard of Physical and Mental Health, Note by the Secretary General', UN Doc A/64/272 (2009) [45].

[30] Committee on the Elimination of Discrimination Against Women, 'Summary of the Inquiry Concerning the Philippines under Article 8 of the Optional Protocol to the Convention on the Elimination of All Forms of Discrimination against Women', UN Doc CEDAW/C/OP.8/PHL/1 (2015) [42].

III. Pregnancy and Childbirth

In the context of pregnancy and childbirth, persistent gender stereotypes that depict women as vessels for reproduction and demean them as incompetent decision-makers have fuelled policies and practices that deprioritise the health needs of persons who are pregnant, subject them to ill-treatment during pregnancy, delivery and in the post-natal period and deprive them of their ability to make informed choices in connection with childbirth and control over their bodies. These stereotyped roles become discriminatory by reinforcing gender hierarchies that regard women as inferior to men, and 'ignore individual women's characteristics, needs, wishes, and circumstances in ways that deny them their rights'.[31] Particularly in the health care context, these gender, as well as medical, hierarchies, combined with broader health system constraints and limitations, may result in the under-prioritisation of and a lack of investment in services only required by women.[32] In turn, this leads to a host of harms, including but not limited to preventable maternal mortality and morbidity.[33] This reflects a grave problem of systemic inequality and discrimination suffered by women on account of their reproductive capacity.

Moreover, these stereotypes may compound with other stereotypes in connection with race, ethnicity or socio-economic status that further deny women access to quality care. For example, the UN Committee on Economic, Social and Cultural Rights has recognised that people living in poverty may face 'pervasive discrimination, stigmatisation and negative stereotyping which can lead to the refusal of, or unequal access to, the same quality of ... health care as others'.[34] Notably, in the 2011 case of *Alyne da Silva v Brazil*, in which Alyne, an Afro-Brazilian woman died as a result of obstetric complications while seeking care in multiple health facilities, the CEDAW Committee found that Brazil had violated the petitioner's rights to health and non-discrimination, among others, and recognised that these violations reached system-level factors of neglect, including the inadequate resources and ineffective implementation of state policies.[35] While the Committee did not explicitly discuss gender stereotypes in analysing the rights violations in this decision, it noted Brazil's failure to address Alyne's 'status as a woman of African descent and her socio-economic background', suggesting that harmful compounded stereotypes about gender, race and socioeconomic background

---

[31] S Cusack and R Cook, 'Stereotyping Women in the Health Sector: Lessons from CEDAW' (2009) 16 *Washington and Lee Journal of Civil Rights and Social Justice* 51; Cook and Cusack (n 12).

[32] United Nations General Assembly 2016 (n 21) [29].

[33] World Health Organization, *Maternal Mortality: Fact Sheet No 348* (2014), at apps.who.int/iris/bitstream/handle/10665/112318/WHO_RHR_14.06_eng.pdf.

[34] *Millicent Awuor Omuya alias Maimuna Awuor and Another v The Attorney General and Four Others* [2015] Petition No 562 of 2012 (High Court of Kenya at Nairobi (Constitutional and Human Rights Division)) [123].

[35] Committee on the Elimination of Discrimination Against Women, 'Views Communication No 17/2008', UN Doc CEDAW/C/49/D/17/2008 (2011) (*Alyne da Silva Pimentel Teixeira v Brazil*).

contributed to the denial of quality care Alyne experienced.[36] The Committee then clearly established that states have an obligation to provide quality maternal health services free from discrimination in order to prevent maternal mortality.

A. Abuse During Childbirth

The gender hierarchies described above impede access to quality care and contribute to the abuse that persons experience while seeking maternal health services across the globe. Such abuse is increasingly documented and recognised by human rights bodies, and is a phenomenon that is now referred to as 'obstetric violence' in some places.[37] The WHO and human rights bodies are increasingly addressing this issue.

i. The World Health Organization

In 2014, noting that 'a growing body of research on women's experiences during pregnancy, and particularly childbirth, paints a disturbing picture', the WHO issued a statement on the prevention and elimination of disrespect and abuse during facility-based childbirth. In its statement, endorsed by over 90 civil society and health professional organisations, the WHO highlighted that:

> Such treatment not only violates the rights of women to respectful care, but can also threaten their rights to life, health, bodily integrity, and freedom from discrimination. This statement calls for greater action, dialogue, research and advocacy on this important public health and human rights issue.

Furthermore, the WHO listed some of the reported abuse including:

> outright physical abuse, profound humiliation and verbal abuse, coercive or unconsented medical procedures (including sterilization), lack of confidentiality, failure to get fully informed consent, refusal to give pain medication, gross violations of privacy, refusal of admission to health facilities, neglecting women during childbirth to suffer life-threatening, avoidable complications, and detention of women and their newborns in facilities after childbirth due to an inability to pay.[38]

---

[36] ibid [7.7].

[37] Oja and Yamin (n 22).

[38] World Health Organization 2015 (n 4). There is a rather long history of the various terms used to explain this issue, which is well documented in a recent article by Sen et al (n 4) 7–8. These authors' explanation of the language they have proposed to use 'disrespect and abuse', provides useful guidance that encompasses the various drivers as well as the conduct needing to be addressed,

'For our purposes of being both inclusive and incisive, we prefer the terminology of D&A [disrespect and abuse] despite the above limitation for provider buy-in. In the context of obstetric care, we define disrespect as the violation of a woman's dignity as a person and as a human being on the basis of her economic status, gender, caste, race, ethnicity, marital status, disability, sexual orientation, or gender identity. Disrespect is often revealed in the biased normative judgements that health workers

The statement recognised the impact of this mistreatment and violence on women, as well as children and families, underscoring that: 'Such practices may have direct adverse consequences for both the mother and infant'.[39] The WHO called for 'greater action, dialogue, research and advocacy on this important public health and human rights issue'.[40]

ii. International Human Rights Bodies and National Courts

A joint statement released by a group of UN and regional human rights experts recognised the ill-treatment that women experience in health care facilities in the context of pregnancy and childbirth, including 'acts of obstetric and institutional violence ... including with respect to forced or coerced sterilisation procedures, refusal to administer pain relief, disrespect and abuse of women seeking health-care and reported cases of women being hit whilst giving birth'.[41]

The Committee against Torture has recognised the abuse and violations that women face in maternal health facilities, when they are detained post-delivery for their inability to pay maternal health bills and when incarcerated women are shackled to beds during labour and delivery.[42] Additionally, the Special Rapporteur

make about women and the resulting acts of omission or commission. Abuse refers to actions that increase the risk of harm to the woman and are not in the best interests of her health or well-being. Such actions may be learned and reproduced through the practices of institutional medicine. They may or may not be intended to cause harm and are often justified by resource constraints that can become a cover for prioritising the convenience of health providers over the well-being of the woman. We identify three important advantages to this definition. It captures both intentional behaviours and unintended consequences. It is open to addressing institutionalised medical practices as well as socio-economic inequalities. And it allows us to identify both manifestations and underlying drivers of the problem.

This definition appears to meet the criteria spelled out by Vogel et al: "Any definition needs to adequately capture the health, human rights, legal and sociocultural dimensions of this problem. It should consider a range of possible acts (whether intentional or not), the risks (or potential risks) of harm or suffering to women, and that these events can occur in different levels of care."

[39] World Health Organization 2015 (n 4).

[40] ibid. The WHO has explicitly taken a human rights approach to framing this mistreatment, recognising that women have the right to the highest attainable standard of health, including 'the right to dignified, respectful health care throughout pregnancy and childbirth'.

[41] Office of the United Nations High Commissioner for Human Rights, Joint Statement by UN Special Rapporteurs [on the Right of Everyone to the Enjoyment of the Highest Attainable Standard of Physical and Mental Health, on the Situation of Human Rights Defenders, on Violence Against Women, its Causes and Consequences, and the Working Group on Discrimination Against Women in Law and in Practice], the Rapporteur on the Rights of Women of the Inter-American Commission on Human Rights and the Special Rapporteurs on the Rights of Women and Human Rights Defenders of the African Commission on Human and Peoples' Rights' (UNHCHR 24 September 2015) at www.ohchr.org/EN/NewsEvents/Pages/DisplayNews.aspx?NewsID=16490&LangID=E.

[42] Convention Against Torture and Other Cruel, Inhuman or Degrading Treatment or Punishment (CAT) Committee, 'Concluding Observations on the Second Periodic Report of Kenya, Adopted by the Committee at its Fiftieth Session (6 to 31 May 2013)', UN Doc CAT/C/KEN/ CO/2 (2013), 27; CAT Committee, Consideration of Reports Submitted by States Parties Under Article 19 of the Convention, Conclusions and Recommendations of the Committee Against Torture, United States of America, UN Doc CAT/C/USA/CO/2 (2006) [33].

on torture and other cruel, inhuman or degrading treatment or punishment has
noted the stereotypes driving such practices,

> [i]n many States women seeking maternal health care face a high risk of ill-treatment,
> particularly immediately before and after childbirth. Abuses range from extended
> delays in the provision of medical care, such as stitching after delivery to the absence
> of anaesthesia. Such mistreatment is often motivated by stereotypes regarding women's
> childbearing roles and inflicts physical and psychological suffering that can amount to
> ill-treatment.[43]

As a result of the stereotype depicting women's role as child bearer, the pain and
suffering that accompanies childbearing may be considered to be a natural consequence of such role, and health care professionals may not provide women with
the same palliative care that they offer to other patients.

Cases that challenge the abuse that women face during childbirth are increasingly being brought to courts. Notably, in a decision from the High Court of Kenya
at Nairobi, the Court recognised the bias of health care providers towards two petitioners 'on account of their status as poor, socially and economically marginalised
women'.[44] Notably, the Court referenced the affidavit of one of the doctors at the
hospital, in which he 'speaks of managing "stubborn" and "rogue mothers," [as]
a clear indication of the attitude that the hospital had towards its patients'.[45] The
Court further elaborated that 'The experience of the petitioners ... demonstrated
the disdain that those charged with the provisions of the services held towards
the poor women'.[46] These stereotypes contributed to the verbal abuse the patients
experienced and the 'deplorable' conditions under which they were held during the
period of detention and their denial of medical care.[47] The court recognised the
ill-treatment and detention that these women experienced in the hospital following their deliveries, which culminated in violations of several of their constitutional
rights, including the rights to freedom from cruel, inhuman or degrading treatment, dignity, health and non-discrimination.[48]

Additionally, in a 2010 case, the High Court of Delhi recognised the denial of
access to maternal health care that poor women experience as a result of harmful
stereotypes that depict them as irresponsible and prone to take advantage of the
health care system. In this case, Shanti Devi, a migrant woman, was repeatedly
denied the medical care, rations and financial support to which she was entitled

---

[43] United Nations General Assembly, 'Report of the Special Rapporteur on Torture and Other Cruel,
Inhuman or Degrading Treatment or Punishment, Note by the Secretariat', UN Doc A/HRC/31/57
(2016) [47].

[44] *Millicent Awuor Omuya alias Maimuna Awuor and Another v The Attorney General and Four
Others* (n 34) [125].

[45] ibid [122].

[46] ibid [123].

[47] ibid [122].

[48] ibid [123].

under various government schemes created to promote maternal health and survival, which resulted in her humiliation, suffering, and ultimately, death.[49] The Court noted that,

> [a]n argument was advanced ... that there is an apprehension that the benefit under the scheme would be 'misused'. This Court finds this apprehension to be misplaced. Given the status of the facilities available in Government hospitals and primary health centers across the country, it is very unlikely that any person who can otherwise afford health care is going to 'misuse' these facilities. On the other hand, when it comes to the question of public health, no woman, more so a pregnant woman should be denied on any rational basis facility of treatment at any stage irrespective of her social and economic background. This is the primary function in the public health services. This is where the inalienable right to health which is so inherent to the right to life gets enforced. There cannot be a situation where a pregnant woman who is in need of care and assistance is turned away from a Government health facility only on the ground that she has not been able to demonstrate her [below the poverty line] status or her 'eligibility'.[50]

IV. Denying Choices During Childbirth

Women are also deprived of the ability to determine the course of their treatment during childbirth, undermining their autonomy. In this context, women have been subjected to over-medicalised procedures, which are invasive and unnecessary, and deny them choices about different ways of giving birth.[51]

---

[49] *Laxmi Mandal v Deen Dayal Harinagar Hospital & Others* WP (C) 8853/2008 and *Jaitun v Maternity Home, MCD, Jangpura and Others* WP No 10700/2009 (High Court of Delhi, 2010).

[50] *Jaitun* (n 49) [48]–[49].

[51] For example, a recent report documenting the experience of women in Slovak health facilities recognised that: '[Several women] mentioned ... that the medical personnel had treated them as objects incapable of autonomous expression and making their own decisions about themselves, their bodies, and proposed procedures. Several women said some of the procedures during the birth had been carried out without their consent, for example, the administration of oxytocin and other medicines, episiotomy, breaking the waters, or fundal pressure applied by a member of the medical staff in order to speed up delivery. There were several procedures the medical personnel had used during the labour and delivery, of which the women learnt only afterwards. They were performed not only without women's consent, but even without their knowledge. In some cases, interventions were even performed against the will of these women': Debrecéniová (n 8) 189. The Association for Improvements in the Maternity Services Ireland (AIMS Ireland) has documented 'numerous cases of rights abuses in the provision of maternal health care that are a product of the Eighth Amendment [which protects a foetus' right to life on an equal footing with a woman's]. In a recent statement they noted: "[T]he Eighth Amendment is repeatedly used in the context of maternity rights to deny women the right to bodily autonomy in terms of decision making in pregnancy, in labour, in birth and in the postpartum period. Women have reported being forced into caesarean births, forced into invasive procedures during labour, threatened with social services and in some cases threatened with the Gardaí [police] and mental health services for trying to assert their right to bodily autonomy." Krysia Lynch, Co-Chair and Spokesperson for AIMS Ireland, characterised the situation as the "quashing of choice from the minute you're pregnant"', in Amnesty International, *She is Not a Criminal: The Impact of Ireland's Abortion Law* (London, Amnesty International, 2015) 47.

In this context, gender stereotypes about the self-sacrificing mother who is willing to prioritise the purported best interests of the foetus and assume the risks of various interventions that may be harmful for her, such as caesarean sections or episiotomies, are prevalent. Additionally, in this context, health care providers often do not seek women's informed consent to such interventions, substituting their beliefs about the best course of treatment for those of the women. Such treatment is often justified on the basis of the purported interests of the foetus and reinforces the stereotype that women are unable to make rational decisions, reducing them to objects of intervention without agency.[52] The CEDAW Committee has noted reports of,

> interference with women's reproductive health choices in hospitals, including the routine application of medical interventions, reportedly often without the woman's free, prior and informed consent or any medical indication, a rapid increase in the caesarean section rate … and patronizing attitudes of doctors which impede the exercise by mothers of their freedom of choice. It also notes reports about women's limited options for delivering their babies outside hospitals.[53]

Notably, the Working Group on Discrimination against Women in Law and in Practice has recognised that 'unnecessary medicalization … [has] functioned as [a form] of social control exercised by patriarchal establishments to preserve the gender roles of women'.[54]

Courts and human rights bodies are increasingly starting to address the over-medicalisation of childbirth, and attendant involuntary procedures, as implicating human rights.[55] They have called on states to respect women's choice of home birth, and to appropriately regulate birthing facilities, as a matter of ensuring their autonomy, privacy, and human dignity.[56] In the 2010 case of *Ternovsky v Hungary*, the European Court of Human Rights recognised that Hungary's lack of comprehensive and effective regulation of home birth, which exposed health care professionals who performed home births to the risk of prosecution, amounted to a violation of the right to private life because it effectively denied the complainant the opportunity to give birth at home.[57] The Court effectively

---

[52] Oja and Yamin (n 22) 77.

[53] Committee on the Elimination of Discrimination Against Women, 'Consideration of Reports Submitted by States Parties under Article 18 of the Convention, Concluding Observations of the Committee on the Elimination of Discrimination Against Women, Czech Republic', UN Doc CEDAW/C/CZE/5 (2010) [36].

[54] United Nations General Assembly 2016 (n 21) [73].

[55] Bulgarian Helsinki Committee, *Gross Violations Against Pregnant Women in Bulgaria* at www. bghelsinki.org/en/news/press/single/gross-rights-violations-against-pregnant-women-bulgaria/; *Case of Dubská and Krejzová v the Czech Republic*, App nos 28859/11 and 28473/12 (European Court of Human Rights 11 December 2014) [56]; Committee on the Elimination of Discrimination Against Women 2010 (n 53); United Nations General Assembly 2016 (n 21) [106].

[56] United Nations General Assembly 2016 (n 21) [106(g)].

[57] The Court noted that it 'conclude[s] that the matter of health professionals assisting home births is surrounded by legal uncertainty prone to arbitrariness. Prospective mothers cannot therefore be considered as freely benefiting from such assistance, since a permanent threat is being posed to health

challenged stereotypes about women's ability to appreciate the risks in connection with their health care choices and make rational decisions in holding that the woman 'is entitled to a legal and institutional environment that enables her choice'. The Court concluded that, 'The lack of legal certainty and the threat to health professionals has limited the choices of the applicant considering home delivery', amounting to a violation of her private life.[58]

In contrast, in 2015, the Court in the case of *Dubská and Krejzová v the Czech Republic* ruled that legislation prohibiting health professionals to assist with home birth did not amount to a violation of the right to private life,[59] although the Court recognised the reports of extensive mistreatment and abuse that women in Czech health facilities experience, including 'patronizing behaviour on the part of hospital staff'.[60] The Court called on the Czech Republic to 'consider taking steps to make midwife-assisted childbirth outside hospitals a safe and affordable option for women'.[61] It acknowledged that 'the majority of the research studies presented to it do not suggest that there is an increased risk for home births compared to births in hospital'; and affirmed that the inability to be assisted by midwifes during home birth was an interference with the petitioners' right to private life. However, it ultimately found that this did not amount to a violation of the right to private life.[62] As such, the Court implicitly accepts assumptions about the benefits of medicalised childbirth, despite acknowledging the prevalence of significant evidence challenging this assumption, and failed to consider the impact of this regulation on women's decisional autonomy, thereby reinforcing prevalent stereotypes in this context.[63]

---

professionals inclined to assist home births by virtue of [a decree sanctioning] health professionals who carry out activities within their qualifications in a manner which is incompatible with the law or their licence': *Case of Ternovszky v Hungary*, App no 67545/09 (European Court of Human Rights 14 March 2011) [26].

[58] ibid [24], [26].

[59] *Dubská* (n 55).

[60] ibid [32]. The Court also noted that, 'the applicants submitted testimonies from numerous mothers who had given birth in maternity hospitals during recent years and who pointed to practices that were – in their view – unacceptable, including the following: medical intervention during delivery without the consent of the mothers and sometimes against their explicitly expressed will, such as artificial rupture of membranes; episiotomy; intravenous infusion of medication for the mother; performing the Kristeller manoeuvre (pushing with the fist or forearm the top of the uterus coinciding with a contraction and pushing by the mother during the second stage of labour); performing Caesarean section without sufficient medical justification; using techniques and medication to speed up the delivery; separation of mothers from their babies for several hours after delivery, ignoring the mother's wishes to have immediate contact with the baby after delivery; routinely placing healthy babies in incubators; administering treatment to babies against the express wishes of the mother; and forcing the mother and baby to stay in hospital for seventy-two hours after delivery even when they were both healthy. There had also been complaints of arrogant, intimidating, disrespectful and patronising behaviour on the part of the hospital staff and of a lack of privacy'.

[61] *Dubská* (n 55) [56], citing Committee on the Elimination of Discrimination against Women, *Concluding Observations: Czech Republic*, UN Doc CEDAW/C/CZE/5 (2010) [37].

[62] *Dubská* (n 55) [96], [101].

[63] Oja and Yamin (n 22) 78, 80.

The dissenting opinion challenged the reasoning of the majority, demonstrating that the wishes and needs of the woman are not the basis for such regulation. Instead, respect for women's decisions are subordinated to other power struggles occurring in the medical context between doctors and midwives. The dissent recognises the detrimental impact of the majority's ruling that questions women's decisions about their reproductive lives by noting that, 'While only relatively few mothers might prefer to give birth at home, I have no reason to doubt that for these women this is a very important matter of personal choice'.[64] This case has been referred to the Grand Chamber and is pending.[65]

A 2013 Czech Constitutional Court decision implicitly recognised that the legislation prohibiting home births effectively reinforces stereotypes that women are incapable of appreciating the risks in connection with their health care choices and making rational decisions. This court questioned the public health rationale preferencing birth in hospitals, and noted that it acted as a de facto ban on home births, which curtailed women's freedom and dignity.[66] The Court recognised that,

> a modern democratic State founded on the rule of law is based on the protection of individual and inalienable freedoms, the delimitation of which closely relates to human dignity. That freedom, which includes freedom in personal activities, is accompanied by a certain degree of acceptable risk. The right of parents to a free choice of the place and mode of delivery is limited only by the interest in the safe delivery and health of the child; that interest cannot, however, be interpreted as an unambiguous preference for deliveries in hospital.[67]

V. Forced Sterilisation

While gender stereotypes about women's primary role as mothers have impeded women's access to contraceptive information and services, such stereotypes have also led to involuntary interventions during childbirth. Many cases covered by human rights bodies and courts concern denying women's choices during childbirth, and appear in the context of sterilisation, which provide further insight into the human rights dimensions of all involuntary practices during childbirth.

Under these circumstances, health care providers substitute their own views and beliefs about their patient's procreation, rather than securing the patient's informed consent to the procedure, often under the guise of medical necessity. The UN Special Rapporteur on Torture has noted the paternalistic assumptions underlying this practice: 'the administration of non-consensual medication or involuntary sterilisation is often claimed as being a necessary treatment for the

---

[64] *Dubská* (n 55) Lemmens, dissenting [4].
[65] ibid. The case was referred to the Grand Chamber on 1 June 2015.
[66] ibid [36].
[67] ibid [36].

so-called best interest of the person concerned'.[68] He references the FIGO ethical guidelines, which note that,

> sterilization for the prevention of future pregnancy cannot be ethically justified on grounds of medical emergency. Even if a future pregnancy may endanger a woman's life or health, she must be given the time she needs to consider her choice. Her informed decision must be respected, even if it is considered liable to be harmful to her health.[69]

The Inter-American Court of Human Rights, in *IV v Bolivia*, in its first case concerning informed consent in a health care context and also the first case concerning involuntary sterilisation, found a violation of the right to be free from discrimination based on the underlying gender stereotypes which led to sterilisation of the petitioner.[70] In 2000, IV, a Peruvian refugee in Bolivia, went to a public hospital to deliver her child. During her Caesarean section, IV was sterilised without her consent. She was only informed that doctors had performed a tubal ligation several days later. The Court recognised that the freedom and autonomy of women in sexual and reproductive health has historically been limited or annulled based on negative and harmful gender stereotypes in which women have been socially and culturally viewed as having a predominantly reproductive function, with men as decision-makers over women's bodies. The Court recognised that non-consensual sterilisation reflects this historically unequal relationship. The Court noted how the process of informed decision-making operated under the harmful stereotype that IV, as a woman, was unable to make such decisions responsibly, leading to 'an unjustified paternalistic medical intervention' restricting her autonomy and freedom.[71] The Court thus found a violation of the right to non-discrimination because she was a woman.[72] It also recognised the particular vulnerability to forced sterilisation facing certain women based on other characteristics, such as socioeconomic status, race, disability, or living with HIV.[73]

While all women may be subject to involuntary practices which could constitute a human rights violation (see above), stereotypes that certain groups of women – particularly marginalised women, such as Roma women, women living with HIV, migrant women, women with disabilities and poor women – are not 'good' mothers, are incapable of making responsible decisions, and therefore should not have children, have led to their involuntary sterilisation.[74]

---

[68] United Nations General Assembly, 'Report of the UN Special Rapporteur on Torture and Other Cruel, Inhuman and Degrading Treatment, Juan E Méndez', UN Doc A/HRC/22/53 (2013) [32].

[69] ibid [33]; see also World Health Organization 2014 (n 15).

[70] *IV v Bolivia*, Series C No 336 (Inter-American Court of Human Rights 30 November 2016).

[71] ibid [246].

[72] ibid [249].

[73] ibid [247]–[248].

[74] See generally World Health Organization 2014 (n 15).

VI. Conclusion

Persons have a right to dignified, respectful health care, free from discrimination, coercion and violence, throughout pregnancy and childbirth, as protected in international and regional human rights law and standards. The abuses against women during facility-based childbirth are serious violations of women's human rights. This mistreatment is a form of discrimination against women prohibited under international human rights law. There is a due diligence obligation to prevent, investigate and punish human rights violations occurring during childbirth.

To combat this and prevent mistreatment and abuse, measures need to be taken to guarantee human rights during childbirth, including adopting the recommendations issued by the UN Special Rapporteur on Violence against Women on the topic.[75] Reviewing and strengthening laws, policies and practices to prohibit mistreatment, violence and discrimination against women during pregnancy and childbirth is key. Laws must ensure, for example, autonomy in health care decision-making; guarantee free and informed consent, privacy and confidentiality; prohibit screening procedures that are not of benefit to the individual or the public; and ban involuntary treatment. The introduction of measures that address the drivers of abuse – including gender stereotyping – so as to prevent further abuses, is also crucial. For example, Ministries of Health at the national level could adopt a version of the FIGO guidelines on 'Harmful Stereotyping of Women in Health Care' (2011).[76] It is only by respecting persons' autonomy, integrity and agency to make informed decisions about their reproductive health, including during childbirth, that gender equality will ever be achieved.

---

[75] United Nations General Assembly 2019 (n 9).
[76] *Ethical Issues in Obstetrics and Gynecology* (n 14) 28–32.

7

How Should the Performance of Periparturient Vaginal Examinations be Regulated?

CHARLES FOSTER

I. Introduction

This chapter asks how the law and various quasi-legal regulatory mechanisms should regulate the performance of periparturient vaginal examinations (PPVEs).

The relevant substantive criminal and tort law is, by and large, well understood and uncontroversial. So far as crime is concerned, the performance of a non-sexually motivated PPVE would, absent consent or other lawful justification, be common assault. The relevant consent, there, is a consent in broad terms to an act of the nature of that done. If sexually motivated, it would be an assault by penetration.[1] Even a (non-sexual and non-maliciously) rough PPVE will often have been performed with the requisite consent. Indeed, in the case law and among practising lawyers it is rare, if not unknown, to hear of cases of unnecessary but non-sexually motivated vaginal examinations. There are, by contrast, plenty of cases where it was said an insufficient number of vaginal examinations were performed.

So far as tort is concerned, there are two possibilities: assault/battery, and negligence. Assault and battery are the application of unlawful force. 'Unlawful', in the case of non-sexually motivated PPVEs performed on a capacitous patient, will usually mean simply that the force (usually penetrative force) has been applied without sufficient consent. Consent here means, again consent in broad terms to an act of the relevant nature. Again, even a (non-sexual and non-maliciously) rough PPVE will often have been performed with the requisite consent.

In *Chatterton v Gerson* Garland J said that:

> Once a patient is informed in broad terms of the nature of the procedure which is intended, and gives her consent, that consent is real, and the cause of action on which to base a claim for failure to go into risks and implications is negligence, not trespass.[2]

[1] Sexual Offences Act 2003, s 2.
[2] *Chatterton v Gerson* [1981] QB 432 at 443.

That is what generally happens in practice. Cases in tort based on inadequate consent are generally pleaded as cases where the clinician has negligently failed to seek or to obtain the requisite consent.

The general law about liability in tort for failure to obtain the requisite consent to medical treatment or investigation is set out in the decision of the Supreme Court in *Montgomery v Lanarkshire Health Board*.[3] I raise *Montgomery* only to dismiss it. In the context of allegations that a PPVE has been performed inappropriately, *Montgomery* will generally be more or less irrelevant, primarily because it is mainly concerned with questions about the notification of risk. Its main focus is to ensure that patients are provided with the information about risks and benefits necessary to ensure that consent to treatment is adequately informed. The dominant view among clinicians and specialists in medical litigation is that in almost all cases of PPVEs there will be little clinical risk associated with the procedure, and the vaginal examination will (absent sexual motivation) have been suggested because it can reasonably be expected to provide information pertinent to the welfare of the woman and her baby.

Montgomery emphasised the importance of patient autonomy: her 'entitlement to decide on the risks to her health which she is willing to run (a decision which may be influenced by non-medical considerations)'.[4] The clinician's duty was 'to take reasonable care to ensure that the patient is aware of any material risks involved in any recommended treatment, and of any reasonable alternative or variant treatments'.[5] There is a two-fold test. The court must ask itself: first, what risks associated with the procedure were or should have been known to the clinician; and second, whether the patient should have been told about those risks by reference to whether they were material. A risk is material, for these purposes, if, in the circumstances of the case, a reasonable person in the patient's position would be likely to attach significance to the risk, or the clinician is or should reasonably be aware that the particular patient would be likely to attach significance to it. *Bolam* is plainly relevant to the first limb. It is not, said the *Montgomery* court, relevant to the second.

Note the reference to the 'reasonable' person in the materiality test. It will be an unusual case where a reasonable patient would find material something that a reasonable doctor would think it was unreasonable for that patient to find material. The views of reasonable patients will generally coincide with those of responsible doctors. Accordingly the concerns addressed by the law of tort (which will not sound in significant damages in the context of PPVEs) will also be those addressed by the regulatory bodies.

Assault/battery, whether in tort or criminal law, or whether framed (in tort) as negligence or as assault, in practice never appear as allegations in relation to PPVEs. A non-sexually-motivated PPVE that some clinicians may say was unnecessary

---

[3] *Montgomery v Lanarkshire Health Board* [2015] UKSC 11.
[4] ibid [84].
[5] ibid [87].

can almost always be justified within the broad ambit of the *Bolam/Bolitho* test as a responsible (or not irresponsible) attempt to monitor the progress of labour.[6] The *manner* in which a PPVE is performed (eg over-rough) could theoretically give rise to civil liability in negligence under the principles set out above, but the damages would be derisory.

Much more commonly the allegation in relation to a PPVE (typically in relation to periparturient brain damage, where it is said that there has been a failure to assess adequately the progress of labour), will be that it has not been performed where it should have been. Such allegations are (legally) straightforward contentions of negligence.

PPVEs, then, generate little legal controversy in practice. There is one exception. It relates to the law of necessity.

II. Necessity

Some PPVEs will be performed when the patient cannot give appropriate consent. This may be: (a) because the patient is constitutionally incapable ever of giving consent; or (b) because capacity is temporarily affected by pain, exhaustion, or the central effects of analgesic agents such as 'gas and air'.

Constitutional incapacity presents no legal difficulty: the Mental Capacity 2005 applies, and the treatment given must be in the patient's best interests. The 'patient', here, is the mother, not the baby.[7] But cases falling into the second category, (b), are arguably more interesting. In such cases it is common to see the common law doctrine of necessity invoked.

The doctrine stipulates that an otherwise unauthorised procedure may be lawful if it is necessary. 'Necessary', here, means that it would be unreasonable (and not merely inconvenient) to delay the procedure until the patient can give consent.

The classic cases of necessity, unsurprisingly, are where procedures for which specific consent has not been given are performed under general anaesthesia. Thus in *Marshall v Curry* the patient underwent an operation for the repair of a hernia.[8] In the course of the operation a grossly diseased testicle was discovered. Without waking up the patient and seeking his consent for the removal of the testicle, the testicle was removed. Two justifications for the removal were cited: first (it was said) the removal was part and parcel of the hernia operation; and, second, the surgeon thought that the testicle was gangrenous and constituted a threat to life and health. The consequent battery action was dismissed. The surgeon was

---

[6] *Bolam v Friern Hospital Management Committee* [1957] 1 WLR 582; *Bolitho v City and Hackney Health Authority* [1998] AC 232.
[7] *Re MB (Caesarean Section)* [1997] EWCA Civ 1361; *St George's Healthcare NHS Trust v S* [1998] 3 WLR 936; *Paton v British Pregnancy Advisory Service Trustees* [1979] QB 276.
[8] *Marshall v Curry* [1933] 3 DLR 260 (Sup Ct Nova Scotia).

justified in acting without consent 'in order to save the life or preserve the health' of the patient.[9]

The courts are rightly reluctant to allow exceptions (or apparent exceptions) to the principle that where consent can (at some time) be given, consent is an absolute requirement. Thus, Lord Goff observed (obiter) in *F v West Berkshire Health Authority*, that a clinician 'should do no more than is reasonably required, in the best interests of the patient, before he recovers consciousness'.[10]

Where it would be medically feasible to allow a patient to return to a position of full (or adequate) capacity, this must generally be done. But, pragmatically recognising that this is sometimes not desirable, the courts have often found that the requisite consent has been implied, and (at least many) modern applications of the law of necessity should be seen as examples of implied consent. The clearest examples are where a consent form has been signed, but does not deal explicitly with the circumstances that eventuate. Thus in *Davis v Barking, Havering and Brentwood Health Authority*, the claimant signed a form consenting to the 'administration of general, local or other anaesthetics,' but was told that a general anaesthetic would be used.[11] It was, but a caudal block was given too, as a result of which the claimant temporarily lost control of her legs and bladder and had some minor residual problems. Her claim in battery was dismissed. The question, said the court (articulating the general principle which we have seen already) was: 'Have the defendants shown that the plaintiff consented to a procedure the nature and effect of which had in broad terms been explained to her?'[12]

What of the position re PPVEs on temporarily incapacitous patients? Is necessity relevant? Several general observations can be made.

(a) there can never be any excuse for an unnecessarily rough PPVE. No one would ever give consent for such an examination, and accordingly no implied consent can arise;

(b) if the incapacity results from the administration of gas and air, it will usually be possible to stop the administration, allow the patient to regain capacity, and then seek consent;

(c) pain and/or distress and/or exhaustion may truncate capacity. Where this is the case, the truncation is likely to last until delivery. Here, there will generally be little difficulty about implying consent or (if that is different) invoking necessity. The patient is in the hospital precisely because she wishes to have a safe delivery, and a clinically indicated PPVE is designed to achieve that result;

---

[9] Per Chisholm CJ at 265; *cp Murray v McMurchy* [1949] 2 DLR 442 (Sup Ct BC), where a patient undergoing Caesarean section was sterilised because she had fibroids which the surgeon thought would make future pregnancies hazardous.

[10] *F v West Berkshire Health Authority* [1990] 2 AC 1 [77].

[11] *Davis v Barking, Havering and Brentwood HA* [1993] 4 Med LR 85.

[12] ibid [91]. See, similarly, *Brushnett v Cowan* [1991] 2 Med LR 271 (Newfoundland CA).

(d) all that said, to deploy necessity/implied consent now seems unnecessarily to complicate the law. The principles relating to the medical (or any) treatment of an incapacitous patient are comprehensively summarised in the Mental Capacity Act 2005 – and practical guidance is given in the associated Code of Practice. Treatment of an incapacitous patient is only justified if it is in the patient's best interests. Autonomous decision-making must be facilitated if and insofar as possible (which may, in the gas and air example, mandate cessation of the administration until consent can be obtained), a bona fide belief that the decision has been made in the patient's best interests amounts to a defence.

III. Relevant Guidelines

The General Medical Council's (GMC) foundational document, *Good Medical Practice* provides that: 'You must provide a good standard of practice and care. If you assess, diagnose or treat patients, you must … where necessary, examine the patient'.[13] And: 'You must treat patients as individuals and respect their dignity and privacy'.[14]

The GMC's supplementary guidance *Intimate Examinations and Chaperones* notes that 'Intimate examinations can be embarrassing or distressing for patients and whenever you examine a patient you should be sensitive to what they may think of as intimate'.[15] It continues, inter alia and in so far as relevant:

5 Before conducting an intimate examination, you should:

a. explain to the patient why an examination is necessary and give the patient an opportunity to ask questions

b. explain what the examination will involve, in a way the patient can understand, so that the patient has a clear idea of what to expect, including any pain or discomfort

c. get the patient's permission before the examination and record that the patient has given it

d. offer the patient a chaperone …

e. if dealing with a child or young person

- you must assess their capacity to consent to the examination
- if they lack the capacity to consent, you should seek their parent's consent

f. give the patient privacy to undress and dress, and keep them covered as much as possible to maintain their dignity; do not help the patient to remove clothing unless they have asked you to, or you have checked with them that they want you to help.

---

[13] General Medical Council, *Good Medical Practice* (London, General Medical Council, 2013) [15].
[14] ibid [47].
[15] General Medical Council, *Intimate Examinations and Chaperones* (London, General Medical Council, 2013) 3.

6 During the examination, you must follow the guidance in *Consent: patients and doctors making decisions together*. In particular you should:

a.   explain what you are going to do before you do it and, if this differs from what you have told the patient before, explain why and seek the patient's permission

b.   stop the examination if the patient asks you to

c.   keep discussion relevant and don't make unnecessary personal comments.[16]

In relation to intimate examination of anaesthetised patients, the guidance states: 'Before you carry out an intimate examination on an anaesthetised patient, or supervise a student who intends to carry one out, you must make sure that the patient has given consent in advance, usually in writing'.[17]

It is not clear that the guidance about chaperones is explicitly recognised as relevant in the perinatal context. In practice, of course, another healthcare professional, or the woman's partner or companion, will usually be present.[18]

The GMC guidance is very general. It makes no specific reference to the exigencies of the perinatal situation. In particular there is no mention of capacity-affecting conditions or substances, or of the urgent need to undertake PPVEs for the safety of the woman and her child. The context envisaged appears to be a GP surgery or a gynaecological clinic rather than the delivery suite. The need for examination is mentioned, but the overall tone, with its emphasis on the obtaining of appropriate consent from presumed capacitous patients, tends towards the discouragement of examination.

The Royal College of Obstetricians and Gynaecologists has issued advice on intimate perinatal examinations in its document Obtaining Valid Consent.[19] This, as one would expect, is tailored far more tightly to the obstetric context. It provides, inter alia:

Care must be taken when obtaining consent from women who are in labour. This applies particularly if they are in pain or under the influence of narcotic analgesics. Women who are pain-free in labour as a result of effective epidural anaesthesia can consent normally. Where possible, women should be informed during the antenatal period about predictable problems that may occur in labour. It is important for carers of women in labour to be aware that the woman may not recall such previously presented information during labour. If a procedure is planned, she should receive a full explanation as if she had not previously had the relevant information. RCOG patient information may be particularly helpful. It is available from: www.rcog.org.uk.

When consent has to be obtained from a woman during painful labour, such as to perform a vaginal examination, episiotomy, operative delivery or to site an epidural,

---

[16] ibid 6 (footnotes omitted).

[17] ibid 7.

[18] Although note General Medical Council (n 15) [10]: 'A relative or friend of the patient is not an impartial observer and so would not usually be a suitable chaperone, but you should comply with a reasonable request to have such a person present as well as a chaperone'.

[19] Royal College of Obstetricians and Gynaecologists, *Obtaining Valid Consent (Clinical Governance Advice No 6)* (London, Royal College of Obstetricians and Gynaecologists, 2015).

information should be given between contractions. If appropriate, upon admission in labour or for induction of labour, consideration should be given to the provision of summarised information concerning possible procedures and interventions. Women should be encouraged to express their views on such procedures so that their carers are aware of the choices made by the women and act accordingly.[20]

The Royal College of Midwives has issued its own guidance. It notes that vaginal examinations are the cornerstone of the assessment of the progress of labour, but that they have shortcomings – notably subjectivity, and the consequent difficulty of drawing meaningful conclusions by comparing the results of PPVEs undertaken by different operators.[21] Its guidance about the indications for PPVEs and the care that needs to be taken when undertaking them is far more holistic and explicit than that of the GMC or the RCOG. It shows up their shortcomings. Here is an extract:

The process of care in labour usually demands a focus on the woman's genitalia, with exposure to people that are strangers (Devane 1996). Midwives have sometimes responded to the embarrassment of this situation by adopting ritualistic semi-sterile procedures, and by using language which infantilises the woman. Such behaviour can now easily be recognised as inappropriate. Midwives should give consideration to the emotional and psychosexual aspects of any procedure, and talk about these issues in a respectful way.

Many women experience vaginal examinations as painful (Bergstrom et al 1992), distressing and embarrassing (Devane 1996) and invasive (Stuart 2000). They bring up issues of sexual intimacy, invasion of privacy and vulnerability (Warren 1999). They also carry a risk of infection (Seaward et al 1997).

Menage (1996) suggests that the physical pain, feelings of powerlessness, lack of information and an unsympathetic attitude by the midwife or the doctor may contribute to psychological trauma; she also points out that this may have medico-legal implications. The GMC has received many complaints about improper or rough behaviour during intimate examinations (RCOG 1997). Lewin et al's (2005) survey of 104 primiparas' experience of vaginal examinations found that the practice needed to be more sensitive to pain and distress, improve on information giving about possible alternative options and obtaining informed consent.

Vaginal examinations must be considered within the context of the woman's individual experience of labour. Examinations carried out with sensitivity, in privacy by one midwife with whom the woman has a good relationship will be experienced as very different from brusque examinations from different professionals whom the woman hardly knows (Clement 1994).

Consent should be obtained for each vaginal examination: it should not be assumed for repeated assessments.[22]

---

[20] ibid [4.1].
[21] Royal College of Midwives, *Evidence Based Guidelines for Midwifery-Led Care in Labour: Assessing Progress in Labour* (London, Royal College of Midwives, 2012).
[22] ibid 4–5.

No less should be expected of doctors than of midwives. Between them, the GMC, the RCOG and the RCM guidance comprise a comprehensive (and commonsensical) code for the performance of PPVEs, but there is no reason why the GMC and the RCOG should not emulate the RCM, and every reason why they should.

Between them, the guidelines from the three bodies summarise the effect of the relevant law and go further. Rough examinations (for instance) that fall short of an assault and which it would be hard to characterise as negligent would fall foul of the guidance and could lead to a finding that a practitioner's practice was impaired. Sanctions guidance (eg of the GMC/the Medical Practitioners Tribunal Service)[23] set out the criteria that should be applied in determining the gravity of a departure from the guidance, and accordingly the sanction that should follow.

The mention in the RCM guideline of reports of complaints to the GMC about 'improper or rough behaviour during intimate examinations' comes from a 1997 RCOG publication.[24] There are no recent published data indicating how many GMC complaints or RCM complaints relate to such examinations. The standard of proof in the relevant disciplinary tribunals (the Medical Practitioners Tribunal Service in the case of doctors, and the Nursing & Midwifery Council in the case of midwives) is the civil standard – the balance of probabilities. The rules of evidence there are much more relaxed than in the criminal courts, and significantly more relaxed than in the civil courts. This enables a detailed inquisition into the propriety of PPVEs, unfettered by legal niceties. The nature of the inquisition has led to complaints by many practitioners.

The sanctions that can be imposed are draconian – including erasure. Erasure has a far more significant effect on a clinician's life than a finding of liability to pay the (usually modest) damages that would be made by a civil court considering allegations of assault or negligence relating to a rough examination.

It follows that in large majority of cases the professional regulators are better placed than the courts to police the performance of PPVEs. The threat of criminal or civil litigation is no doubt present in the minds of many clinicians. The actual danger of civil or criminal proceedings is remote, but it probably does little harm, and perhaps does some good.

Local disciplinary procedures can and sometimes do play an important part in detecting and eliminating inappropriate practice. They are faster than the statutory process and can take offenders quickly out of the clinic, but there are widespread concerns amongst practitioners about the fairness of those procedures. They often produce findings adverse to practitioners in circumstances noted for their lack of

---

[23] General Medical Council and Medical Practitioners Tribunal Service, *Sanctions Guideline: For Members of Medical Practitioners Tribunals and for the General Medical Council's Decision Makers* (London, General Medical Council, 2017), in effect from February 2018.

[24] Royal College of Obstetricians and Gynaecologists, *Intimate Examinations: Report of a Working Party* (London, RCOG Press, 1997).

transparency and independence, and for the difficulty of challenge. Those criticisms apply decreasingly to the statutory regulators. The speed with which local procedures can take potential offenders out of the clinic is not in itself a reason to prefer those procedures to the statutory scheme: the statutory regulators do have an (often used) power of interim suspension, pending a final determination.

The civil and criminal law, then, have little meaningful impact on the regulation of PPVEs. The regulators do. Not only is this the case, it should be the case.

8

Including the Victim's Perspective: Can Vaginal Examinations Ever be Sexual Assaults?

CATARINA SJÖLIN

I. Introduction

Vaginal examination involves the insertion of one or more fingers into a woman's vagina by a medical professional. Vaginal examination is routinely done to determine the dilation of the cervix to assess the onset and progress of labour, but it is not always medically necessary.[1] It is a standard part of maternity care, particularly in labour, and even when medically justified can be unpleasant, painful and sometimes traumatic for the examined woman.[2] Critically, it is not always the subject of valid consent.[3] This chapter examines whether a criminal offence may be committed when a medical professional conducts a non-consensual vaginal examination, examining first common assault and then sexual assault. Gynaecological examinations have often been used in case law and legal literature as examples when considering what makes conduct 'sexual' or 'indecent', but the conduct is rarely analysed from the examined woman's perspective. Consideration is given here to that neglected perspective and what difference it makes when the examined woman considers her violation to be beyond the physical. The chapter concludes that neither common

---

[1] H Dahlen et al, 'Vaginal Examination during Normal Labor: Routine Examination or Routine Intervention?' (2013) 13 *International Journal of Childbirth* 142; S Downe et al, 'Routine Vaginal Examinations for Assessing Progress of Labour to Improve Outcomes for Women and Babies at Term' (2013) 7 *Cochrane Database of Systematic Reviews* Art No CD010088.

[2] In one study of first-time mothers across three labour wards, the findings were that 'Painful and distressing vaginal examinations were reported at some stage by almost half the women. Two-fifths felt, on balance, that they could not really refuse an examination even if they wished to do so, and about one-third wished the staff had provided additional information about vaginal examination': D Lewin et al, 'Women's Experiences of Vaginal Examinations in Labour' (2005) 21 *Midwifery* 267.

[3] J Marshall et al, 'An Observational Study to Explore the Power and Effect of the Labor Ward Culture on Consent to Intrapartum Procedures' (2011) 1 *International Journal of Childbirth* 82.

nor sexual assault adequately cover most non-consensual vaginal examinations, and suggests ways to better mark them in substantive or sentencing law.

II. Common Assault

The term 'common assault' encompasses both technical assault and battery. Both are defined at common law although the sentence is set by statute.[4] For technical assault, the defendant (D) intentionally or recklessly causes the victim (V) to apprehend immediate and unlawful personal violence.[5] For battery, D intentionally or recklessly inflicts unlawful force on V.[6] 'Force' and 'violence' in these definitions do not connote a high level or severe type of force: the most minor of touches will suffice, by person or object and the contact need not be hostile.[7] Unlawfulness means, for present purposes, lack of V's consent, lack of D's genuine belief in V's consent, that the conduct does not fall within the exception for conduct within 'generally acceptable standards' and D cannot successfully claim the defence of necessity.[8]

A vaginal examination may involve a technical assault (if V is conscious and aware of D's intentions to carry out the examination) but as touching is always involved, a vaginal examination is more likely to be considered as a battery. The fact that the touching is in a medical context does not prevent the vaginal examination from amounting to an offence.[9] The intentional touching in a vaginal examination is thus capable of amounting to a battery, but unlawfulness must also be made out.

Lack of consent is assumed for the purposes of this chapter and so it is also assumed that V has capacity to give or refuse consent.

The exception for conduct which falls within generally acceptable standards is used to avoid everyday contact (such as being jostled on a busy bus) and perhaps also less common contact (such as receiving CPR when struck down by a heart attack in the street) being categorised as batteries in the absence of V's consent.[10]

---

[4] Criminal Justice Act 1988, s 39.

[5] *R v Ireland* [1998] AC 147 (HL).

[6] ibid.

[7] See for minor touches sufficing: W Blackstone *Commentaries on the Laws of England* (1765–9) Book 3, Chapter 8 and *Cole v Turner* (1704) 87 ER 907; regarding types of objects consider V stabbed herself on D's concealed hypodermic needle in *DPP v Santa-Bermudez* [2003] EWHC 2908 (Admin) and in *DPP v K* [1990] 1 WLR 1067 (DC) V was sprayed with acid by a hand drier into which V had poured the acid; regarding hostility see D Ormerod and K Laird, *Smith, Hogan and Ormerod's Criminal Law*, 15th edn (Oxford, Oxford University Press, 2018) 658–59; C Sjölin, 'The Need to Kill of Zombie Law: Indecent Assault, Where It Went Wrong, and How to Put It Right' (2017) 81 *Journal of Criminal Law* 50.

[8] *R v Jones* (1986) 83 Cr App R 375 (CA); *Collins v Wilcock* [1984] 1 WLR 1172 (DC) per Goff LJ; and *F v West Berkshire Health Authority* [1990] 2 AC 1 (HL) per Lord Donaldson MR; *F v West Berkshire Health Authority* per Lord Goff.

[9] *F* (n 8) and *Airedale NHS Trust v Bland* [1993] AC 789 (HL) per Lord Keith 857 and per Lord Brown-Wilkinson 882 (*cf* Lord Mustill in *Bland* 891).

[10] *F* (n 8) per Lord Donaldson MR.

What the exception covers is obviously context dependent: the CPR example could not fall within the exception if the person having the heart attack was not a stranger in the street but a patient in hospital who had given instructions not to be resuscitated. Outside the emergency maternity context (unconscious woman in labour rushed into maternity department), a vaginal examination does not sit comfortably within this exception; our paradigm situation of a vaginal examination without consent is not everyday, unavoidable contact but a medical procedure on an individual who is able to choose whether or not to consent.

It may be argued that medical procedures do not fall comfortably within the exception at all. Lord Goff, whose analysis originally recognised the exception, was emphatic that medical treatment does not fall within it and must instead be justified by consent or under the defence of necessity unless it is to be unlawful, in order to respect V's right to self-determination: 'Every human being of adult years and sound mind has a right to determine what shall be done with his own body; and a surgeon who performs an operation without his patient's consent commits an assault'.[11]

Lord Goff's conception of necessity can only apply where V is incapable of giving consent and has two requirements:

> [N]ot only (1) must there be a necessity to act when it is not practicable to communicate with the assisted person, but also (2) the action taken must be such as a reasonable person would in all the circumstances take, acting in the best interests of the assisted person.[12]

Necessity is a defence much-avoided judicially, but where it has been recognised in modern times it has tended to be in medical situations.[13] Lord Goff's model of necessity is a more attractive way of dealing with medical situations than the generally acceptable conduct exception as it makes a sharp distinction between the non-capacitous V and the capacitous but unconsenting V which may be lost when the focus is the general acceptability of the conduct. Could the necessity defence apply in the non-consensual vaginal examination situation?

Necessity looks unlikely to avail D in our vaginal examination situation because V has capacity and is not consenting, so (1) is not made out. Could D still claim the defence on the basis that V is not acting in her own best interests by refusing consent? Lord Goff firmly, and with respect rightly, rejects this argument:

> [O]fficious intervention cannot be justified by the principle of necessity. So intervention cannot be justified when another more appropriate person is available and willing to act; nor can it be justified when it is contrary to the known wishes of the assisted person, to the extent that he is capable of rationally forming such a wish.[14]

---

[11] ibid, per Lord Goff 73 quoting with approval the words of Cardozo J in *Schloendorff v Society of New York Hospital* (1914) 105 NE 92, 93.

[12] ibid, per Lord Goff 75.

[13] For example *F* (n 8) (per Lord Goff and Lord Brandon), *R v Bournewood Community and Mental Health NHS Trust* [1998] 2 WLR 764 (CA) and *Re A (Children) (Conjoined Twins: Medical Separation)* [2001] Fam 147 (CA) per Brooke LJ.

[14] *F* (n 8) 76.

This view is reflected in the Mental Capacity Act 2005 (used to determine in civil law whether V has the capacity to make a particular decision) which specifically states that 'A person is not to be treated as unable to make a decision merely because he makes an unwise decision'.[15] And if able to make a decision, that decision must be respected as V's own decision to make.

While self-determination might be collapsed into autonomy, Jonathan Herring and Jesse Wall argue that bodily integrity is a separate principle which recognises the 'integrated body' and provides for 'the exclusive use and control over our own bodies on the basis that our bodies are the "site" and "location" of where our subjectivity engages with the world'.[16] Case law has also recognised the principle of bodily integrity, although not as clearly or analytically as Herring and Wall argue it:

> Every human being's right to life carries with it, as an intrinsic part of it, rights of bodily integrity and autonomy – the right to have one's own body whole and intact and (on reaching an age of understanding) to take decisions about one's own body.[17]

Both self-determination and bodily integrity thus provide strong arguments against ignoring V's refusal of consent to the bodily interference inherent in a vaginal examination.

Could D claim that V's failure to act in the best interests *of the foetus* makes it necessary for the vaginal examination to take place? In law the foetus is not a person (with attendant rights) until s/he is born, but is also not an adjunct of the mother: it is a 'unique organism'.[18] Because of that unique status, however, simply to apply 'the principles of a law evolved in relation to autonomous beings is bound to mislead'.[19] As the Court of Appeal rhetorically asks in *St George's Healthcare NHS Trust v S* when considering the legality of a Caesarean section on a competent woman who was refusing it: 'how can a forced invasion of a competent adult's body against her will even for the most laudable of motives (the preservation of life) be ordered without irremediably damaging the principle of self-determination?'[20]

Approaching the issue from the aims of medical intervention, Lord Keith, again in the House of Lords, in *Airedale NHS Trust v Bland* states that 'The object of medical treatment and care is to benefit *the patient*' (emphasis added).[21]

---

[15] Mental Capacity Act 2005, s 1(4).

[16] J Herring and J Wall, 'The Nature and Significance of the Right to Bodily Integrity' [2017] *Cambridge Law Journal* 566.

[17] *Re A* (n 13) [258] per Walker LJ.

[18] *Attorney-General's Reference (No 3 of 1994)* [1998] AC 245 (HL) per Lord Mustill 256 and applied with approval in *CP (A Child) v First-tier Tribunal (Criminal Injuries Compensation)* [2014] EWCA Civ 1554.

[19] ibid.

[20] *St George's Healthcare NHS Trust v S* [1998] 3 WLR 936 (CA).

[21] *Bland* (n 9) 857.

For Butler-Sloss LJ (albeit in obiter comments) in *Re MB (Caesarian Section)*, the patient is the woman, not the foetus:

> A competent woman who has the capacity to decide may, for religious reasons, other reasons, for rational or irrational reasons or for no reason at all, choose not to have medical intervention, even though … the consequence may be death or serious handicap of the child she bears, or her own death … The foetus up to the moment of birth does not have any separate interests capable of being taken into account when a court has to consider an application for a declaration in respect of a Caesarean section operation.[22]

The Court of Appeal in *St George's* accurately sums up the position in a paragraph worth quoting at length:

> In our judgment while pregnancy increases the personal responsibilities of a woman it does not diminish her entitlement to decide whether or not to undergo medical treatment. Although human, and protected by the law in a number of different ways set out in the judgment in *In re MB (An Adult: Medical Treatment)*, an unborn child is not a separate person from its mother. Its need for medical assistance does not prevail over her rights. She is entitled not to be forced to submit to an invasion of her body against her will, whether her own life or that of her unborn child depends on it. Her right is not reduced or diminished merely because her decision to exercise it may appear morally repugnant.[23]

V's right to be the object of medical intervention together with her rights to self-determination and bodily integrity cannot be overborn in the name of necessity in the foetus' best interests.

All that remains in the way of criminal liability for D is a claim that D had a genuine belief in consent. D will be a medical professional with the requisite training and time in practice and s/he will be aware of the requirement to obtain informed consent for all examinations.[24] Despite this, s/he may rely on the common nature of vaginal examinations in general practice as a basis for a genuine belief in consent and/or a claim that a vaginal examination is generally accepted in the antenatal and particularly labour context, despite incomplete or non-existent steps taken to obtain consent. As examined above, the best interests of V and the foetus cannot in themselves legitimise a non-consensual vaginal examination. Nevertheless, D could rely on them to claim a genuine belief that V was consenting based on a belief that V would prioritise the best interests of herself and the foetus. As there is no reasonableness requirement to the belief in consent, it is possible that the prosecution could struggle to disprove a genuine belief in consent were this argument deployed.

---

[22] *Re MB (Caesarean Section)* [1997] EWCA Civ 1361.

[23] *St George's Healthcare NHS Trust* (n 20) 957.

[24] See Department of Health, *Reference Guide to Obtaining Consent for Examination or Treatment*, 2nd edn (London, Central Office of Information, 2009).

In conclusion, it is possible to make a case for a non-consensual vaginal examination to amount to common assault in both forms (depending on whether V apprehends she is about to be touched) but the prosecution might struggle, depending on the evidence, to prove that D did not have a genuine belief in consent.

III. Sexual Assault

Despite use of the term 'assault' in the Sexual Offences Act 2003, sexual assaults are not simply aggravated forms of common assault; they are new creatures, of statute, defined in a way both specific and broad. Two forms of sexual assault under the Act could be engaged here: section 2 sexual assault by penetration and section 3 sexual assault. (For rape (section 1) penile penetration of the vagina is required, so this does not cover a vaginal examination.)[25]

For section 2 the vaginal penetration can be by anything, so penetration by finger or object would be covered.[26] As penetration is a continuing act, if consent were withdrawn during penetration any continuing penetration could amount to the offence.[27]

For section 3, 'touching' is required, which can be with anything (including a body part) and includes penetration, so section 3 includes conduct also caught by section 2.[28] The apprehension V has of being touched in a vaginal examination (the technical assault) does not involve a touch and so is not caught by sections 2 or 3.

Beyond the specific physical act involved, the elements of the offences under sections 2 and 3 are identical: D intended to do the physical act, the act was sexual, V was not consenting and D did not reasonably believe that V was consenting.[29] In a vaginal examination situation there will be intentional touching which amounts to penetration of V's vagina. As we are assuming a lack of consent, the elements which call for discussion are lack of a reasonable belief in consent and the sexual nature of the act.

A. Reasonable Belief in Consent

The reasonableness of D's belief in V's consent is determined having regard to all the circumstances, including any steps taken by D to ascertain whether V was consenting.[30] Compared to a normal sexual encounter, the steps are clearer

---

[25] Sexual Offences Act 2003, s 1 also covers penile penetration by mouth or anus, but only vaginal penetration is relevant here.
[26] Sexual Offences Act 2003, s 2(1)(a).
[27] Sexual Offences Act 2003, s 79(2).
[28] Sexual Offences Act 2003, s 79(8).
[29] Sexual Offences Act 2003, ss 2(1) and 3(1).
[30] Sexual Offences Act 2003, ss 2(2) and 3(2).

in the medical professional-patient relationship: there is an expectation that medical professionals will seek *explicit* informed consent from patients before examinations/procedures are commenced and there is a framework for seeking that consent.[31] Even if there was a genuine belief in consent (as examined above in relation to common assault), the failure to take the specified steps to obtain actual consent should make it easier to prove that this belief was not reasonable.

The reality may be different. In routine sexual offence cases the impact of the reasonable belief requirement has been limited, it is argued, because in most sexual offence cases V's conduct is questioned far more than D's, such that D's belief is more easily found reasonable.[32] The problem in the medical professional-patient context is unlikely to be this, but instead an absence of evidence due to lack of accurate medical notes reflecting the failure to obtain consent and/or unwillingness of other medical professionals present during the vaginal examination to admit their colleague's (and perhaps their own) failure to follow the proper procedure. Assuming such evidential problems could be overcome, the remaining issue is whether the vaginal examination is sexual.

B. Sexual

'Sexual' is defined in the Sexual Offences Act 2003:

> For the purposes of this Part ..., penetration, touching or any other activity is sexual if a reasonable person would consider that—
>
> (a) whatever its circumstances or any person's purpose in relation to it, it is because of its nature sexual, or
> (b) because of its nature it may be sexual and because of its circumstances or the purpose of any person in relation to it (or both) it is sexual.[33]

The forerunner of sections 2 and 3, abolished by the Sexual Offences Act 2003, was indecent assault. The Home Office review which led to the 2003 Act suggested using the term 'sexual' in the new offences instead of 'indecent', stating that 'sexual' was a narrower term, although the review made no attempt to define it.[34] The two-part definition in the final Act was intended by the government to update but not differ in any material way from the way 'indecent' had been defined by the House of Lords case of *R v Court*.[35]

---

[31] See Department of Health (n 24).

[32] E Finch and V Munro, 'Breaking Boundaries? Sexual Consent in the Jury Room' (2006) 26 *Legal Studies* 303; A Carline and C Gunby, '"How an Ordinary Jury Makes Sense of it is a Mystery": Barristers' Perspectives on Rape, Consent and the Sexual Offences Act 2003' (2011) 32 *Liverpool Law Review* 237.

[33] Sexual Offences Act 2003, s 78.

[34] UK Home Office, *Setting the Boundaries Reforming the Law on Sex Offences* (London, Home Office, 2000) [2.14.2]–[2.14.4].

[35] *R v Court* [1989] AC 28 (HL). See the Explanatory Notes to s 78 and ministerial statement by Paul Goggins MP, Hansard, HC Standing Committee B, 8th Sitting, 18 September 2003, col 312.

Indecent assault was an aggravated version of both forms of common assault – aggravated by the indecency. What amounted to 'indecency' was not necessarily clear cut, as the case of *Court* had to grapple with. Court had spanked a 12-year-old girl 12 times (over her clothes) and when asked by police why he had done this said 'I don't know – buttock fetish'. He argued at trial that this answer should not have been put before the jury for them to consider when determining whether his actions were indecent. The trial judge disagreed, as did the judges in the Court of Appeal and all bar one of the judges in the House of Lords. The Court of Appeal concluded that the indecent assault involved an assault in circumstances of indecency and required as its mental element that D intentionally assaulted V 'with knowledge of the indecent circumstances or being reckless as to the existence of them'.[36] An act which was not indecent could not be made indecent by an indecent motive, but the motive *could* be relevant where the act was capable of being indecent.[37] The majority in the House of Lords agreed that acts which were not indecent could not be made indecent by D's motive. Where the act was ambiguous, they required that D *must* intend that the act be indecent. Where the act was unambiguously indecent D must be aware of the indecent circumstances but need not have an indecent intention. Lord Goff, dissenting, stated that indecent motive must always be irrelevant; it could not be an element of the offence on some occasions but not others.

The approach of the majority of the House of Lords in *Court* can be distilled into three categories of conduct each of which required different treatment of D's knowledge and intentions:

(1)   inherently non-indecent activity – could not be rendered indecent by D's indecent motive;
(2)   inherently indecent conduct – could amount to an indecent assault only if D was *aware of* the circumstances which make the conduct indecent (but s/he need not have *intended* to act indecently);
(3)   conduct capable of being indecent – could only amount to an indecent assault if D *intended* indecency.

Despite the government's intention, there are important differences between the *Court* categorisation and section 78. First, section 78 does not explicitly state that some acts cannot be sexual. The Explanatory Notes assert that the fact that a particular individual may obtain sexual gratification from carrying out an activity would not make it sexual, so 'obscure fetishes do not fall within the definition of sexual activity', but the statutory language does not support this.[38] Activity may be sexual under section 78 if the reasonable person considers that by 'its nature it may be sexual', not that they themselves consider it sexual. If any person (whether D or someone else) considers the activity sexual, then it is obviously *capable* of

---

[36] *R v Court* [1987] QB 156 (CA) 162.
[37] *R v George* [1956] Crim LR 52 (Lincoln Assizes), Streatfeild J.
[38] Explanatory Notes to the Sexual Offences Act 2003, [146].

being sexual. With the inexorable spread of the internet, no fetish is truly obscure anymore. The reasonable person can be considered more sexually aware now, not only because it is more acceptable to talk about sexual matters and judgemental attitudes to matters of personal morality continue to ebb away, but also because many and varied sex abuse scandals mean that there is also a growing awareness of the awful things which some people will do to others.[39] The reasonable person does not consider a baby in a sexual way, but knows that there are those who do, so the defendant's wiping of a baby's bottom may or may not actually be sexual, but it is certainly *capable* of being sexual. The Court of Appeal's suggestion in *R v H* that, when considering section 78, the jury ask themselves first, whether the activity is *capable* of being sexual and second whether it *was* sexual, is unnecessarily complicated: the first of these question is, it is submitted, pointless.[40] The approach the Court suggests for the judge on a submission of no case to answer, which is to consider section 78(a) and then (b) (is it by nature sexual, or by circumstances/purposes sexual), is more helpful and grounded in the statute.[41]

At the other end of the scale is conduct which is by its nature sexual (section 78(a)). Although it has been argued that no touching is inherently sexual,[42] touching under the Act includes penetrative activity and it is difficult to see how penile penetration of another's vagina, mouth or anus could not be sexual and the same goes for oral sex whether involving vagina or anus.[43] There is no *Court* requirement in section 78(a) that D be aware of the sexual circumstances for the conduct to be sexual in this category. There may be non-sexual purposes for inherently sexual activity, for example, punishment or humiliation. Simester et al argue that such punishment or humiliation would be of a 'particularly intimate, sexual sort' and so would be sexual in any event,[44] but the point is that section 78(a) leaves no room for non-sexual purposes, or indeed sexual ones, to be considered if the conduct is by its nature sexual. This is not unfair on D as it is difficult to see how D could be intentionally doing one of the inherently sexual acts listed above without being aware of the circumstances which make it inherently sexual, even if D's purpose was not sexual.

This leaves the vast majority of conduct dealt with by sections 2 and 3 in the ambiguous category governed by section 78(b) and here there is a more radical

---

[39] Disapproval of same-sex relationships and sex before marriage continues to decrease: K Swales and E Attar Taylor, 'Moral Issues; Sex, Gender Identity and Euthanasia' in E Clery et al (eds), *British Social Attitudes: The 34th Report* (London, The National Centre for Social Research, 2017). In pretty much any sphere people will do awful things to others. Scandals over the last decade have ranged from the world of entertainment, religion, sport, politics and children's homes.

[40] *R v H* [2005] 1 WLR 2005 (CA) [13]; A Simester et al, *Simester and Sullivan's Criminal Law: Theory and Doctrine*, 6th edn (London, Bloomsbury, 2016) 471–72.

[41] *H* [2005] 1 WLR 2005 (CA) [12].

[42] I Bantekas, 'Can Touching Always be Sexual When There is No Sexual Intent?' (2008) 72 *The Journal of Criminal Law* 251.

[43] See [145] and [146], Explanatory Notes to the Sexual Offences Act 2003; Ormerod and Laird (n 7) 783; Simester et al (n 40) 469–70.

[44] Simester et al (n 40) 469.

divergence from *Court*. Under the Act, D need not have a sexual intent or purpose for the ambiguous act to become sexual: D's purpose is just one factor to consider in making the determination, which is objective.[45] As section 78(b) does not require that the activity be *exclusively* sexual, a non-sexual purpose or description of the act would not prevent the jury concluding that there is also a sexual aspect to the act; neither description need oust the other.[46] On a strict reading of section 78, D need not even be aware of the circumstances which make the ambiguous act sexual, as long as they make the reasonable person find that the act was sexual. On this reading, D could be convicted of a sexual offence without intending to do a sexual act, unaware that s/he was doing something which would be considered a sexual act and even positively believed the act was not sexual, as long as the reasonable person would consider the act sexual in the circumstances.

There are two direct responses to this strict reading. Ilias Bantekas accepts it but argues that it is against Parliament's intention and so a defence of necessity must be invoked to negate the sexual character of the offending and make the offence fair on D.[47] But the necessity defence would not negate the sexual label, it would apply to the *conduct* which was either necessitated or not. If the conduct was not necessary, then there has still been an assault which could still be described as sexual. If the conduct is, in the all the circumstances, in the view of a reasonable person, sexual, then it is not unfair to label it as such. Indeed, it is more strongly arguable that it is inaccurate *not* to label it as sexual, a point which we will return to below.

A different approach is taken by Simester et al, who do not accept the strict reading, instead asserting that section 78 leaves open what D's mens rea must be as to the sexual nature of the conduct. To fill this statutory gap they argue that the offence should require that D is aware of the circumstances which make the activity sexual, even if s/he does not him/herself consider it to be sexual.[48] But the wording of section 78 together with sections 2 and 3 is clear. While D must intend the touching, or penetration, there is no need for a subjective mental state to be proved in relation to the conduct's sexual nature. Section 78(b) refers to D's purpose as one of the factors which may be taken into account, but is explicit that it can be the other circumstances alone which make the conduct sexual; limiting the other circumstances which can be considered to those within D's subjective awareness is contrary to this wording. Section 78(a) in the same objective vein expressly excludes D's purposes and other circumstances from preventing inherently sexual conduct from being labelled such. An objective approach to D's culpability was Parliament's intention throughout the Sexual Offences Act 2003, demonstrated, for example, in the strict liability as to V's age in the child sex offences in sections 5–8 and the reasonable belief in consent requirement in sections 1–4. The appellate

---

[45] Confirmed by Hughes LJ in *R v Heard* [2008] QB 43 (CA) [15].
[46] *cf* query raised in Ormerod and Laird (n 7) 784.
[47] Bantekas (n 42).
[48] Simester et al (n 40) 472.

courts have embraced the objective approach and have thus far taken a similar approach to section 78, the Court of Appeal accepting in *Heard* that section 78 is objective and section 78(b) only *allows* D's mental state to be considered – it does not require it.[49]

There is another, softer alternative reading of section 78(b) which gives a modified objective test akin to the reasonable bystander test in unlawful act manslaughter: the reasonable person is aware only of what D is, or could reasonably be expected to be, aware of.[50] This softer reading of section 78 would require a court to take the reasonable person to be in the position of the bystander at the scene rather than a juror equipped with hindsight, which is possible within the statutory wording. In favour of this reading is that it would keep the essence of the *Court* approach but would reflect something of the objective approach in the Sexual Offences Act 2003 – D would only be branded a sex offender on the basis of what D was or should have been aware of but would not be saved by a reckless indifference to the context of his/her actions. It would be similar to how reasonable belief in consent works in practice: as reasonable belief is about the reasonableness of D's actual state of mind, the only circumstances likely to make any difference to that are ones of which D is or should have been aware. That said, section 78(b) requires an objective assessment of the *act* rather than D's state of mind, so D's knowledge or expected knowledge is relevant but not determinative. Parliament was aware that it was taking a more objective, and thus stricter, approach throughout the Act and nonetheless did so. The softer reading places unnecessary limits on the accurate labelling of the act by inserting a mens rea requirement where Parliament chose not to place one. D's lack of sexual intent can properly be reflected in sentence.

Strong adherents to the correspondence principle (that an offence's mens rea must extend to the whole of the actus reus) might argue that that principle is breached by the strict reading, as D can be guilty without any mens rea as to the sexual nature of the act.[51] Deviation from the correspondence principle in criminal law is as much a rule as the exception (although the deviation should be justifiable) but it is arguable that there is no real deviation here in any event. D does an act which D intends to do.[52] D is not held liable for a further consequence of his/her act, but only for the descriptive label of the act (sexual). Liability is not strict in respect of this label as the jury must be sure that a reasonable person would consider the act sexual (*cf* strict liability as to V's age in sections 5–8). Further, D would not be convicted on the basis that the act *could* be sexual, only on the basis that in the assessment of the reasonable person it *was* sexual. In practice it is

---

[49] See *R v M (M)* [2011] EWCA Crim 1291 and *R v B (MA)* [2013] EWCA Crim 3; *Heard* [2008] QB 43 (CA) [15].

[50] *R v Lamb* [1967] 2 QB 981 (CA); *DPP v Newbury* [1977] AC 500 (HL); and *R v Dawson* (1985) 81 Cr App R 150 (CA).

[51] See, for example, A Ashworth, *Principles of Criminal Law*, 7th edn (Oxford, Oxford University Press, 2013).

[52] From murder downwards through the offences against the person, for instance; Simester et al (n 40) 206–207.

very unlikely that D would be found guilty of a sexual offence if s/he was wholly unaware of the sexual nature of it, or indeed had a different, particularly if benign, motive for his/her actions.

Which reading should be preferred determines the importance of the final difference to *Court*. The use of the term 'circumstances' and the reference not just to D's purpose but to 'the purpose of any person' enables V's attitude to and experience of D's act to be considered when making the section 78(b) determination. This interpretation is partially supported by the Explanatory Notes to the Act, which state that when determining the status of an ambiguous act, the reasonable person would need to consider, amongst other things, 'the purpose of any of the participants'.[53] The Notes confuse by then illustrating with the example of a vaginal examination, saying 'if the doctor's purpose is medical, the activity will not be sexual; if the doctor's purpose is sexual, the activity also is likely to be sexual' but without reference to V and her state of mind.[54] It is the Act rather than the Notes which must be interpreted, however, and on the wording of section 78 V's response to the act – an experiencing of it as sexual – is a circumstance which is capable of being considered by the reasonable person under section 78. The extent to which V's state of mind can be used to determine the sexual nature of the act will depend on the reading of section 78 discussed above; an uncommunicated state of mind would always be relevant on the strict reading but could not be taken into account on the softer reading unless it would be reasonable to expect D to have been aware of it or the possibility of it (for example if D was aware that V had post-traumatic stress disorder due to previous penetrative sexual abuse).

The cases and the literature on indecent assault are generally silent about V's state of mind.[55] The experience of V had no role in determining the nature of indecent assault, but that is not true of sexual assault (despite the continuing silence in the literature). The specific use of the words 'any person' rather 'the defendant' provides further support for the strict reading of section 78: why include reference to purposes other than D's if they are only to be considered if D is aware of them? Limiting the circumstances which the jury may consider limits their ability to make a fair and complete assessment of D's act. Their ability to make an assessment in the round enables a fair and accurate label to be attached to D's conduct, and that label may or may not be 'sexual'. If the victim of a *Court*-like assault were told of D's comments about a buttock fetish, the victim may well consider that s/he had been the victim of a sexual rather than a physical assault and that is surely part of the reason that Court's actions were more than a mere physical assault.

---

[53] Explanatory Notes to the Sexual Offences Act 2003 [146].
[54] ibid.
[55] The only reference is in G Williams, *Textbook of Criminal Law*, 2nd edn (London, Stevens, 1983) 231 where he states 'An assault is not indecent if it is neither intended by the defendant nor interpreted by the other party as having a sexual purpose', though this may well have been more about exculpating the defendant than about giving importance to the victim's experience.

So, if V's experience is sexual notwithstanding D's lack of sexual motive, that should also be considered when making an objective determination of the sexual nature of the act. The strict reading should be preferred and with it the ability to take all circumstances, including V's state of mind, into account.

The practical effect may be marginal where the only reason an otherwise innocent-looking touch is alleged to be sexual is V's unexpectedly sexual reaction to it as it is highly unlikely in this situation that a jury would be sure such a touch was sexual. It *is* capable of making a difference in vaginal examinations because it is easier to conclude that a vaginal examination is sexual. It is time to consider the nature of vaginal examinations.

IV. What Kind of Act is Vaginal Examination?

To decide how vaginal examinations should be treated under the Sexual Offences Act 2003 we must determine first whether they are inherently sexual or just capable of being sexual. Ashworth and Temkin in their important and wide-ranging article on the 2003 Act considered vaginal examinations and reached no conclusion as to whether they were inherently or just possibly sexual.[56] A vaginal examination has been used as an example repeatedly in texts, articles and cases on the topic of indecent assault and conclusions have been reached but they have not been consistent. There are three strands of thought.

A. Vaginal Examination for a Genuine Medical Purpose cannot be Indecent

The Court of Appeal in *Court* together with Lords Griffiths, Ackner and Goff in the House of Lords and Glanville Williams agree that a vaginal examination carried out by a medical professional for a genuine medical reason cannot be indecent, even if D had a secret indecent intention.[57] In 2006 the Court of Appeal in *Kumar* provided lukewarm support for this conclusion, emphasising that the manner and circumstances must be in accordance with the genuine medical purpose.[58] This would put a vaginal examination in the category of inherently non-indecent conduct.

The Court of Appeal and Lord Goff's conclusions are driven by the view that D's indecent intention is irrelevant to the offence, but a decent purpose can

---

[56] A Ashworth and J Temkin, 'The Sexual Offences Act 2003 (1): Rape, Sexual Assault and the Problems of Consent' (2004) *Criminal Law Review* 328, 331–32.

[57] *Court* (n 36) 162; *Court* (n 35) 35, 43–4, 50.

[58] *R v Kumar* [2006] EWCA Crim 1946 [16], [17], [26].

be evidentially relevant (a view in which he was fortified by the fifth edition of Smith and Hogan).[59] Lord Griffiths and Glanville Williams do consider D's intention to be relevant, which leads them to the second strand of thought.

B. Although Vaginal Examination for a Genuine Medical Purpose cannot be Indecent, without Such Purpose it is Capable of Being Indecent

Lord Griffiths and Glanville Williams both state that a vaginal examination can be indecent if there is no genuine medical purpose *and* D has an indecent intention.[60] This would put a vaginal examination in the ambiguous conduct category where D's intention does make a difference. It is difficult to follow how D's non-indecent purpose makes the act *inherently* non-indecent such that D's sexual intention is irrelevant, but a change in D's purpose makes the conduct ambiguous and D's sexual intention relevant.

Although they both agreed on a narrow, sexual meaning of indecency (Glanville Williams stating that it means 'overtly sexual' and Lord Griffiths 'an affront to the sexual modesty of a woman') this does not explain how a vaginal examination can be both inherently non-indecent and ambiguous. It does explain *why* they concluded as they did, however.[61] It is submitted that they baulked at the idea of a medical professional being guilty of a sexual crime for a poorly performed vaginal examination but wanted to be able to convict a medical professional conducting a non-necessary vaginal examination for sexual gratification.

The sexual definition of indecency was too narrow for most, though. Lords Ackner and Goff define 'indecent' as 'so offensive to contemporary standards of modesty and privacy' and 'an affront to modesty' respectively.[62] The Court of Appeal in *Court* concludes similarly.[63] Cases have favoured the wider meaning when the issue has arisen, as seen, for example, in *Parsons* (D's indecent conduct towards his step-daughters was 'jocular horseplay' rather than for sexual gratification, but conviction for indecent assault upheld), *DPP v H* (drunken adult D should have been convicted of indecent assault for inserting thumb into baby's anus despite intention to cause pain rather than desire for sexual gratification) and *Lemmon* (25 year old D was convicted of indecent assault for trying to show an 11-year-old boy his penis, baring his bottom and then sitting on the boy's face to bully, humiliate and disgust but not for sexual gratification).[64] It is not only the width of the term 'indecent' which is important here, it is that the other motives

---

[59] *Court* (n 35), 52 and Ormerod and Laird (n 7) 424.

[60] *Court* (n 35), 35 and Williams (n 55) 231.

[61] Williams (n 55) 231; *Court* (n 35) 34.

[62] *Court* (n 35) 42, 50.

[63] ibid 164.

[64] *R v Parsons* [1993] Crim LR 792 (CA). The appeal was allowed on other grounds; *DPP v H* [1992] COD 266 (DC) (case stated by prosecution after magistrates acquitted); *R v Lemmon* [2005] EWCA Crim 994.

did not oust the indecent label. This explains how the third strand of thought about a vaginal examination was underpinned.

C. Vaginal Examination without a Genuine Medical Purpose is Inherently Indecent

Lords Ackner and Goff are as keen as Glanville Williams to avoid the midwife or doctor being guilty of indecent assault, but only where the vaginal examination is done for proper medical purposes. Lord Goff and the Court of Appeal point to the requirement that the vaginal examination be done 'in a manner and in circumstances consistent with [the genuine medical] purposes'.[65]

Lord Goff of course considers D's indecent intention to be irrelevant for the offence, so it follows that digital penetration done other than in the correct medical manner would have to be indecent, otherwise it would be impossible for him to argue that *any* digital penetration is indecent.

Lord Ackner's analysis is based on the centrality of V's consent. Where D had made false representations about its necessity to V, the vaginal examination would be an indecent assault without any need for D to have an indecent intention.[66] This approach was echoed by the Court of Appeal in *Tabassum* which found that examination of women's breasts amounted to an indecent assault despite a lack of proven indecent intent on the part of D because: 'The nature and quality of the defendant's acts in touching the breasts of women to whom, in sexual terms he was a stranger, was unlawful and an indecent assault unless the complainants consented to that touching'.[67]

i. If Vaginal Examination is Inherently Indecent would that Mean that it is also Inherently Sexual?

As noted above, indecency is best understood to cover more than sexual misconduct, but it also arguably failed to cover some sexual conduct, for example where the affront to modesty was simply too minor.[68] 'Indecent' is thus not wider than 'sexual' but different, albeit with some overlap. As a result, it would not necessarily follow that inherently indecent conduct is inherently sexual.

ii. Is Vaginal Examination Inherently Sexual?

Sullivan believes that Lord Ackner's conclusion on inherent indecency was correct on the basis of his reasoning in *Court* but Sullivan criticises the whole approach,

---

[65] *Court* (n 36) 164.
[66] *Court* (n 35), 42, 44.
[67] *R v Tabassum* [2000] 2 Cr App R 328 (CA) [37].
[68] See discussion in Williams (n 55) 232.

asserting that the wrong in vaginal examination is not to V's sexual integrity; she is wronged as a patient.[69] This type of assertion about Vs' views is not uncommon and highlights the need for women's different experiences to be heard; if a woman experiences a non-consensual vaginal examination as a violation of her sexual integrity there should be, and now is, a space for this to be recognised in the criminal law. Sullivan's analysis of V as purely a patient and the violation to her only as a patient ignores several points: (1) that pregnancy and childbirth are not illnesses but human processes (although there may be medical issues which arise) so she is not a patient in the normal sense; (2) a vaginal examination involves a part of the female body which is used for menstrual blood and sex but also for birth (a huge change for a woman undergoing pregnancy for the first time); and (3) vaginal penetration is a particularly intrusive form of bodily interference in a world where interference with women's bodies has been common and controlling. Thus, there is some benefit from considering, as Simester et al do, the comparator of a man having a prostate examination conducted by an oncologist but it is limited.[70]

Looking from V's perspective, a vaginal examination is not inherently sexual. Although some Vs may consider themselves sexually violated, not every woman who has had a vaginal examination without giving valid consent would consider herself sexually violated. If a woman gives valid consent to a vaginal examination, she probably would not consider herself having consented to a sexual act, but to a medical procedure or examination. Just as it is too extreme to say a vaginal examination cannot be sexual, it is also too dogmatic to say that it is *always* sexual.

There are legal problems with concluding that a vaginal examination is inherently sexual too. If it is inherently sexual, how could a genuine medical purpose and V's consent prevent D from committing a child sex offence if V is under 16 (as consent is irrelevant to the child sex offences in sections 5–12)? A parent or carer could not give consent for child V to be examined any more than s/he could give legally relevant consent to V having sex. JC Smith, in his commentary on the Court of Appeal decision in *Court*, suggests that the genuine medical purpose could be analysed as providing a defence to the otherwise indecent nature of the act.[71] This seems rather too open to abuse and is not included in the Act; the Sexual Offences Act 2003 expressly deals with medical purposes enabling limited, specified medical purposes to be claimed as a defence by secondary parties (so limited that the consenting parent or carer in our example would not be able to claim it).[72] Lord Goff's necessity defence discussed earlier would be the more likely defence to succeed, but that would have to be squared with section 78(a) expressly excluding consideration of any person's purposes in relation to the act in considering whether it is sexual meaning that on the face of it D's genuine medical purpose

---

[69] G Sullivan, 'The Need for a Crime of Sexual Assault' (1989) *Criminal Law Review* 331.
[70] Example used in Simester et al (n 40) 471.
[71] [1987] Crim LR 134.
[72] Sexual Offences Act 2003, s 73.

could not prevent the act from being sexual if a vaginal examination was put in the inherently sexual category.[73]

It is unrealistic and inaccurate to label a vaginal examination as inherently sexual.

iii. Vaginal Examination as Possibly Sexual under Section 78(b)

The activity of digitally penetrating another's vagina is capable of being sexual; indeed, without more information it would be presumed to be sexual. The medical setting may make it less likely to be considered sexual by the reasonable person, but it should not prevent it.

What Sullivan's argument does do is highlight the heart of the problem with requiring a sexual purpose to make a vaginal examination sexual, and indeed the softer reading of section 78: the sexual nature of the act would be defined by D, or at best some external person, with limited reference to V and her experience. This is not a sustainable argument. As examined above, the description 'sexual' is a non-exclusive one. An act could have both sexual and medical aspects to it.[74] The defendant in *Lemmon* could have been convicted of sexual assault, as he was of indecent assault, if his actions took place a few months later because his humiliation purpose does not oust the sexual nature of his conduct. V may experience the vaginal examination as sexual, at least in part because of the intimate nature of the contact. She may feel so even more if her consent has not been validly given or because she later learns that there was no genuine medical purpose. But V may not experience the vaginal examination in that way, in which case, in the absence of a sexual intention on the part of D, a non-consensual vaginal examination would not be sexual within section 78 and thus no offence under sections 2 and 3. This leaves only common assault as a charge for most non-consensual vaginal examinations.

iv. Between 'Sexual' and 'Indecent'

Lord Ackner recognises the problem in categorizing a vaginal examination as simply common assault, so concludes that a vaginal examination is inherently indecent, enabling a conviction for indecent assault with the lack of indecent motive reflected in sentence.[75] While this may have been arguable for indecency, which as Simester et al argue involves a moral pejorative implying wrongfulness, it is not possible for the descriptive term 'sexual'.[76]

The binary choice between common assault and sexual assault is the problem here both at substantive and sentencing levels. To call a non-consensual vaginal

---

[73] Ashworth and Temkin (n 56) refer to clinical necessity although they do not refer to Lord Goff.
[74] *cf* Williams (n 55) 470.
[75] *Court* (n 35) 44.
[76] Simester et al (n 40) 470.

examination a mere common assault ignores the difference between this violation and a push in a pub. Herring and Wall's concept of bodily integrity – the integration of subjective self and body – helps to understand the different wrongs V may experience in a non-consensual vaginal examination, which may be physical, sexual, intimate, personal, dignity-sapping, depersonalising, political. Beyond the perspective of V's experience, D has abused a position of power and trust at a time when V is particularly vulnerable, to conduct an extremely invasive touching of and in V's body. Common assault is an insufficient and unrepresentative label for V, for communicating to D the nature of his/her wrongdoing and for informing others in society what D has done (whether D's patients or employers or simply members of the public).[77] Some may baulk, for the same reasons, at the label 'sex offender' with the notification requirements (ie inclusion on the sex offenders register) which would follow such a conviction for a vaginal examination by D acting without a sexual purpose (although this is a weaker criticism as neither indecent nor sexual assault has ever required an indecent/sexual purpose in all cases).[78]

Turning to procedure and sentence, the difference between the offences is stark. Common assault is a summary offence, triable in the magistrates' court (where proceedings must be issued within six months of the incident) with a maximum sentence of six months.[79] Sexual assault by penetration under section 2 carries a maximum sentence of life (albeit with a sentencing guideline range of a community order up to 19 years) and is triable only on indictment.[80] Sentencing guidelines fail to recognise the particular nature of a vaginal examination as an aggravating factor of common assault (although there are general headings of V's vulnerability and D's abuse of position) and the lack of a sexual motive on D's part means that it is difficult to apply the sexual offences guidelines which assumes such a motive (a weakness in the guidelines as a whole).[81]

How to deal with this failure to reflect a vaginal examination properly? To label such violation now as 'indecent' feels outdated, carrying with it some notion of tarnish to V as well as D; the moral connotations are not helpful now for D or V or for the jury trying to apply it to the facts. Where a vaginal examination is experienced as sexual it might be charged under section 2, but in other cases the term 'intimate' might be used to bridge the gap at substantive and sentencing levels, providing a term which better enables the experiences of Vs to be understood and reflected. Intimacy might be made into an aggravating factor for common assault as racial or religious motive already is, changing the offence label and increasing

---

[77] For an in-depth discussion of fair labelling see J Chalmers and F Leverick, 'Fair Labelling in Criminal Law' (2008) 71 *Modern Law Review* 217.

[78] Sexual Offences Act 2003, s 81 and schedule 3.

[79] Criminal Justice Act 1988, s 39.

[80] Sexual Offences Act 2003, s 2(4); Sentencing Council, *Sexual Offences: Definitive Guideline* (London, Sentencing Council, 2013).

[81] Sentencing Council, *Assault: Definitive Guideline* (London, Sentencing Council, 2011); Sentencing Council, *Sexual Offences: Definitive Guideline* (London, Sentencing Council, 2013).

the maximum sentence.[82] Failing that, sentencing guidelines could recognise the intimate nature of the assault as a specific aggravating factor in common assault, as it does for domestic violence. For sexual assault, the lack of sexual motive could be noted with counterbalancing reference to the breach of trust, professional standards and the fact that D could only commit the offence because of his/her good character and standing as a medical professional (and so to expect no great reduction to sentence because of those).[83]

It may be possible to bring non-consensual vaginal examinations within the current law, but it would be even better to recognise this particular form of misconduct and to label and sentence it accurately.

---

[82] Crime and Disorder Act 1998, s 29. The maximum sentence is increased to two years.

[83] *Attorney-General's Reference (No 68 of 2003)* [2004] EWCA Crim 620 noted these, although the case was dealing with doctors acting from a sexual motive.

9

When 'Battery' is not Enough: Exposing the Gaps in Unauthorised Vaginal Examinations During Labour as a Crime of Battery

CAMILLA PICKLES

I. Introduction

The ever-growing body of research reveals that violence and abuse during labour and childbirth is a rather common phenomenon and one that occurs around the world.[1] However, facility-based abuse and violence is not new and activists have been working to address this issue for decades.[2] The World Health Organization's researchers identify several types of 'mistreatment' including verbal, physical and sexual abuse, discrimination on the basis of sociodemographic characterises, and a failure of healthcare professionals to meet professional standards of care.[3] Their typology offers a neat categorisation of a disturbing trend that is extremely complex in terms of its social and cultural roots and thus very difficult to understand when one is first confronted with the fact that some healthcare professionals abuse women during facility-based childbirth.

In the context of researching facility-based abuse and its different manifestations, I came across a reoccurring theme: many women from around the world

---

[1] World Health Organization, *The Prevention and Elimination of Disrespect and Abuse During Facility-Based Childbirth: WHO Statement* (Geneva, WHO, 2015) WHO/RHR/14.23 at apps.who.int/iris/bitstream/handle/10665/134588/WHO_RHR_14.23_eng.pdf;jsessionid=7EF7E3BCE5C835388AC1E38224611D44?sequence=1.

[2] This is particularly evident within the Latin American context. See P Quattrocchi, 'Obstetric Violence Observatory: Contributions of Argentina to the International Debate' (2019) 38 *Medical Anthropology* 762.

[3] M Bohren et al, 'The Mistreatment of Women During Childbirth in Health Facilities Globally: A Mixed-Methods Systematic Review' (2015) 12(6) *PLoS Medicine* e1001847.

have reported that healthcare professionals subjected them to vaginal examinations during labour in legally questionable circumstances. For instance:

> She said she wanted to do one more cervical check. I consented and when she did it, she grabbed my cervix and pinched it. She would not let go until I consented to letting her break my water. I was in tears from the pain, screaming, begging and sobbing for her to let go and get her hand out of my vagina. She would not let go until I consented, which I finally did.[4]

> The five medical students came to the room. The senior doctor on the morning shift asked them to examine the case and give him a report about each one. But what happened was completely inhuman. Instead of one student examining a woman and giving a report about her, each one examined all the women … If someone got a different report from the others he would go back to examine the woman again to be sure of his examination … It was like a queue, when one finished with the woman, the other one took his turn. Suddenly the five women were screaming and crying at the same time.[5]

> On arrival at the hospital I was given a very painful internal exam. I don't know what they were looking for … There seemed to be a stream of men doing painful internal exams without asking my permission.[6]

> They never said anything to me; she was inserting her finger without saying a word. They yelled at me. I felt pain and burning. Then I stopped feeling anything because of the contractions.[7]

> [T]he door was open and I was exposed [during the examination]. I asked her to cover me up, she refused. I asked her to close the door, she refused.[8]

Some women frame these violations as sexual violations and they sometimes equate their experience to rape and 'birth rape'.[9] However, when confronted with these types of violations, a typical response is that these experiences fall within the realms of the crime of battery or medical negligence. These responses can be located on social media platforms and in professional and academic literature. For instance, according to US-based blogger, Lindsay Beyerstein, 'birth rape' is unhelpful and misleading, and she contends: 'If a doctor performs a procedure without informed consent, *that's malpractice and possibly a crime*, but it's not a sexual assault' (emphasis added).[10] Some healthcare professionals take the same

---

[4] R Reed et al, 'Women's Descriptions of Childbirth Trauma Relating to Care Provider Actions and Interactions' (2017) 17(1) *BMC Pregnancy Childbirth* 21, 27.

[5] S Abed Almajeed Abdallah Hussein et al, 'Women's Experiences of Childbirth in Middle Eastern Countries: A Narrative Review' (2018) 59 *Midwifery* 100, 108.

[6] C Tatano Beck, 'A Secondary Analysis of Mistreatment of Women during Childbirth in Health Care Facilities' (2018) 47(1) *Journal of Obstetric, Gynecologic & Neonatal Nursing* 94, 99.

[7] S Hassan et al, 'The Paradox of Vaginal Examination Practice During Normal Childbirth: Palestinian Women's Feelings, Opinions, Knowledge and Experiences' (2012) 9(1) *Reproductive Health* 16, 23.

[8] ibid.

[9] This is discussed in more detail below.

[10] L Beyerstein, '"Birth Rape" Rhetoric is Ugly, Misleading' (*Big Think*, 10 September 2010) at bigthink.com/focal-point/birth-rape-rhetoric-is-ugly-misleading.

approach. Susan Bewley, an obstetrician, published a warning in the *British Medical Journal* that teaching vaginal examinations on anesthetised women without their consent amounts to the crime of battery.[11] This approach is confirmed in the criminal law literature. According to Jonathan Herring, intimate examinations without consent may amount to the crime of battery.[12] He explains, a doctor may be committing a battery if they were to insert their fingers or an instrument into a person's vagina or anus without getting that person's consent.[13] I, myself, have argued elsewhere that, from a South African perspective, touching women without their consent during facility-based childbirth constitutes the crime of assault.[14]

Assault and battery or common assault form the basis for many aggravated offences and some medical interventions without consent might constitute more serious crimes, such as assault occasioning actual bodily harm.[15] Nevertheless, in this chapter I focus on the crime of battery because the theme of this collection is concerned with vaginal examinations, which involves actual touch or applied force without consent and because battery forms the basis for the more serious crimes that might be relevant. But more specifically, I focus on criminal battery because critical reflection of the appropriateness of 'battery' is warranted given that this is the crime that others tend to identify as being relevant to unauthorised touch or examination in the medical context.[16]

In this chapter I question whether battery is adequate in the context of unauthorised vaginal examinations during labour. The chapter starts with a brief discussion about the crime of 'battery' and its scope. Then I reflect on what makes unauthorised examinations something more than mere battery and I make three claims in this regard. First, battery hides the fact that unauthorised vaginal examinations are manifestations of a form of gender-based violence: obstetric violence. Second, battery fails to capture the seriousness of the violation that women experience when healthcare professionals subject them to vaginal examinations without their consent and it is thus an inadequate and unfair label. Finally, that battery lacks expressive effect within the maternity care context. Before moving onto the three claims, I will explore the basis for which the crime of battery is deemed relevant in this context.

[11] S Bewley, 'The Law, Medical Students, and Assault' (1992) 304 *British Medical Journal* 1551.

[12] J Herring, *Criminal Law: Text, Cases, and Materials*, 8th edn (Oxford, Oxford University Press 2018) 433, fn 78. Also see, G Laurie et al, *Law and Medical Ethics*, 10th edn (Oxford, Oxford University Press 2015) 111.

[13] Herring (n 12) 433, fn 78.

[14] C Pickles, 'Eliminating Abusive "Care": A Criminal Law Response to Obstetric Violence in South Africa' (2015) 54(1) *South African Crime Quarterly* 5, 10.

[15] D Ormerod and K Laird, *Smith, Hogan and Ormerod's Criminal Law*, 15th edn (Oxford, Oxford University Press, 2018) 659.

[16] Herring (n 12) 433, fn 78; Bewley (n 11) 1551; Pickles (n 14) 10. The issue of proof of consent will not be discussed, as this issue is covered in Chapter 8, by C Sjölin, 'Including the Victim's Perspective: Can Vaginal Examinations ever be Sexual Assaults?'.

II. Unauthorised Vaginal Examinations
as the Crime of Battery

Women's narratives of sexual violation (as depicted above) are usually replaced with the sanitised discourses of crime of battery. Here, we are directed towards framing this issue as an unlawful and unwanted contact with the body of another.[17]

Contrary to Charles Foster's position in Chapter 7 above, I find it unsurprising that the criminal law is brought into this context. The criminal law demonstrates the wrongs that our society deems especially significant and to not apply the criminal law would suggest that the wrongs that women suffer during unauthorised vaginal examinations are not serious enough to capture the criminal law's attention.[18] This cannot be so. Amel Alghraniet et al remind us that medical practice can involve wrongs that should be the concern of the criminal law because they contravene defining values that the state endeavours to safeguard to ensure the good of its citizens.[19] They argue that there is almost an *inevitability* about the inclusion of criminal law within this space because our criminal laws reflect society's basic values and it helps to punish those who culpably cause harm or risk of harm.[20]

In the context of battery, we are concerned with the fundamental principle that every person's body is inviolate; so much so that even the slightest touch of another may amount to battery.[21] However, battery concerns more than that because this crime does not necessarily involve the harming of the *body*; the Court of Appeal accepts that touching another's clothing while they wear the item is the equivalent to touching them.[22] Thus, the crime of battery includes a recognition that personal space is something that we value in our society and that it should not be intentionally or recklessly penetrated without justification.[23]

Battery's broad and gender-neutral definition renders it a crime that encompasses the touching of any person in any context, and we can and should expect the birth room to be included here. Thus, it has the beneficial potential for universal application.[24] This might prove helpful in some instances, but I argue that its neutrality, universal applicability and general disregard for context are problematic in the context of unauthorised vaginal examinations. This is because these characteristics hide key features of what makes unauthorised vaginal examinations something different and more serious than mere unauthorised touch.

---

[17] Definition of battery taken from Herring (n 12) 310.

[18] A Alghrani et al, 'Introduction: When Criminal Law Encounters Bioethics: A Case of Tensions and Incompatibilities or an Apt Forum for Resolving Ethical Conflict' in A Alghrani et al (eds), *Bioethics, Medicine and the Criminal Law: The Criminal Law and Bioethical Conflict: Walking the Tightrope*, vol 1 (Cambridge, Cambridge University Press, 2013) 1.

[19] ibid.

[20] ibid.

[21] *Collins v Wilcock* [1984] 1 WLR 1172 [1177].

[22] *R v Emrys Thomas* (1985) 81 Cr App 331 [334].

[23] Herring (n 12) 316.

[24] S Walby et al, *The Concept and Measurement of Violence Against Women and Men* (Bristol, Policy Press, 2017) 44.

III. Reflections on Why Battery is not Enough

Technically speaking, battery is applicable because quite obviously an unwanted vaginal examination during labour is the touching of another's body without consent. However, I argue that battery is inadequate in this context. To make my point I situate unauthorised vaginal examinations within the broader context of obstetric violence and demonstrate that the crime of battery paints an incomplete and incorrect picture of the nature of the problem we need to tackle. I look at how women describe the harm that they experience and I make the case that battery is an unfair label because it does not capture the seriousness of the harms that healthcare professionals cause when they penetrate women's vaginas without consent. Finally, I argue that the crime of battery has failed to effectively signal to healthcare professionals what is expected of them and thus it has failed to shape their behaviour accordingly. In other words, this particular crime lacks expressive effect within the maternity care context.

A. Claim 1: The Crime of Battery Fails to Confront Obstetric Violence and Hides it

If we apply the decontextualised definition of 'battery' to vaginal examinations during labour without consent it suggests that unauthorised vaginal touches are random and isolated incidences of inappropriate healthcare provider behaviour. However, this issue is far more complex, and without the inclusion of some of these complexities we are left with an incomplete and therefore incorrect picture of the nature of the problem we face.

Battery focuses on one individual actor. However, the violence we see here is not an indiscriminate act of a rogue healthcare provider. Women's experiences reveal that it sometimes involves coordination between multiple actors and between actors and institutional structures. Some actors coerce or convince refusing and reluctant women, or some actors restrain women who may physically resist the violation while another performs the vaginal examinations. Sometimes, a room will be filled with healthcare professionals and no one will step in to prevent an examination without consent. In this case, those in a position to prevent harm do nothing. At times, maternity care units indirectly support this behaviour either by enabling this behaviour via prescriptive hospital protocols or by failing to act when healthcare professionals violate women in this way.[25] These circumstances reveal that things are going wrong on an individual level because institutional structures and broader social norms about women and pregnancy allow healthcare professionals and maternity care to function in this way. Therefore, it is unsurprising that

---

[25] For example, requiring women to undergo vaginal examinations for the purposes of being admitted into facilities to give birth: see Chapter 2, by R Brione, 'Non-Consented Vaginal Examinations: The Birthrights and AIMS Perspective'.

scholars and activists identify unauthorised vaginal examinations as one manifestation of a much bigger issue: obstetric violence.

The term 'obstetric violence' originates from Latin American contexts, where it is included in laws directed at eliminating gender-based violence.[26] Feminist activists use this concept to contextualise and connect what are sometimes perceived to be isolated acts of abuse within the context of facility-based childbirth.[27] Contextualising makes the underlying reasons why women are abused during facility-based childbirth more apparent, and it serves to render visible some of the unseen linking factors that shape maternity care contexts and women's experiences therein.

Some of the legal definitions of obstetric violence are vague and sometimes contradictory.[28] However, there is growing consensus in the literature that obstetric violence occurs when health care personnel or healthcare facilities (through their hospital protocols or training, for instance) appropriate women's bodies and reproductive processes during childbirth and cause women to experience a loss of autonomy by denying them their right to decide freely about their bodies and sexuality.[29] Most of the time, incidents of obstetric violence are expressed as 'dehumanised treatment' or 'abuse of medication', and the incidents often highlight those medical processes that pathologise the natural or physiological process of childbirth.[30]

The violence in obstetric violence is not limited to our conventional understanding of violence, being the intentional use of force that causes physical harm. It is much broader than that and it takes women's experiences as its starting point. While there has been very little theorising on what constitutes 'violence' in obstetric violence, I argue that the 'violence' lies in the violation of women's bodily and psychological *integrity* during labour and childbirth.[31] The violence concerns the process of reducing women to lesser beings in physical and/or psychological terms during their maternity care.[32] Behaviour typically recognised as obstetric violence includes performing procedures on women that lack an evidence-base; performing procedures with force or without informed consent; physically, verbally, and emotionally abusing women, and so on.[33]

---

[26] R D'Gregorio, 'Obstetric Violence: A New Legal Term Introduced in Venezuela' (2010) 111 *International Journal of Gynaecology and Obstetrics* 201; Grupo de Información en Reproducción Elegida, *Obstetric Violence: A Human Rights Approach* (2015) at gire.org.mx/en/wp-content/uploads/sites/2/2015/11/ObstetricViolenceReport.pdf.

[27] M Sadler et al, 'Moving beyond Disrespect and Abuse: Addressing the Structural Dimensions of Obstetric Violence' (2016) 24 *Reproductive Health Matters* 47.

[28] Grupo de Información en Reproducción Elegida (n 26).

[29] This conceptualisation originates, in part, from the Venezuelan Organic Law of the Right of Women to a Life Free of Violence (2007). See D'Gregorio (n 26) 201.

[30] ibid.

[31] C Pickles, 'Leaving Women Behind: The Application of Evidence-Based Guidelines, Law, and Obstetric Violence by Omission' in C Pickles and J Herring (eds), *Childbirth, Vulnerability and Law: Exploring Issues of Violence and Control* (London, Routledge, 2019) 140, relying on V Bufacchi, *Violence and Social Justice* (Basingstoke, Palgrave Macmillan, 2007) 13.

[32] Bufacchi (n 31) 41.

[33] See generally Bohren et al (n 3).

The gender-neutral framing of battery obscures the lived reality that the overwhelming majority of victims of this form of violence are women. Consequently, we are concerned with a form of gender-based violence.[34] Sara Cohen Shabot explains that obstetric violence is clearly a gender-based violence because 'women are its main victims and it has its origins primarily in how women (and their (dis) abilities) are perceived … in Western patriarchal societies'.[35]

Patriarchal perceptions of women and their abilities seep into maternity care settings and gendered expectations shape the normative beliefs of healthcare professionals therein.[36] In this regard, Joanna Erdman explains that a health system 'wears the inequalities of the society in which it functions'.[37] This means that women's treatment in childbirth tends to reflect their social status within their particular societies.[38] Within patriarchal societies, depictions of acceptable manifestations of femininity may vary according to class, age, sexual orientation, race and historical periods but it has generally involved expectations of cooperativeness, passivity, and availability for the purposes of objectification.[39] Maria Bastos argues that these gender expectations are incorporated into medical thinking as if they were acceptable explanations of women, and are used to justify and legitimise provider-lead decision-making.[40] Accordingly, oppressive social constructions of femininity are intertwined in maternity care, rendering the interaction between women and their doctors or nurses subject to the reproduction and reinforcement

[34] S Cohen Shabot, 'Making Loud Bodies "Feminine": A Feminist-Phenomenological Analysis of Obstetric Violence' (2016) 39 *Human Studies* 231, 233. The Committee on the Elimination of Discrimination against Women defines gender-based violence as 'violence which is directed against a woman because she is a woman or that affects women disproportionately' and which violates her human rights. See Art 1 of Committee on the Elimination of Discrimination against Women General Recommendation 35 (CEDAW/C/GC/35).

[35] Cohen Shabot (n 34) 233. Many support this understanding: see R Castro and J Erviti, 'Violations of Reproductive Rights during Hospital Births in Mexico' (2003) 7 *Health and Human Rights* 91; A Wolf, 'Metaphysical Violence and Medicalized Childbirth' (2013) 27 *International Journal of Applied Philosophy* 101; S Sánchez, 'Obstetric Violence: Medicalization, Authority Abuse and Sexism within Spanish Obstetric Assistance. A New Name for Old Issues?' (Master's thesis, Utrecht University 2014); F Diaz-Tello, 'Invisible Wounds: Obstetric Violence in the United States' (2016) 24(47) *Reproductive Health Matters* 56; R Chadwick, 'Obstetric Violence in South Africa' (2016) 106 *South African Medical Journal* 423; Sadler et al (n 27).

[36] M Bastos, 'Abuse in Health Care: The Trivialisation of Violence in Maternity Care in Brazil' in B Wijma et al (eds), *GEXcel Work in Progress Report: Gender Violence – Mechanisms, Anti-Mechanisms, Interventions, Evaluations* (Centre of Gender Excellence, 2011) 57. See also Chapter 5, by Stella Villarmea, 'When a Uterus Enters the Room, Reason Goes out the Window' and Chapter 4, by Neda Taghinejadi and Brenda Kelly, 'Female Genital Examination and Autonomy in Medicine'.

[37] J Erdmann, 'Bioethics, Human Rights, and Childbirth' (2015) 17 *Health and Human Rights Journal* 43, 48. Also see S Montesanti and W Thurston, 'Mapping the Role of Structural and Interpersonal Violence in the Lives of Women: Implications for Public Health Interventions and Policy' (2015) 15 *BMC Women's Health* 100, 103.

[38] L Dixon, 'Obstetrics in a Time of Violence: Mexican Midwives Critique Routine Hospital Practices' (2015) 29 *Medical Anthropology Quarterly* 437, 447.

[39] For instance, see Cohen Shabot (n 34); S Walby, *Theorizing Patriarchy* (Oxford, Blackwell, 1990) 90–108.

[40] Bastos (n 36) 57.

of hierarchical relationships of power, with certain groups of marginalised women being right at the bottom.[41]

The complexity of the hierarchical relationship that exists between a woman and her healthcare professionals is exacerbated/intensified when it intersects the privileged standing of medical authority within our society. Healthcare professionals' level of education and technical biomedical knowledge confer superior social status on them in relation to their female 'patients' and this power imbalance influences how healthcare professionals behave towards women.[42] Joanna Erdmann explains that the power of authoritative knowledge allows healthcare professionals to perceive themselves as entitled or obligated to speak for women and women's interests and to employ harmful practices to ensure (what they perceive to be) 'healthy' birth outcomes for women.[43]

An obstetric violence perspective highlights what it is about unauthorised vaginal examinations that the crime of battery does not capture. We are dealing with a gendered issue and this form of violence takes place within a very particular setting and within a particular relationship where one would expect trust to be a core feature. Recognising that obstetric violence occurs within a clinical setting is not simply about pointing out where the abuse occurs; it reveals that this is a location that is shaped by 'a set of norms, hierarchies, and conventions through which acts of abuse and disrespect are rationalized, even normalized'.[44] Thus, we are dealing with something much more than mere intentional or reckless touching without consent.

B. Claim 2: Battery is an Inadequate Label that does not Capture the Seriousness of the Harm that Women Experience

When women report that healthcare professionals subjected them to unauthorised vaginal examinations they also explain that their violation took place at an

---

[41] Montesanti and Thurston (n 37) 103.

[42] A Miltenburg et al, 'Disrespect and Abuse in Maternity Care: Individual Consequences of Structural Violence' (2018) 26(53) *Reproductive Health Matters* 88, 102.

[43] See generally, S Irwin and B Jordan, 'Knowledge, Practice, and Power: Court-Ordered Cesarean Section' (1987) 1 *Medical Anthropology Quarterly* 319; B Jordan, 'Authoritative Knowledge and its Construction' in R Davis-Floyd and C Sargent (eds), *Childbirth and Authoritative Knowledge: Cross-Cultural Perspectives* (Berkeley, University of California Press, 1997) 56–58. Susan Irwin and Brigitte Jordan explain that despite there being multiple kinds of legitimate knowledge (or ways of knowing), some knowledge is deemed more powerful and authoritative than others. The authoritative nature of certain types of knowledge originates from the perception that these types of knowledge can explain things better because they are associated with a stronger power base. The generation of authoritative knowledge is a social process. It builds from and reflects power relationships within a community of practice which creates a hierarchy of knowledge structures that cause the devaluation or outright dismissal of other forms of knowledge. Authoritative knowledge is the knowledge that participants to a community of practice agree counts in certain circumstances; they see it as consequential in that it serves as the basis to make certain decisions and it can be used justify particular conduct; Erdmann (n 37) 48.

[44] Erdmann (n 37) 47.

extremely intimate level, and some women equate their experience to sexual viola-tion.[45] For instance:

> The most terrifying part of whole ordeal was being held down by 4 people and my genitals being touched and probed repeatedly without permission and [I had] no say in the matter, this is called rape, except when you are giving birth. My daughter's birth was more sexually traumatising than the childhood abuse I'd experienced.[46]

> Touching is like raping: they just put their hand in there almost without warning.[47]

> So then after he yelled at me he cut my Vagina twelve times … I could not believe after explaining I was raped twice that I was going to experience Birth Rape under your care.[48]

> I am amazed that 3 1/2 hours in the labor and delivery room could cause such utter destruction in my life. It truly was like being the victim of a violent crime or rape.[49]

Feelings of sexual violation are unsurprising. Aside from the fact that childbirth concerns women's genitalia, researchers and maternity care specialists have docu-mented behavioural, emotional, and physiological similarities between women's sexual excitement and labour and childbirth, causing some to conclude that childbirth forms part of women's broader 'reproductive and sexual cycle'.[50] Lorel Mayberry and Jacqueline Daniel explain:

> Childbirth and sexuality are two aspects of the same phenomenon. The sequence of events that encompass a woman's broader reproductive and sexual cycle, from menstru-ation through to ovulation and conception, followed by pregnancy, labour, birth, and breastfeeding *are sexual acts* (emphasis added).[51]

Thus, women's sexual experiences extend far beyond having sex with men; labour and childbirth are seen to be deeply sexual events too.[52]

Women's accounts of sexual violation tell us that we are dealing with something more than mere touch without consent. There certainly appears to be an awakening

---

[45] Reed et al (n 4) 27; B Bradby, 'Like a Video: The Sexualisation of Childbirth in Bolivia' (1998) 6(12) *Reproductive Health Matters* 50, 53; G Güneş and Z Karaçam, 'The Feeling of Discomfort During Vagi-nal Examination, History of Abuse and Sexual Abuse and Post-Traumatic Stress Disorder in Women' (2017) 26 *Journal of Clinical Nursing* 2362; S Kitzinger, 'Birth as Rape: There Must be an End to "Just in Case" Obstetrics' (2006) 14 *British Journal of Midwifery* 544.

[46] Reed et al (n 4) 27–28.

[47] X Morales et al, 'Neither Medicine nor Health Care Staff Members are Violent by Nature: Obstetric Violence from an Interactionist Perspective' (2018) 28 *Qualitative Health Research* 1308, 1312.

[48] Hermine Hayes-Klein is quoting Kimberly Turbin, see H Hayes-Klein, 'Forced Episiotomy: Kelly's Story' (10 September 2014) at www.opendemocracy.net/en/transformation/forced-episiotomy-kellys-story/.

[49] C Beck, 'Birth Trauma: In the Eye of the Beholder' (2004) 53 *Nursing Research* 28, 32.

[50] See S Buckley, 'Sexuality in Labour and Birth: An Intimate Perspective' in D Walsh and S Downe, *Essential Midwifery Practice: Intrapartum Care* (Oxford, Blackwell Publishing, 2010) 213. Also see L Mayberry and J Daniel, '"Birthgasm": A Literary Review of Orgasm as an Alternative Mode of Pain Relief in Childbirth' (2016) 34 *Journal of Holistic Nursing* 331; T Postel, 'Childbirth Climax: The Revealing of Obstetrical Orgasm' (2013) 22(4) *Sexologies* e89; S Kitzinger, *Birth and Sex: The Power and the Passion* (London, Pinter and Martin, 2012) 15–29, 58–61.

[51] Mayberry and Daniel (n 50) 331.

[52] Sarah Buckley gives a short literature review, Buckley (n 50) 213–14.

consciousness of the underlying sexual nature of the type of violation that women experience when healthcare professionals subject them to vaginal examinations without their consent. 'Rape' and 'sexual violation' seem to give adequate expression because these terms possibly resonate most closely with women's feelings of physical restriction, betrayal, objectification, forced exposure, forced penetration, powerlessness, or total violation of the body and mind.[53]

It is not the aim of my chapter to make the case for unauthorised vaginal examinations to be considered a form of sex-based crime. Instead, I use these shared descriptions of bodily and psychological violation to demonstrate that the crime of battery does little to capture fully the experiences of the specific types of violations that women experience in the contexts of childbirth. This is not the mere touch of clothing or a finger; we are concerned with the touch and penetration of an intimate part of a woman's body during a vulnerable time by those who are in a position of trust.

The broad scope of the crime of battery trivialises the harm inflicted on women and hides the fact that only a particular group of people (healthcare professionals) cause this harm. Consequently, it does not capture the differences in harm we might experience when different people touch different body parts in different settings or contexts. These characteristics render battery an inadequate label in this context. Karen Brennan suggests that we need a suitably labelled offence in the context of obstetric violence for three reasons: to draw attention to this issue; to allow for the identification of specific harms that women experience; and to resist the minimisation of women's experiences.[54] Thus, the name we use in law must speak directly to the harms that healthcare professionals cause women during childbirth and, to this end, I find the literature on fair labelling in criminal law helpful.

The principle of fair labelling requires that the description of the crime must match the wrong done.[55] A fair label is important to the offender, victims, and society more generally.[56] Fair labelling in criminal law prevents us from describing defendants in ways that overstate the gravity of the kind of conduct they have engaged in, and it prevents society from being misled about the seriousness of their behaviour.[57] Here, inaccurate labels might stigmatise offenders and severely affect

---

[53] S Kitzinger, 'Birth and Violence against Women' in H Roberts (ed), *Women's Health Matters* (London, Routledge, 1992) 68–77. Broader literature on birth-related trauma supports claims that abuse during childbirth has serious and long-lasting effects on women. For instance, see A Horsch and S Garthus-Niegel, 'Posttraumatic Stress Disorder following Childbirth' in Pickles and Herring (n 31) 49.

[54] K Brennan, 'Reflections on Criminalising Obstetric Violence – A Feminist Perspective' in Pickles and Herring (n 53) 226.

[55] Herring (n 12) 13.

[56] There are several reasons to explain why fair labelling is important. Most of these are considered in J Chalmers and F Leverick, 'Fair Labelling in Criminal Law' (2008) 71 *Modern Law Review* 217. However, the authors do not necessarily accept some of these explanations.

[57] V Tadros, 'Fair Labelling and Social Solidarity' in L Zedner and J Roberts, *Principles and Values in Criminal Law and Criminal Justice: Essays in Honour of Andrew Ashworth* (Oxford, Oxford University Press, 2012) 68.

their reputation within their society, profession, or employment more generally.[58] Fair labelling is important for non-perpetrators because a label holds a symbolic function; it symbolises the degree of condemnation that should be assigned to the offender and it tells us how to regard the offender.[59] Thus, if the label fails to adequately reflect the wrong done, society will have no clear reason to exclude perpetrators from positions of trust, and members of society will not perceive perpetrators to be a form of danger to particular members of society.

Further, and more significantly, fair labelling is important for victims. The label must reflect adequately the wrong that a victim suffers.[60] Jeremy Horder argues:

> Particularly where moral wrongdoing is or may be concerned (as it is in the case of non-fatal violence), what matters is not just that one has been convicted, but of what one has been convicted. If the offence in question gives too anaemic a conception of what that might be, it is fair neither to the defendant, nor to the victim. For the wrongdoing of the former, and the wrong suffered by the latter, will not have been properly represented to the public at large.[61]

This aspect of fair labelling has not received much attention in the literature, and James Chalmers and Fiona Leverick question the 'fairness to the victim' arguments that do exist.[62] They suggest that the magnitude of the sentence might be more important than the name of the offence.[63]

The magnitude of the sentence imposed is an important factor but this factor should not overshadow the fact that law performs a communicative function. According to Wibren van der Burg, the law communicates normative standards to society, it provides a framework in which communication can take place, and it tells citizens how to behave in certain contexts.[64] From a feminist perspective, Lucinda Finley explains:

> Law is a language of power, a particularly authoritative discourse. Law can pronounce definitively what something is or is not and how a situation or event is to be understood. The *concepts, categories, and terms* that law uses … has a particularly potent ability to shape popular and authoritative understandings of situations. Legal language does more than express thoughts. It reinforces certain world views and understandings of events (emphasis added).[65]

---

[58] Chalmers and Leverick (n 56) 225–26.

[59] ibid.

[60] Tadros (n 57) 68.

[61] J Horder, 'Rethinking Non-Fatal Offences Against the Person' (1994) 14 *Oxford Journal of Legal Studies* 335, 351.

[62] Chalmers and Leverick (n 56) 236.

[63] ibid.

[64] W Van Der Burg, 'The Expressive and Communicative Functions of Law, Especially with Regard to Moral Issues' (2001) 20 *Law and Philosophy* 31.

[65] L Finley, 'Breaking Women's Silence in Law: The Dilemma of the Gendered Nature of Legal Reasoning' (1989) 64 *Notre Dame Law Review* 886, 888 (footnotes omitted). Also see L Kelly, *Surviving Sexual Violence* (Oxford, Polity Press, 1993) Ch 6.

In this regard, a lengthy sentence should not detract from the importance of a label for victims, especially when we are concerned with conduct that rarely attracts a criminal law gaze. The imposition of a lengthy sentence (on its own) does not refer to a crime that offers a communicative framework that provides *a language* that women can use to describe their harms in legal terms or demand that others recognise their harms as a serious harms. It does not offer enough information regarding the sort of behaviour that should be avoided, and who the target audience might be.

Battery misses the mark in very important ways. It does not capture the seriousness of the harm that women experience when healthcare professionals examine them without their consent. Its focus on unauthorised touch does not speak directly and more specifically to *healthcare professionals* and the fact that they have violated women's rights during the course of their *professional duties*. This gap in legal language makes it difficult for women to claim in legal terms that they have been seriously harmed and it makes it difficult for society to know how to respond to the offending healthcare professionals. Women need a new, adequate label in law.

C. Claim 3: The Crime of Battery has Limited Expressive Effect in Medical Contexts

Technically, there seems to be little reason to question the applicability of the crime of battery to unauthorised vaginal examinations during labour but this technical understanding does not translate into this crime being applied within the maternity care context. The very fact that women continue to experience unauthorised vaginal examinations across time reveals that the crime of battery does not influence healthcare professionals' behaviour. Further, it seems that others (eg police, prosecuting authorities, healthcare institutions) are not applying the crime of battery to this context either. This suggests that the crime of battery has limited expressive effect within this context.

Law is regarded as an influential social tool that has the power to influence our beliefs, emotions or behaviour by what it expresses.[66] Richard McAdams lists four possible reasons why legal expression shapes our behaviour: the law might impose sanctions for non-compliance; it is perceived by the majority as a legitimate authority and thus worthy of obedience; it provides a focal point that helps to solve co-ordination problems within our society; and it provides information regarding risks or the beliefs and values of a society.[67] These four theories represent a contested space in that there is no unified expressive theory used to explain

---

[66] R McAdams, *The Expressive Powers of the Law: Theories and Limits* (Cambridge, Harvard University Press, 2017).
[67] ibid 12.

the law's effect on us and indeed the word 'expressive' is not a constant in the literature on this subject.[68] Nevertheless, whichever theory one might be inclined to support, it can be accepted that the law will fail to shape behaviour in cases where the intended audience (those to whom this law is directed) fail to understand what the law means and that it is applicable to them; that is, there is no 'uptake'.[69]

> Any expressive theory of *effects* invariably turns on audience meaning. If there were no audience meaning because the audience is unaware of the law, it could not possibly affect their behaviour ... If the audience does not perceive the law, its effect on their behaviour will surely depend on *its* actual understanding of the law and not the lawmaker's intended meaning nor on some sentence a third party could construct from the relevant conventions.[70]

There seems to be a gap in the communication between the lawmaker and healthcare professionals and third parties who are required to apply the law. The gap may comprise of a lack of knowledge of the crime of battery. Alternatively, healthcare professionals and third parties may know of the crime of battery (or common assault) but the lawmakers' intention for it to be applicable to *all* contexts *including the maternity care context* might not be adequately internalised. While empirical research is needed to explain where things might be going wrong here, I think the latter is the most likely explanation.

The ongoing debates regarding the teaching of vaginal examinations on anesthetised female patients helps to demonstrate the point that healthcare professionals consider themselves to be beyond this law's reach. In 1992, Susan Bewley made that case that teaching examinations on anesthetised patients without their consent is battery.[71] She explains that vaginal examinations are 'no different from any other form of touching' and that doctors and students may face a charge of battery if they touch their patients without consent.[72] In a letter to the editor, Linda Cardozo responds to Bewley as follows:

> By taking such a negative attitude towards vaginal examination of anaesthetised patients ... Susan Bewley is instilling into us the views of an articulate and vociferous minority who will, if allowed to continue, undermine the education of future generations of doctors. It is hard enough to encourage medical students to come to the operating theatre without making them feel that if they examine patients [without consent] they may be committing a criminal offence ... Personally, I would prefer to see a new generation of well-trained doctors who are able to relate appropriately to women who require gynaecological examination rather than a nation of women whose vaginas are protected from battery by medical students.[73]

---

[68] ibid.
[69] ibid 20.
[70] ibid.
[71] Bewley (n 11).
[72] ibid.
[73] L Cardoza, 'Letters: Teaching Vaginal Examination' (1992) 305 *British Medical Journal* 113 (footnote omitted).

This quote represents a very clear detachment from the dictates of the law. One might argue that Cardoza places healthcare professionals above the law. While this exchange took place nearly three decades ago and guidelines have since been introduced, recent studies show that this practice is likely to be alive and well.[74]

There is a continued breach of the criminal law but there are no criminal cases reported on this issue. Susan Bewley and James McGarry recognise that the risk of doctors being charged with battery is minimal.[75] I believe that this remains the position today, especially in light of the fact that there is anecdotal evidence that a woman has been turned away from a police station because her unauthorised vaginal examination during labour was considered to be a private/civil issue rather than a criminal one. This is a particularly alarming application of the criminal law: the touch of clothing without consent will attract criminal responsibility but not the insertion of a finger into another's vagina without their consent. These circumstances suggest that third parties fail to see the relevance of battery within this particular context. Again, while I recognise that questions regarding third party perceptions of the applicability of battery can only be answered through empirical research, I argue that the privileged and authoritative position of healthcare professionals within society might be a major influence here.

Joanna Erdman argues that legal rules 'are read through and subordinated to a system of medical authority'.[76] In the context of court-order Caesarean sections, Susan Irwin and Brigitte Jordan argue that courts have ordered Caesarean sections without considering the reasons why women refused the surgery and the orders were provided even though the law clearly did not support this approach.[77] Women's voices were silenced in these cases and the law lost its authority; they argue that this is a consequence of authoritative knowledge:

> The power of authoritative knowledge is not that it is correct but that it counts. In spite of the fact that medical opinions change over time and that doctors often disagree with one another, assertions made by medical professionals are consistently respected by the members of this society, including the legal establishment.[78]

The Special Rapporteur on Torture and other Cruel, Inhuman or Degrading Treatment or Punishment highlighted this very same issue in his 2013 report on abuse in healthcare settings. He recognised that we face 'unique challenges' in stopping abuse in healthcare facilities because, while not justified in other contexts, healthcare professionals successfully defended certain practices on the grounds of

---

[74] P Friesen, 'Educational Pelvic Exams on Anesthetized Women: Why Consent Matters' (2018) 32 *Bioethics* 298; Y Coldicott et al, 'The Ethics of Intimate Examinations: Teaching Tomorrow's Doctors' (2003) 326 *British Medical Journal* 97, 98.

[75] Bewley (n 11); J McGarry, 'Letters: Teaching Vaginal Examination' (1992) 305 *British Medical Journal* 113.

[76] Erdmann (n 37) 47.

[77] Irwin and Jordan (n 43) 330. See also Wolf (n 35) 101.

[78] Irwin and Jordan (n 43) 330.

administrative efficiency, behaviour modification, and *medical necessity*.[79] Erdman emphasises that 'Medical authority can thus foster a culture of impunity, where human rights violations do not only go unremedied, but unnoticed'.[80] I would like to add that the extent of the culture of impunity would be informed (in part) by broader gender norms that devalue women has human beings. The more we undervalue women in our society, the more likely it is that we will not harness the power of the law to support their rights more generally.

Battery is too loosely defined to have any meaningful sway when confronted with the formidable social powers of medical authority and harmful gender norms. On the face of it, it says absolutely nothing about protecting *women* from *healthcare professionals* during *childbirth*. Thus, it leaves too much room for medical authority and harmful gender norms to colour the views of the people making decisions about the applicability of battery to the very particular context of unauthorised vaginal touch/penetration during childbirth.

One might argue that battery's lack of expressive effect indicates that we need to dedicate more resources and time to public awareness raising and training of relevant decision-makers. While this might be helpful in the short term, this response will do little to make it clear that unauthorised vaginal examinations are gendered experiences of highly traumatic interactions that take place within a system that sometimes facilitates these types of abuses. This point supports the call for law reform: women need a name that clearly and fairly labels this issue in law.

IV. Concluding Reflections on Moving Forward

Demands for law reform are getting louder as we learn more about the normalised nature of abuse during facility-based childbirth and as we realise how little the law in its current form speaks to women's lived experiences. This chapter provides a glimpse into where some of the gaps might be found. The crime of battery is an ineffective behaviour-shaping tool in the context of unauthorised vaginal examinations during labour. It glosses over the unique types of harms women experience during facility-based abuse and its continued application to this context hides important, behaviour-shaping norms that explain why abuse occurs. Harmful gender norms and the privileged position of medical authority in society have a chilling effect when it comes to applying loosely-defined crimes, and we need a crime that speaks directly to dismantling the perception that women are not valued and that healthcare professionals can do what they deem best. We need something more explicit, that dissolves the need for discretion in law-related decision-making and that shifts the power from the hands of healthcare professionals back into the hands of women.

---

[79] United Nations General Assembly, 'Report of the UN Special Rapporteur on Torture and Other Cruel, Inhuman and Degrading Treatment, Juan E Méndez', UN Doc A/HRC/22/53 (2013) [13].
[80] Erdmann (n 37) 48.

10

Implied Consent and Vaginal Examination in Pregnancy

JONATHAN HERRING

I. Introduction

In many cases of unwanted vaginal examinations in pregnancy, the medical profes-sional will have acted on the basis of what they believe is implied consent.[1] They will believe they have followed the Royal College of Obstetricians and Gynaecologists' guidance on obtaining consent, which states 'You should give information and obtain consent at a time and in a manner that is appropriate', but they have not obtained proper consent.[2] There may be a tiny number of cases where the profes-sional is acting maliciously or out of sexual motivation. However, most will simply be assuming there is consent from the fact the woman has consented to receive care during pregnancy and this is taken to include consent to vaginal examinations; or that it can be implied that a woman is happy to receive whatever examinations the professionals will think will promote her foetus's wellbeing. This chapter explores whether relying on implied consent in this way is appropriate in either moral or legal terms.

Although the law does recognise the concept of implied consent to medical procedures in some contexts, I explore the philosophical and legal literature on implied consent and argue that it should not be seen as providing a moral or legal justification for a vaginal examination. To make this argument I will proceed as follows. In section II I explain why consent is required at all in law for a vaginal examination, because that is not as obvious to some academic commentators as it may seem to others. Section III explores how consent works in a moral and legal sense. In other words, to explain what it is about consent that provides a justifica-tion for an otherwise wrongful act. In section IV, I outline what precisely is meant

---

[1] That seems to be the case with pelvic examinations on women under anaesthesia: see S Barnes, 'Practicing Pelvic Examinations by Medical Students on Women under Anesthesia: Why not Ask First?' (2012) 120 *Obstetrics and Gynecology* 941.

[2] Royal College of Obstetricians and Gynaecologists, *Obtaining Valid Consent (Clinical Governance Advice No 6)* (London, RCOG, 2015).

by the term 'implied consent'. It is in section V that I make the case that implied consent cannot do the work it needs to do to provide a legal and moral justification for vaginal examinations. The conclusion, section VI, will be that explicit consent is required for all vaginal examinations for there to be legal and moral justification.

Before starting this task I note two limitations to the chapter. First, I will not be considering the case of women who are unable to consent (eg because they are unconscious or lack mental capacity). Those cases raise different issues. Second, I emphasise that I am not saying that where the medical professional has proceeded without explicit consent they will be guilty of a criminal offence. They may be able to rely on a defence that they reasonably believed there was consent. I will not be able to explore that in any detail, because that too raises some complex issues.

II. When is Consent Needed?

Consent is a complex philosophical issue, as evidenced by the vast range of publications on the issue.[3] The starting point is to consider when in moral and legal terms consent is required. Consent operates to justify an act which is prima facie wrong. It can (or can help) render a prima facie wrongful act justified 'all things considered'. There are many instances in the law where an act is prima facie unlawful but can become lawful if there is consent and sometimes other conditions are satisfied. A trespass can be rendered lawful by an invitation to tea; cutting someone's hair can be rendered lawful by a request for a smart bob; and so forth.

Consent is not required in moral terms if the act is not prima facie wrongful. Normally, looking at someone or walking past someone or even talking to someone does not require consent because those acts are not prima facie unlawful. Indeed, it would seem positively odd to ask someone if they minded you looking at them! That is because it is not a prima facie wrong merely to look at someone. Conversely, the fact an act is only lawful if performed with consent indicates that the act is a prima facie wrong, which requires some justification.

What makes an act prima facie wrongful? One reason is that the act will adversely affect a person's wellbeing. That is often in terms of pain, injury or distress, but is broader than that. Remember that we are talking at a prima facie level here. So an activity may – all things considered – promote the person's wellbeing even though the act itself causes pain. So, an injection would be a prima facie wrong – it requires a justification – even though very often it will be justified because the patient has consented and the injection will be beneficial. The point is that the person giving the injection needs a justification. They could not simply go around injecting people for the heck of it.

---

[3] See, eg, J McGregor, *Is it Rape?* (Aldershot, Ashgate, 2005); A Wertheimer, *Consent to Sexual Relations* (Cambridge, Cambridge University Press, 2003); P Westen, *The Logic of Consent* (Aldershot, Ashgate, 2004); F Miller and A Wertheimer (eds), *The Ethics of Consent* (Oxford, Oxford University Press, 2010).

So, is a vaginal examination a prima facie wrong of the kind that calls for a justification?[4] I will be very brief on this as other chapters in this collection explore this issue and manifestly support that conclusion. I think there is no difficulty if the examination involves the application of force on the woman's body. That would be a typical example of an act which is a prima facie wrong.[5] It is less straightforward where the medical professional is simply looking at a woman's vaginal area.

Lawyers and ethicists have struggled to explain the common intuition that such an act must be a prima facie wrongful. The debate at the theoretical level has arisen in particular in relation to voyeurism.[6] It is the particular interest in privacy of genital areas which seems key here. Even if hard to articulate in our society, there is a particular attention paid by most, but of course not all, people to keeping genital areas covered. In this sense non-consensual examination of a person's genital area may be seen as showing a lacking of respect for their personhood.[7] I think it ties to a very particular interest in bodily privacy. Although we seek to control access to information and our property, there is a special place for controlling access to bodies. Gerald Dworkin explains:

> One's body is irreplaceable and inescapable. If my architect doesn't listen to me and this results in a house I do not like, I can always move. I cannot move from my body. In addition, because my body is me, failure to respect my wishes concerning my body is a particularly insulting denial of autonomy.[8]

In an interesting discussion of pelvic examinations on anesthetised women without consent, Phoebe Friesen notes a view among some doctors that an examination of a genital area is equivalent to checking a pulse or looking into a patient's mouth. She argues that this does not accord with the views of patients, who in surveys have said they would want to be asked for consent about an intimate examination.[9] And if we are looking at a matter of bodily privacy it should be the understanding of the person viewed, not that of the person viewing, which determines the nature of the act.[10]

---

[4] M Plaxton, 'Privacy, Voyeurism, and Statutory Interpretation' *Criminal Law Quarterly* (forthcoming).

[5] M Dempsey and J Herring, 'Why Penetration Requires Justification' (2007) 27 *Oxford Journal of Legal Studies* 467.

[6] Department of Justice Canada, *Voyeurism as a Criminal Offence: A Consultation Paper* (2002) 8 at www.justice.gc.ca/eng/cons/voy/voy.pdf.

[7] S Benn, 'Privacy, Freedom, and Respect for Persons' in J Pennock and R Chapman (eds), *Nomos XIII: Privacy* (New York, Atherton Press, 1971); J Moor, 'The Ethics of Privacy Protection' (1997) 39 *Library Trends* 69. See, for a contrary view, T Doyle, 'Privacy and Perfect Voyeurism' (2009) 11 *Ethics and Information Technology* 181.

[8] G Dworkin, *The Theory and Practice of Autonomy* (Cambridge, Cambridge University Press, 1988) 113.

[9] P Friesen, 'Educational Pelvic Exams on Anesthetized Women: Why Consent Matters' (2018) 32 *Bioethics* 298.

[10] Catarina Sjölin, Camilla Pickles and Andrea Mulligan discuss this further in this volume so I will not explore that here.

III. What does Consent do?

While it is claimed that consent is 'morally transformative' little attention is given on why that is so.[11] What is it that consent is doing in moral terms to have its impact? Only once we understand what it is that consent does, can we consider what the requirements for consent are.[12]

The model of consent I will adopt here is that propounded by Michelle Madden Dempsey.[13] In outline, the argument is as follows. Consent becomes relevant when an actor (A) wrongfully harms another person's (B) wellbeing thereby rendering the act a prima facie wrong. That requires A to provide a reason justifying acting in the way he or she did. Consent can operate as providing a justifying reason. It gives A an option to decide to set aside the reasons against acting in a particular way which rest in B's wellbeing. Consent does that by allowing A to assume that the act is not, all things considered, contrary to the wellbeing of the victim B. That is because A is permitted to rely on B's assessment that the act is overall in B's best interests. In effect where consent is effective Madden Dempsey claims that A is entitled to say:

> This is [B]'s decision. He's an adult and can decide for himself whether he thinks the risk is worth it. In considering what to do, I will assume that his decision is the right one for him. After all, he is in a better position than I to judge his own well-being. And so, I will not take it upon myself to reconsider those reasons. Instead, I will base my decision of whether to [harm] him on the other relevant reasons.[14]

There is, of course, much more that could be said about this, and no doubt it needs a more sophisticated justification than given here. But this one will be adopted in this chapter.

The significance of this approach for the issue of vaginal examinations is four-fold. These points will be elaborated on in section V:

(1) consent is a 'positive' notion. The legal issue is whether or not the patient consented to the procedure, not whether the patient failed to oppose the treatment.[15] A patient who responds passively to a medical professional's proposal for an examination is not giving the medical professional sufficient evidence that they have assessed the examination as in their welfare. In its nature an omission in the face of a proposal is at most ambiguous;

---

[11] A Wertheimer, 'Consent to Sexual Relations' in F Miller and A Wertheimer (eds), *The Ethics of Consent* (Oxford, Oxford University Press, 2010).

[12] T Dougherty, 'On Wrongs and Crimes: Does Consent Require Only an Attempt to Communicate?' (2019) 13 *Criminal Law and Philosophy* 409.

[13] M Dempsey, 'Victimless Conduct and the Volenti Maxim: How Consent Works' (2013) 7 *Criminal Law and Philosophy* 11, building on J Herring and M Madden Dempsey, 'Rethinking the Criminal Law's Response to Sexual Penetration' in C McGlynn and V Munro (eds) *Rethinking Rape Law* (London, Routledge, 2010). For a different view see R Healey, 'Consent, Rights, and Reasons for Action' (2019) 13 *Criminal Law and Philosophy* 499.

[14] Dempsey (n 13) 20.

[15] *St George's Healthcare NHS Trust v S* [1998] 3 WLR 936 (CA).

(2)   consent can only do its work where there is full consent. As we shall see in the remainder of this chapter, there may be cases of apparent consent in vaginal examinations which will not be true consent because it cannot do the moral work required. The consent must be sufficiently 'rich' for the medical professional to be able to rely on it as an assessment by B as to their own wellbeing;

(3)   it is important not to exaggerate the significance of consent. Heidi Hurd has famously argued that consent has moral magic and that it can transform 'trespasses into dinner parties … and rape into lovemaking'.[16] That is clearly an exaggeration because as Michelle Madden Dempsey points out, 'turning a trespass into a dinner party requires, at least, dinner – while turning rape into lovemaking requires, at least, love'.[17] So not only must any vaginal examination be done with consent, for it to be lawful it must also comply with professional standards in relation to respect for privacy; medical justification and so forth;

(4)   on the model outlined only the patient can provide the medical professional with the exclusionary permission to do the act. Fairly obviously, a third party cannot provide an adequate assessment of the patient's best interests, and the professional should seek consent from the patient.

Before developing these points in the context of vaginal examinations, more needs to be said about the nature of implied consent.

IV. The Concept of Implied Consent

Consent is generally seen as falling into one of three categories:

(1)   express consent: this is where A has proposed a course of action (X) and B has consented to that action. In this context it would be where the healthcare professional proposes undertaking a vaginal examination and the patient has explicitly agreed. The consent may be in writing (by signing a consent form) or by giving oral agreement;

(2)   implicit consent:[18] this is where A has proposed a course of action (X) and that course of action necessarily involves (Y) and B has explicitly consented to X. B has also implicitly consented to Y. In this context this might be said to arise where the healthcare professional has offered to take care of the pregnant woman during her labour and this is taken to necessarily involve undertaking regular vaginal examinations, although the patient has not explicitly agreed to this. Of course, much depends here on whether the vaginal examination

---

[16] H Hurd, 'The Moral Magic of Consent' (1996) 2 *Legal Theory* 121, 122.

[17] Dempsey (n 13) 12.

[18] Archard prefers the terminology 'tacit' consent: see D Archard, *Sexual Consent* (London, Routledge, 2019) 8.

is necessarily involved in the care. There is room for disagreement because much depends on whether consenting to X is 'generally taken';[19]

(3)   implied consent: this is where A has proposed a course of action (X) and although B has not explicitly consented with words, their conduct is taken as evidence of a consenting state of mind. In our context it might be said that if a healthcare professional proposed a vaginal examination and the patient opened their legs to facilitate that or moved clothing to enable it, this could count as implied consent. Their failure to voice any opposition and perform an act which might indicate consent is used to imply consent.

In the literature sometimes reference is made to the concept of imputed intent. This is where A has proposed a course of action (X) and although B has not explicitly consented with words, their conduct is evidence of a consenting state of mind, which causes A to believe B has consented, even if B has not. Peter Singer writes that 'under certain circumstances, actions or failures to act may justify us in holding a person to be obliged as if he had consented, whether or not he actually has'.[20] Jean McHale explains 'where the patient conducts himself such that it is reasonable to imply that he consented to the treatment or procedure, the law merely prohibits the patient because of his conduct from denying that he consented even though, in fact, he did not'.[21] I would argue that this is not consent. At most it is an argument that the medical professional should not be found legally accountable because they reasonably believed there to be consent. To see it as a species of consent simply invites confusion.[22]

In the next section I develop an argument that of these three kinds of consent only the first should be effective in the context of vaginal examinations.[23]

V. Implicit Consent cannot do the Work of Morally Transformative Consent

We are now in a position to see why positive consent should be required for an act which is a serious invasion of sexual and bodily privacy, remembering that for consent to operate it must be sufficient for the medical professional to be able to rely on it as an assessment by the patient that the examination is for her wellbeing. Relying on implied or imputed consent cannot be sufficient for the medical

---

[19] ibid 10.

[20] P Singer, *Democracy and Disobedience* (New York, Oxford University Press, 1974) 47.

[21] J McHale, 'Consent to Treatment: The Competent Patient' in J Laing and J McHale (eds), *Principles of Medical Law* (Oxford, Oxford University Press, 2017) 434.

[22] ibid.

[23] R Wheeler, 'Presumed or Implied: It's Not Consent' (2010) 16 *Clinical Risk* 1.

professional to be secure that the patient has determined that the examination is in their best interests. The fact there is no opposition or an act that might possibly indicate consent, does not give warrant to the defendant acting on it in a way which is a prima facie wrong. To explain further why, I explore four themes.

A. 'Ambiguous Consent' is not Morally or Legally Effective

Recall that the medical professional in seeking to do a vaginal examination will be embarking on a prima facie wrongful act. The consent of the patient must be sufficient for the medical professional to take the patient to have assessed the examination to be for their wellbeing. If the behaviour of the patient is ambiguous, that cannot provide sufficient authorisation to perform the prima facie wrongful examination.[24] In cases of implicit or implied consent the medical professional has, at best, evidence that the patient *might have* assessed the examination to be in their best interests, but they cannot be sure.

This argument mirrors the change in approach in many jurisdictions to the law and social attitudes towards sex. Now a positive expression of consent is generally taken to be consent. The view that it can only be rape where there has been positive resistance, or that silence can be taken as consent, is outdated and based on patriarchal assumptions. Modern sex education is based on the idea that 'young people learn that sex must begin with a "yes" – for sex to be consensual, both parties must affirmatively communicate their willingness to participate in the activity on offer'.[25] A Canadian judge who in 2017 asked a rape victim 'why couldn't you just keep your knees together' was rightly forced to resign.[26] It is not for the rape victim to demonstrate that she did enough to stop the rape, it is for the would-be rapist to demonstrate he had sufficient justification to have sex.

The same is true in cases of vaginal examination. Consent should not be implied or assumed from the basis of a failure to consent, or from actions which are in their nature ambiguous. This rejection of implied consent is important because there is a real danger that 'implied consent' can look very like a patient who is complying but not genuinely consenting. Writing generally on obtaining consent to procedures, Marc Stauch et al state that the concept of presumed consent 'is not relevant in respect of patients who are in a position to provide consent: here,

---

[24] S Schulhofer, *Unwanted Sex: The Culture of Intimidation and the Failure of Law* (Cambridge, Harvard University Press, 1998) 272–73, in the context of sex.

[25] J Gilbert, 'Contesting Consent in Sex Education' (2018) 18 *Sex Education* 268.

[26] M Lessard, 'Why Couldn't You Just Keep Your Knees Together?' *The Guardian* (London, 10 March 2017).

assumptions (on the part of doctors) as to their wishes will be unnecessary and potentially highhanded'.[27]

A medical professional should not perform a prima facie wrongful act on a patient based on guesses or assumptions about what the patient wants,[28] especially where any ambiguity could be resolved by asking the patient whether they consent. Indeed, if the professional proceeds on the basis of assumptions or implications, then it must be asked why they did not obtain the full consent?[29] Is it that they fear what answer will be given if they ask for full consent? Or do they not really care whether the victim consents or not? Clearly they do not have the autonomy-respecting state of mind that Madden Dempsey describes as necessary for consent to be morally and legally effective.

B. Only 'Rich' Consent is Morally and Legally Effective

If we return to the Michelle Madden Dempsey discussion of the role of consent, it is clear this requires a 'rich consent'. The patient must be informed and have made the decision free from undue pressure. If the medical professional knows that the patient would not be consenting if they knew all the facts, or would only consent if the professional applied pressure, then they cannot rely on the apparent consent as an assessment of best interests. In effect, in such a case a medical professional is claiming to know better than the patient about what will be in their best interests. A medical professional who is withholding facts from the patient is applying pressure on them, or seeking otherwise to manipulate them; they are clearly not seeking to discover the patient's own assessment of their best interests but are seeking to impose their assessment on the patient. So, it is not simply a matter of getting the patient to say the words 'yes' to the examination, it is about ensuring that patient is able to make an effective assessment of their best interests.

It should also be emphasised that the English courts have quite rightly rejected an argument that foresight can equate to consent. In *H v Crown Prosecution Service* a teacher was attacked by a pupil at a school for children with behavioural problems.[30] The defence argued that by taking the job the teacher must have foreseen that he might be subjected to violence and so could be taken to consent to any violence. Quite rightly, this argument was given short shrift by the court. Foreseeing that one is going to be subjected to violence is hardly consent to the violence. Similarly, foreseeing that there might be vaginal examinations in the course of medical intervention is not consent to them.

---

[27] M Stauch et al, *Text, Cases and Materials on Medical Law and Ethics*, 4th edn (London, Routledge, 2012) 84.

[28] T Dougherty, 'Affirmative Consent and Due Diligence' (2018) 46 *Philosophy & Public Affairs* 90.

[29] ibid.

[30] *H v Crown Prosecution Service* [2010] EWHC 1374 (Admin).

C. Consent should be Understood Relationally

In determining whether or not consent is effective it is important generally to understand the relational context of the encounter. There are two aspects to this. The first is that a medical professional should not see consent as simply a matter of a 'yes' or 'no' but understand the patient's views in light of the history of their relationships. This approach requires the professional, so far as is possible, to consider the patient's whole story and place it in the context of her values and relationships. The birth plan, life values and relational context should all be considered. Where a patient's consent or refusal is inconsistent with this, the professional will need to be especially careful to determine whether the consent or refusal does reflect an assessment of their own wellbeing, rather than being a momentary decision.

Second, we must recall that consent to a vaginal examination involves an encounter between the two people, and must be interpreted in light of the relationship between them. This inevitably involves an acknowledgement of the power differential between a patient and a medical professional. The question becomes less 'was there a yes?' or 'was there an intellectual understanding of the issues?', and, rather, 'was an interaction marked by mutuality and respect?', 'was the medical professional truly seeking to find out and respect what the patient wanted or seeking to produce the answer the professional wanted?'[31]

An important aspect of this is an acknowledgement that there is ample evidence that we are bad decision makers. Neil Levy refers to a wide range of psychological studies which reveal 'fallibilities of human reasoning' (including 'myopia for the future', 'motivated reasoning' and 'biases' in 'assessing probabilities ... exacerbated ... under cognitive load').[32] He concludes that 'Human beings are, under a variety of conditions, systematically bad reasoners, and many of their reasoning faults can be expected to affect the kind of judgements that they make when they are called upon to give informed consent'.[33]

However, it should be noted that this works two ways. While the professional must acknowledge the ways in which the patient's consent may be flawed, so too must the professional appreciate the ways in which their own assessment of whether there is valid consent is potentially flawed. We hear what we want to hear. We like to think we know better than others about what is good for them. We want people to like us and to agree to what we want. Consent, then, must to be treated

---

[31] A Donchin, 'Autonomy, Interdependence, and Assisted Suicide: Respecting Boundaries/Crossing Lines' (2000) 141 *Bioethics* 187, 192.

[32] N Levy, 'Forced to be Free? Increasing Patient Autonomy by Constraining it' (2014) 40 *Journal of Medical Ethics* 293.

[33] ibid.

by both parties with an awareness of their vulnerabilities. The approach advocated in this chapter seeks to do this. It is line with what Kim Atkins argues:

> Respect for autonomy is an acknowledgment of the limitations of our knowledge of other people and a willingness to incorporate that understanding into our worldviews. When we respect autonomy we don't simply observe another's freedom from a distance, as it were; we accede to our fundamental fallibility and epistemological humility. It is in recognition of the fact that we cannot experience from another's perspective that we normally refrain from judging what will make another's life good *for them*.[34]

It encourages us, in our interactions with others, to seek to engage with them, accepting their values.

D. Consent should be Understood in its Social Context

Feminist writing has done much to show how societal pressures impact on women's sense of self. Feminism is 'centrally concerned with freeing women to shape their own lives' and to 'define' themselves 'rather than accepting the definition given by others (men and male-dominated society, in particular)'.[35] This is particularly relevant in relation to consent in the context of decisions made during labour and pregnancy.

First, there is an extensive literature on the pressures on women to set aside their own interests for 'the good of the baby'. It is hard to underestimate the pressure on a woman to make a decision which is seen to promote what is best for the child. There is extensive literature on this and in other chapters in this book so I will not discuss that further.

Second, we should recall that in labour and pregnancy the agenda is set by the medical professional. Nicola Lacey, writing in the context of sexual behaviour, highlights the problems in simply asking whether the victim consented to 'the act'. She writes:

> The victim's consent responds to power by conferring legitimacy, rather than shaping power in its own terms: consent is currently understood not in terms of mutuality but rather in relation to a set of arrangements initiated, by implication, by the defendant, in an asymmetric structure which reflects the stereotypes of active masculinity and passive femininity.[36]

---

[34] K Atkins, 'Autonomy and the Subjective Character of Experience' (2000) 17 *Journal of Applied Philosophy* 71.

[35] S Boyd, 'Motherhood and Autonomy in a Shared Parenting Climate' in J Jones et al (eds), *Gender, Sexualities and Law* (London, Routledge, 2011) 121.

[36] N Lacey, *Unspeakable Subjects: Feminist Essays in Legal and Social Theory* (Oxford, Hart Publishing, 1998) 114.

There is a similar point to be made in relation to the professional/patient relationship, particularly in relation to labour. Here it is the professional who sets the agenda, and who determines the questions the patient must answer. This limits the role of the woman's autonomy to confirming the plan of the professionals, rather than giving her a voice to set her own agenda.[37] Proper respect for autonomy requires more than making a demand and limiting the other person's response to either yes or no. It can be a politician's favourite trick to claim 'you are either for us or against us', a trick which forecloses a range of more nuanced positions.[38]

Third, the social context is relevant when considering what might be taken as implied consent.[39] Drawing again on the literature on rape, there is ample discussion on what makes a 'good' rape victim, whose account is believable and acceptable, in contrast to the 'bad' rape victims whose choices over clothes, previous partners, social venues, and personality are taken to imply consent and make her account unreliable.[40] The same is probably true in the context of gynaecological care.

E. There is a Responsibility to Ensure Consent is Effective

Implied with what has been said under the previous heading is a further claim. Not only must A truly respect B's autonomy, A has a responsibility to take reasonable steps to enable B to exercise autonomy and to ensure they are not doing anything that might impede B's autonomy.

It must be recalled that we are dealing with a situation where the medical professional is planning to do an act to the patient which is a prima facie wrong. They are always free not to act in that way, but if they decide to commit the wrong, relying on the consent of the patient, then they have responsibilities to ensure that the consent is effective in the way explained above. This will mean doing what they can to ensure the patient has the time, information, trust and atmosphere to consent. The use of deceptions, withholding information, threats, manipulation or exploitation are not consistent with a professional seeking to respect the bodily and sexual autonomy of a patient.

It is important to note here that the professional and patient might interpret what is said or done differently. So, what to the professional might appear to be

---

[37] J Flanigan, 'Obstetric Autonomy and Informed Consent' (2016) 19 *Ethic Theory Moral Practice* 225.

[38] See eg President Bush's remarks on the War on Terror: 'You are either with us or against us' *CNN Online*, 6 November 2001.

[39] E Schneider, *Battered Women and Feminist Lawmaking* (New Haven, Yale University Press, 2000).

[40] M Randall, 'Sexual Assault Law, Credibility, and "Ideal Victims": Consent, Resistance, and Victim Blaming' (2010) 22 *Canadian Journal of Women and the Law* 397; J Benedet, 'The Sexual Assault of Intoxicated Women' (2010) 22 *Canadian Journal of Women and the Law* 435, 440–41.

advice or information may be interpreted as a threat. Empathy is therefore key. As Catriona Mackenzie claims, in a medical context,

> [t]he principle of respect for autonomy … gives rise to an obligation to try to empathically engage with the other's experience, to imagine what the other person's situation is like for her, given her cares, values and concerns. In the context of patient care, it requires carers and medical staff to try to understand, from the patient's perspective, her experience of illness, or of particular treatment options.[41]

A proper respect for a patient's authority over their sexual and bodily integrity will take positive steps to ensure there is effective consent, and not merely evidence of a 'yes'.[42]

VI. Conclusion

This chapter has explored the jurisprudential and ethical literature to make the case that only explicit consent should be sufficient for vaginal examinations, and implied, inferred or imputed consent is insufficient. I have argued that consent gets its moral significance because it allows the medical professional to do what would otherwise be a prima facie wrongful act by allowing them to take the patient's consent as an assessment that the examination would be for their welfare. However, that approach requires the professional to have a particular attitude towards the consent: recognising that this is the patient's decision, and that they must be confident that the patient has made an assessment of their own wellbeing which is genuine. This requires much more than ensuring the patient says 'yes'; it requires the professional to give the patient the time, confidence, information and space to make their own assessment. It means that ambiguous consent is insufficient to justify the examination. Patient consent is not a bauble, which the professional must grab in any way they can.

I am confident that the majority of professionals do seek to act in the way described in this chapter. However, I suspect that in many cases where there has not been genuine consent – but the professional believes there has been – are ones where implied or inferred consent are improperly used, and the approach promoted in this chapter has not been followed.

---

[41] C Mackenzie, 'Relational Autonomy, Normative Authority and Perfectionism' (2008) 39 *Journal of Social Philosophy* 512.
[42] Dougherty (n 28).

11

Troubling Consent: Pain and Pressure in Labour and Childbirth

CLAIRE MURRAY

I. Introduction

In *Montgomery v Lanarkshire Health Board* the UK Supreme Court confirmed the importance of autonomy and communication in healthcare decision-making, and emphasised that pregnancy does not dilute the legal protections available to an individual.[1] It is well-established that informed consent is the principal mechanism through which autonomy is protected in the healthcare context and this legal principle is reflected in professional and clinical guidance, including those related to the provision of maternity care.[2] Standard maternity care in the UK includes obstetric vaginal examinations to monitor the progress of labour as an element of ensuring safe births for women and babies.[3] The NICE Clinical Guidance on 'Intrapartum Care for Healthy Women and Babies' states that women should be offered vaginal examinations if the clinician is of the opinion that the examination is necessary and will add useful information to the decision-making process.[4] The Guidance document also emphasises the importance of obtaining informed consent from the woman; ensuring her dignity, privacy and comfort is respected; explaining the reason for the procedure and what is involved to her; and

---

[1] *Montgomery v Lanarkshire Health Board* [2015] UKSC 11.

[2] See Royal College of Obstetricians and Gynaecologists, *Obtaining Valid Consent: Clinical Governance Advice No. 6* (London, RCOG, 2015); Royal College of Midwives (RCM), *Evidence Based Guidelines for Midwifery-Led Care in Labour: Assessing Progress in Labour* (London, RCM, 2012).

[3] For further detail on progress of labour see the discussion in Chapter 2 above, by R Brione, 'Non-Consented Vaginal Examinations: The Birthrights and AIMS Perspective'. The terms 'woman' and 'women' are used throughout this chapter while recognising that trans* and non-binary people can become pregnant, and so these terms are intended to include all those who may become pregnant and require care during labour and childbirth. The term 'baby' or 'babies' is used, rather than foetus, to reflect that for most women who have carried a pregnancy to term and who are in labour that is generally how they think about and speak of the foetus. This is also usually the terminology used by those who care for women in labour and childbirth.

[4] National Institute for Health and Care Excellence, *Intrapartum Care: Care of Healthy Women and Their Babies during Childbirth: Clinical Guideline 190* (London, NICE, 2014) [1.4.5].

communicating the outcome of the examination to her and any impact that may have on her birth plan.[5] However, despite this clear emphasis in law and clinical guidance on the importance of consent, some women are experiencing unwanted vaginal examinations during labour and childbirth. The circumstances in which this occurs may vary, but the focus in this chapter is on the impact of pain and pressure in labour on the validity of consent.[6]

This chapter will begin by briefly locating the discussion of consent, pain and pressure in labour within the broader legal context in the UK. The chapter is primarily grounded in case law on consent and treatment refusal involving pregnant women, but there is no existing body of case law on vaginal examinations and treatment refusal in labour, which indicates that these issues are, to date, being addressed (or not) in locations outside of the courts. Section II will outline the interconnectedness of pain and pressure and highlight the role of *Montgomery* in normalising the pregnant subject. Section III will focus on decision-making in labour and childbirth and will seek to trouble the current binary model of consent which struggles to accommodate the pregnant woman in labour who does not neatly fit within the existing binary framework. This discussion will briefly refer to the existing narratives and stereotypes of pregnant women, illustrated by the enforced Caesarean section case law, which further complicate the recognition of women's autonomy in labour and childbirth. At the centre of section III is a discussion of *ML v Guys and St Thomas' National Healthcare Foundation Trust*, where the High Court considered the impact of pain in labour on decision-making in the context of a request for a Caesarean section.[7] The chapter will conclude with reflections on the need for a more flexible model of consent, one which stretches the temporal context, if the recognition of autonomy for pregnant women in labour is to be meaningful. It also acknowledges the challenges and risks associated with the suggestions put forward.

II. Consent

Consent to any healthcare treatment or intervention must be voluntary, informed and provided by someone with decision-making capacity.[8] The absence of any

---

[5] ibid.

[6] See discussion on 'implied consent' in Chapter 10, by J Herring, 'Implied Consent and Vaginal Examination in Pregnancy', and on forced vaginal examinations in Chapter 9 by C Pickles, 'When "Battery" is Not Enough: Exposing the Gaps in Unauthorised Vaginal Examinations During Labour as a Crime of Battery'.

[7] *ML v Guys and St Thomas' National Healthcare Foundation Trust* [2018] EWHC 2010 (QB).

[8] This principle was reaffirmed in *Freeman v Home Office* [1984] 2 WLR 802 (CA). In this case the trial court and the Court of Appeal rejected claims that the plaintiff had been physically restrained and had medical treatment forcibly imposed on him in prison. The Court of Appeal did, however, accept that some situations, including a prison setting, would require a closer examination of consent to establish voluntariness. In *Montgomery* (n 1) the approach of the law to information disclosure was characterised as one which recognises patients as adults who are capable of understanding that medical

one of those elements will vitiate consent.[9] The courts have acknowledged that pain (unrelated to labour) can have an impact on the capacity of a person, and therefore on the validity of consent. In *Re T (Adult: Refusal of Medical Treatment)* Lord Donaldson stated that a person may be deprived of capacity or have it reduced 'by reason of temporary factors, such as unconsciousness or confusion or other effects of shock, severe fatigue, pain or drugs being used in their treatment'.[10] This can be contrasted with *NHS Trust v T*, where the court adopted a more absolute approach and stated that only where confusion, shock, fatigue, pain or drugs 'completely erode capacity' should it be found that there is no consent.[11] The Irish Supreme Court in *Fitzpatrick v White* also recognised that pain or stress can have an impact on the ability of a person to fully comprehend and make an informed decision on a proposed medical intervention.[12]

A. Interconnectedness of Pain and Pressure

For the purposes of this chapter, pain and pressure, and their impact on decision-making in labour, will be considered together. This is because they are interconnected – the presence of pain can make someone more susceptible to pressure or 'heavy duty persuasion'.[13] The links between pain and pressure were recognised in

---

treatment contains certain risks, who accept responsibility for taking risks which affect their own lives, and who then live with the consequences of those decisions: [81]. The Supreme Court set out the test for informed consent in the following terms: 'An adult person of sound mind is entitled to decide which, if any, of the available forms of treatment to undergo, and her consent must be obtained before treatment interfering with her bodily integrity is undertaken. The doctor is therefore under a duty to take reasonable care to ensure that the patient is aware of any material risks involved in any recommended treatment, and of any reasonable alternative or variant treatments. The test of materiality is whether, in the circumstances of the particular case, a reasonable person in the patient's position would be likely to attach significance to the risk, or the doctor is or should reasonably be aware that the particular patient would be likely to attach significance to it': [87]. It is a core principle of medical law that an adult with capacity has an absolute right to consent to or to refuse medical treatment. This is the case even if the decision, for example to refuse treatment, will lead to the death of the patient. This has led Donnelly to describe capacity as the 'gatekeeper for autonomy': see M Donnelly, *Healthcare Decision-Making and the Law: Autonomy, Capacity and the Limits of Liberalism* (Cambridge, Cambridge University Press, 2010) 90.

[9] For a more detailed discussion on the moral and legal underpinnings of consent see Herring (n 6).

[10] *Re T (Adult: Refusal of Medical Treatment)* [1992] EWCA Civ 18 [27]. However, while pain was a factor in this case it was not relied on to find that the consent of the young woman in *Re T* was not valid. While the pain may have been a contributing factor to her will being overborne by her mother, the court was more focused on the pressure and undue influence that had been applied.

[11] *NHS Trust v T* [2004] EWHC 1279 (Fam).

[12] *Fitzpatrick v White* [2008] 3 IR 551. At [565] the Court considered that 'There are obvious reasons why, in the context of elective surgery, a warning given only shortly before an operation is undesirable. A patient may be stressed, medicated or in pain in this period and may be less likely for one or more of these reasons to make a calm and reasoned decision in such circumstances'. On the facts the court found that there was no evidence that the plaintiff had been affected in any of the ways outlined above and so the timing of the warning and disclosure was not found to be a breach of the duty of care.

[13] R Scott, *Rights, Duties and the Body* (Oxford, Hart Publishing, 2002) 236–45 makes the case for persuasion as a mechanism to deal with treatment refusal by pregnant women, and suggests the use of 'sympathetic discussion and counselling'. At 243 she argues that in relation to pregnant women who

the Court of Appeal in *Re T.* This case involved the refusal of a blood transfusion by a young woman who had been brought up by her mother as a Jehovah's Witness, although she had not been practising her faith prior to her illness. She signed a written refusal of a blood transfusion following a number of visits from her mother, who was a devout Jehovah's Witness.[14] However, prior to signing the refusal form she had also sought reassurance from the clinical staff that alternatives to blood products were available.[15] While the Court of Appeal upheld the right of a competent patient to refuse treatment, even life-sustaining treatment, on the facts the court found that the right did not apply for reasons of undue influence, her weakened and medicated state, and a failure of the medical staff to provide her with accurate information.[16]

Lord Donaldson noted that the strength of will of the patient is of crucial importance in determining whether the decision was truly their own. In this respect he observed that 'one who is very tired, in pain or depressed will be much less able to resist having his will overborne than one who is rested, free from pain and cheerful'.[17] This is significant in the context of labour and childbirth, where being tired and in pain is – for many women – a central feature of the process. In Lord Donaldson's approach to undue influence in a healthcare context there are two important factors – the strength of will of the patient and the relationship of the persuader.[18] Justice Butler-Sloss in *Re T* also observed the interplay between pain and pressure and consent and stated

> Although the issues of capacity and genuine consent or rejection are separate, in reality they may well overlap, so that a patient in a weakened condition may be unduly influenced in circumstances in which if he had been fit, he would have resisted the influence sought to be exercised over him.[19]

Given that the presence of pain or tiredness or a weakened condition is a significant element in the case law where pressure impacts on the validity of consent in

---

refuse treatment 'heavy duty persuasion' should only be used in circumstances where the treatment being refused 'does not involve significant pain or risks' and where the reasons for refusal are 'insufficiently serious', 'trivial', 'irrational/inappropriate and purposeless' or 'non-existent'.

[14] In circumstances where the full consequences of that action were not clearly explained to her.

[15] She was also advised by hospital staff that the likelihood of her requiring a blood transfusion was very low.

[16] The undue influence was exercised by the young woman's mother. Lord Donaldson stated that 'the influence of her mother was such as to vitiate the decision which she expressed': *Re T* (n 10) [22]. The issue of undue influence has rarely come before the courts in the medical context since *Re T*. One such case is *Mrs U v Centre for Reproductive Medicine* [2002] EWHC 36 (Fam). This involved the applicant seeking to overturn her husband's signed refusal of consent to the posthumous use of his sperm. She argued that the refusal had been made as a result of the undue influence of a staff member at the fertility clinic the couple had been attending. Mrs U was unsuccessful in her action and the decision in *U* was applied in *Evans v Amicus Healthcare Ltd and Others* [2004] EWCA Civ 727. See also S Pattinson, 'Undue Influence in the Context of Medical Treatment' (2002) 5 *Medical Law International* 305.

[17] *Re T* (n 10) [32].

[18] Lord Donaldson also stated that 'some relationships more readily lend themselves to overbearing the patient's independent will than do others': *Re T* (n 10).

[19] *Re T* (n 10) [41].

a healthcare context, I am going to address pain and pressure together throughout the chapter.

B. Normalising the Pregnant Subject: *Montgomery v Lanarkshire Health Board*

Nadine Montgomery was not in labour when she was given inadequate information about the risks of vaginal delivery in her particular circumstances and the alternative possibility of Caesarean section.[20] There was no question that pain or pressure were factors impacting on her decision-making ability. However, the significance of *Montgomery* for the purposes of this chapter is that it reaffirmed the importance of autonomy and consent in healthcare decision-making in a case centred on a pregnant woman. It included a discussion of harm to the woman, as well as to the baby, as a factor to be taken into consideration in weighing up the risks of choosing one delivery option over the other.[21]

It is worth noting that the clear and strongly-worded principle set out by the House of Lords in *Airedale NHS Trust v Bland* that 'it is unlawful, so as to constitute both a tort and the crime of battery, to administer medical treatment to an adult, who is conscious and of sound mind, without his consent ... Such a person is completely at liberty to decline to undergo treatment, even if the result of his doing so will be that he will die' has on many occasions wavered in cases involving pregnant women.[22] This was acknowledged by Lady Hale in *Montgomery* when she stated 'Gone are the days when it was thought that, on becoming pregnant, a woman lost, not only her capacity, but also her right to act as a genuinely autonomous human being'.[23] The strong statement in *Montgomery* that pregnancy does not dilute existing autonomy rights was particularly significant because it co-existed with a recognition of the uniqueness of pregnancy. Unlike many other healthcare decisions that people are required to make, deciding not to choose any of the options presented to you is generally not a possibility. Lady Hale succinctly

---

[20] The consequence of what the Supreme Court found to be a negligent failure to disclose relevant information to her was that her son was born with severe disabilities following a very traumatic birth.

[21] The court noted that 'shoulder dystocia is itself a major obstetric emergency, requiring procedures which may be traumatic for the mother, and involving significant risks to her health. No woman would, for example, be likely to face the possibility of a fourth degree tear, a Zavanelli manoeuvre or a symphysiotomy with equanimity': [94]. See also Lady Hale at [111]: 'In this day and age, we are not only concerned about risks to the baby. We are equally, if not more, concerned about risks to the mother. And those include the risks associated with giving birth, as well as any after-effects. One of the problems with this case was that for too long the focus was on the risks to the baby, without also taking into account what the mother might face in the process of giving birth'.

[22] *Airedale NHS Trust v Bland* [1993] AC 789; see discussion of Caesarean section cases below and S Halliday, *Autonomy and Pregnancy: A Comparative Analysis of Compelled Obstetric Intervention* (London, Routledge, 2016).

[23] *Montgomery* (n 1) [116].

captured it as follows: 'Once a woman is pregnant, the foetus has somehow to be delivered. Leaving it inside her is not an option'.[24]

III. Decision-Making in Labour and Childbirth

The core issue then is how to best protect the autonomy of pregnant women in labour while recognising that pregnancy is different to other healthcare contexts and decision-making in labour is complicated by factors such as pain and pressure. This section first briefly outlines the factors that might give rise to questions about the validity of consent in labour and broadly categorises the women affected. It then moves on to problematise the existing model of consent. This is followed by a discussion on Caesarean section case law, which illustrates the stereotypes and narratives which complicate any discussion of decision-making in labour. Finally, the decision of the High Court in *ML* will be considered in detail because, while it was not concerned with vaginal examinations, it did specifically consider the impact of pain in labour on capacity, decision-making and communication.

A. What Factors Impact on the Validity of Consent?

Where consent has been provided by a woman in labour but there is a concern regarding the validity of that consent there are a number of factors that can give rise to that concern. In reality these factors can be interlinked, but they are unpacked here for the purposes of analysis. The first is that inadequate information was provided to the woman, or there was a failure to effectively communicate adequate information to her. While acknowledging that it can be challenging to clearly and effectively communicate what may be quite complex information in the dynamic context of labour and childbirth, as noted in *Montgomery* one of the purposes of legal obligations in relation to informed consent is to ensure 'that even those doctors who have less skill or inclination for communication, or who are more hurried, are obliged to pause and engage in the discussions which the law requires'.[25]

The second is that the woman's decision-making capacity *may* be in question. This can be for reasons unrelated to labour, for example because she has an intellectual disability or a pre-existing serious mental illness, where labour and the associated pain exacerbate the underlying issues.[26] The final factor is that the

---

[24] ibid [110].

[25] ibid [93].

[26] For further discussion on the challenges for women with intellectual disabilities in the context of reproduction see C Kong, 'Constructing Feminine Sexual and Reproductive Agency in Mental Capacity Law' (2019) 66 *International Journal of Law and Psychiatry* (doi.org/10.1016/j.ijlp.2019.101488); A Arstein-Kerslake, 'Gendered Denials: Vulnerability Created by Barriers to Legal Capacity for Women

pain of labour, perhaps in addition to pressure or persuasion, leads the woman to consent to something that she perhaps was not completely happy with. This includes women whose decision-making capacity was not in question up until the point of labour.

B. Troubling Consent

As noted above, a valid consent must be informed, voluntary, and provided by someone with capacity. From these requirements the current model of consent has been built around a series of binaries: capacity/incapacity, voluntary/involuntary, and informed/not-informed. Some of these binaries are more rigid than others – the boundary between informed consent and not-informed consent is perhaps the most porous, as it relies so much on communication and circumstances. The capacity/incapacity binary, in contrast, is quite rigid, and this is very significant in the context of this paper. For some healthcare decisions this binary model of consent is workable – standard consent to routine medical procedures where there are limited risks, plenty of time to consider the decision, good information-sharing and communication, and no pre-existing conditions that would raise considerations about capacity.[27] However, as the situation becomes more complex the model is less effective.

The uniqueness of pregnancy and labour must be recognised here, because by considering consent through the prism of labour we begin to identify shortcomings in the current model. Labour is both natural and normal, and simultaneously dangerous for women and babies.[28] The pain of labour is very real, but not necessarily incapacitating. Women in labour are both powerful and vulnerable. Because pregnancy and labour occupy a space like no other, when we consider the pregnant woman in labour, she may not always sit clearly within one or other side of the binaries which underpin the legal framework for consent. In some cases she may occupy the unexplored spaces in-between the binaries. However, because we

and Disabled Women' (2019) 66 *International Journal of Law and Psychiatry* (doi.org/10.1016/j. ijlp.2019.101501). For a discussion of capacity and sexual agency see L Series, 'The Use of Legal Capacity Legislation to Control the Sexuality of People with Intellectual Disabilities' in T Shakespeare (ed), *Disability Research Today: International Perspectives*, (London, Routledge, 2015); A Arstein-Kerslake, 'Understanding Sex: The Right to Legal Capacity to Consent to Sex' (2015) 30 *Disability and Society* 1459.

[27] That is not to suggest that these types of situations do not also give rise to issues in relation to consent, but in general the model is a better fit for these kinds of scenarios.

[28] The following is a very small selection of recent cases illustrating some of the risks associated with childbirth. It is important to note that in some of these cases there was no finding of negligence on the part of the healthcare providers, and the negative outcome was understood as being as a result of the ordinary risks of childbirth. See *Montgomery* (n 1) (finding of negligence); *DS v Northern Lincolnshire and Goole NHS Foundation Trust* [2016] EWHC 1246 (QB) (no finding of negligence); *Re (A Minor) and Others v Calderdale and Huddersfield NHS Foundation Trust* [2017] EWHC 824 (QB) (finding of negligence); *ML* (n 7) (no finding of negligence); *YAH v Medway NHS Foundation Trust* [2018] EWHC 2964 (QB) (finding of negligence).

are familiar with the existing binary model of consent it is difficult to concede that pain or pressure might have an impact on decision-making because to do so *feels like* defeat and *appears to be* accepting that pregnant women in labour are less autonomous than other subjects. This is because within the current model it moves the woman from the capable to the incapable category. The challenge is to begin to look beyond the binaries and to explore those in-between spaces where we can perhaps recognise that pain and pressure impact on decision-making ability without that equating to a finding of incapacity. This chapter is intended as one response to that challenge.[29]

i. Caesarian Section Case Law – The Pregnant Woman as a Less than Autonomous Subject

The lack of fit between the model of consent and the reality of the pregnant woman in labour is further complicated by a stereotypical perception that pregnant women refusing treatment are not thinking clearly, because if they were they would do what is best for the baby. The narrative here is of the pregnant woman as a less than fully autonomous subject, and also an unreliable subject who cannot be trusted to make the 'correct' decisions.[30] These narratives and stereotypes are apparent in many of the enforced Caesarean section cases.[31] Clearly a Caesarean section performed on a woman without consent is a profound violation of bodily autonomy and yet the courts have regularly sanctioned such interventions, and continue to do so.

There is a significant body of case law in this area and so the discussion here is focused on a selection of cases, beginning with an older case which foregrounded the role of pain and/or pressure in the finding that the woman lacked capacity. This is followed by a brief discussion of *St George's*, as this is the clearest illustration of the narratives around pregnant women and autonomy in action. The post-*St George's* case law is then briefly outlined.

In *Norfolk and Norwich NHS Trust v W*, W was in arrested labour, but denying that she was pregnant.[32] She had a previous history of mental illness, but at the relevant time she did not satisfy the criteria to be detained under the Mental Health Act 1983. The hospital sought a declaration to permit a forceps delivery, or if necessary a Caesarean section, and permission to restrain W in order to do so. This approach was deemed necessary 'to preserve the life of the foetus, which was

---

[29] See also S Villarmea Requejo and G Fernandez Guillén, 'Fully Entitled Subjects: Birth as a Philosophical Topic' (2011) 11 *Ontology Studies* 211.

[30] For a thoughtful analysis of this issue see Chapter 5 above by, S Villarmea, 'When a Uterus Enters the Door, Reason Goes out the Window'.

[31] For further discussion on stereotypes of women in the context of reproductive rights and childbirth see Chapter 6 above, by C Zampas, 'Human Rights and Gender Stereotypes in Childbirth'.

[32] *Norfolk and Norwich NHS Trust v W* [1996] 2 FLR 613.

in danger of suffocating, and also to avoid the risk of the patient's earlier Caesarean scars reopening and so endangering the life of the foetus. There was also a risk to W's own life'.[33] W was found to lack competence because she did not satisfy the third step of the *Re C* test as, according to the psychiatrist, she was unable to weigh information in the balance to arrive at a choice.[34] The court noted that 'she was called upon to make that decision at a time of acute emotional stress and physical pain in the ordinary course of labour, made even more difficult for her because of her own particular mental history'.[35]

ii. *St George's Healthcare NHS Trust v S*

In *St George's* the Court of Appeal awarded damages in trespass (alongside declaratory relief) to a woman who had a Caesarean section performed on her without her consent.[36] The complex circumstances of this case involved S being involuntarily admitted for the purpose of assessment to a psychiatric hospital under the Mental Health Act 1983, transferred to the maternity ward of the hospital to have the Caesarean section against her wishes, then returned to the psychiatric hospital and subsequently discharged. At no point did she receive any treatment for a mental illness.

This case was also significant because the court held that the existence of a judicial declaration permitting the Caesarean section in this case did not provide a defence to the claim of trespass because the circumstances in which the declaration had been obtained were unacceptable. Mary Donnelly describes the declaration being obtained 'in circumstances of startling procedural inadequacy, due largely to the behaviour of the healthcare trust'.[37] This included the court being advised that S had been in labour for 24 hours at the time of the application, when in fact labour had not yet begun. The court was therefore mistakenly under the impression that it was an urgent life-or-death situation. There was no discussion of the issue of S's capacity or competence in the hearing, including the fact that there were no concerns about S's capacity prior to her admission for assessment or that S was thought to have capacity throughout. The court was also not informed that S had instructed solicitors and that neither she nor the solicitors were aware that the application was taking place. What occurred in this case appears to have been

---

[33] Halliday (n 22) 48.

[34] *Re C (refusal of medical treatment)* [1994] 1 FLR 31.

[35] *Norfolk and Norwich NHS Trust v W* (n 32). In some of the early cases the finding that the woman did not have capacity to refuse the Caesarean section was complicated by pre-existing mental health issues: see *Tameside and Glossop v CH* [1996] 1 FLR 762; *Re L (Patient: Non-Consensual Treatment)* [1997] 2 FLR 837 and *Re MB (Caesarean Section)* [1997] EWCA Civ 1361, both of which involved needle phobias.

[36] *St George's Healthcare NHS Trust v S* [1998] 3 All ER 673. For discussion of the decision see R Bailey-Harris, 'Pregnancy, Autonomy and the Refusal of Treatment' (1998) 114 *Law Quarterly Review* 550.

[37] Donnelly (n 8) 56. For further detail see [682]–[683] of the judgment in *St George's* (n 36).

a complete overriding of the autonomy rights of a pregnant woman because she was not complying with medical advice. While there was no issue around pain or pressure impacting on capacity in this case, S was not in labour, the significance of the case lies in the clear violation of autonomy in the actions of the hospital and the strong response from the Court of Appeal reiterating the continuation of autonomy in pregnancy.[38] Judge LJ stated 'while pregnancy increases the personal responsibilities of a woman it does not diminish her entitlement to decide whether or not to undergo medical treatment'.[39]

iii. Post St George's

The Caesarean section cases post *St George's* have come before the courts by way of a variety of legal frameworks: the Mental Health Act 1983, the Mental Capacity Act 2005, and the inherent jurisdiction of the High Court. Each of these is problematic, but detailed consideration is outside the scope of this discussion.[40] There does appear to be a recurring thread in the more recent case law of orders being sought to permit Caesarean sections to be performed on women with underlying mental health issues or learning difficulties.[41] In some instances the woman is not being treated for her mental illness while pregnant and her condition is deteriorating. In many others the suggestion appears to be that Caesarean delivery would ensure safe delivery of the baby and this is important for the mental health and

---

[38] The consequences of such an approach are encapsulated in the following extract from the Court of Appeal judgment in *St George's* (n 36) at [684] outlining the aftermath of the Caesarean section: '[S] was very angry that the hospital had gone against her wishes and complained of physical assault. When she was told that it was done for her benefit and that of her baby she remarked that is was "a matter of opinion"'. Judge LJ in the Court of Appeal encapsulated the narratives underpinning the approach of the hospital at [692]: 'The prohibited reasoning is readily identified and easily understood. Here is an intelligent woman. She knows perfectly well that if she persists with this course against medical advice she is likely to cause serious harm, and possibly death, to her baby and to herself. No normal mother-to-be could possibly think like that. Although this mother would not dream of taking any positive steps to cause injury to herself or her baby, her refusal is likely to lead to such a result. Her bizarre thinking represents a danger to their safety and health. It therefore follows that she must be mentally disordered and detained in hospital in her own interests and those of her baby. The short answer is that she may be perfectly rational and quite outside the ambit of the Act, and will remain so notwithstanding her eccentric thought process'.

[39] *St George's NHS Trust v S* (n 36) 692.

[40] For a detailed discussion see Halliday (n 22).

[41] *Re AA (Mental Capacity: Enforced Caesarean)* (unreported 24 August 2012); *Re P* [2013] EWHC 4581 (COP); *Great Western Hospitals NHS Foundation Trust v AA, BB, CC & DD* [2014] EWHC 132 (Fam); *Royal Free NHS Foundation Trust v AB* (unreported 31 January 2014); *The NHS Acute Trust & The NHS Mental Health Trust v C* [2016] EWCOP 17; *NHS Trust v JP* [2019] EWCOP 23; *Guys and St Thomas' NHS Foundation Trust v X* [2019] EWCOP 35. For a discussion of the role of mental illness in cases of court-ordered obstetric intervention see S Halliday, 'Court-Ordered Obstetric Intervention: Insight and Capacity, a Tale of Loss' in C Pickles and J Herring (eds), *Childbirth, Vulnerability and Law: Exploring Issues of Violence and Control* (London, Routledge, 2019) 178. For many women with mental illness court-ordered obstetric intervention is just one of a series of interventions they will experience as mothers. For further discussion see P Weller, 'Mothers and mental illness: Breaking the silence about child loss' (2019) 66 *International Journal of Law Psychiatry* (doi.org/10.1016/j.ijlp.2019.101500).

recovery of the woman (even in circumstances where she is resisting a Caesarean delivery). There also appears to be a move away from emergency applications (which was recommended by the Court of Appeal in *MB*) and so most of the findings of incapacity are not related to pain and pressure in labour.[42]

C. Impact of Pain in Labour on Decision-Making

In *ML v Guys and St Thomas' National Healthcare Foundation Trust* a minor (ML) took a case (by his Litigation Friend and mother, SL) as a result of the circumstances surrounding his birth in 2010.[43] In the minutes before delivery he suffered deprivation of oxygen to the brain and this left him with devastating brain damage and profound disability – the judgment of the court notes that he is tube-fed, will always need 24-hour care, has no prospect of independent living and his life expectancy is limited.[44] The judgment relates to the trial of a preliminary issue, namely liability and causation.

According to the judgment SL experienced a spontaneous rupture of membranes and went to the hospital. She was initially sent home but then returned and was admitted. She was induced and was actively monitored throughout labour because there were some pathological CTG readings. On two occasions foetal blood samples were taken, because of the CTG readings, and the results of these samples were normal. On this basis, and because there were other indications of satisfactory progression of labour, the plan was to proceed to a vaginal delivery.[45] Unfortunately there was a sudden deterioration in ML's condition (most likely as a result of cord occlusion) and a decision was made to perform an emergency Caesarean section. There was a slight delay in transferring SL to theatre as both theatres were already occupied with Caesarean deliveries.[46] During this period ML was deprived of oxygen and suffered brain damage. SL contended that she asked for a Caesarean section at an earlier point in labour because she was worried about the safety of ML and had a Caesarean section been carried out shortly after she requested it the injuries to ML would have been avoided.

Spencer J identified two issues for consideration: first, whether the plaintiff's mother, SL, had requested a Caesarean section during labour, and second, whether the hospital responded appropriately to that request.[47] SL's evidence was that at a particularly painful moment in labour she requested a Caesarean section. Her account of the circumstances around the request was that she said 'I was worried and in pain and I clearly remember saying, Please, just chop me, what are you

---

[42] *Re MB* (n 35).
[43] *ML* (n 7).
[44] ibid [1].
[45] ibid [22].
[46] ibid [30]–[33].
[47] ibid [52].

waiting for? Meaning that I wanted a Caesarean section'.[48] The response of the staff attending to her in labour was to give her an epidural. This appeared to provide her with considerable relief and in a statement provided in the course of litigation she said 'after about 20 minutes I felt much more coherent and relaxed as the pain disappeared and I started talking and joking with my husband and sister'.[49]

Spencer J found that it was most likely that SL was motivated by pain in making the request for a Caesarean section at the point she did, rather than from concern for the wellbeing of the baby. He stated that this finding was supported by evidence which demonstrated that shortly before she requested the Caesarean section a foetal blood test had been conducted which showed that the baby's condition was not a cause for concern at that point.[50] In those circumstances he found that the correct course of action was to address the issue of pain, which was done, and if after that SL had continued to request a Caesarean section then the healthcare practitioners would have been required to discuss this with her further. This did not arise in this case, as once SL was given the epidural she relaxed and did not raise the issue of a Caesarean section again.

His comments on pain and decision-making in labour are worth setting out in some detail. He first drew a distinction between a request for a Caesarean section in the ante-natal period and one made in the 'throes of labour pain'. In the first instance such a request should be 'considered carefully and fully by the obstetric staff with the risks and benefits being fully discussed and with time for thought and reflection being given'.[51] However where the request comes when the woman is in labour and in pain

> the appropriate response, as here, is to deal with the pain and then review the matter and see whether the request was or was not 'serious'. By that I do not intend to suggest that any request for a Caesarean section is not serious but an obstetrician or midwife would be failing in their duty to both mother and baby if they simply took every such request at face value without exploring and addressing the underlying reason.[52]

A lot of weight was attached to SL's account that after the epidural she felt more 'coherent'. Spencer J interpreted this as 'a tacit admission that, before the epidural and given the pain she was in, she was less than coherent and I suspect this will be the case for many women undergoing labour for the first time or, indeed, not for the first time'.[53]

---

[48] ibid [36].
[49] ibid.
[50] This finding does not appear to consider the possibility that SL's concern for the wellbeing of the baby would not be completely alleviated by the results of the foetal blood tests in circumstances where the foetal CTG trace was repeatedly assessed as 'suspicious' and the midwives were calling for doctors to review the trace throughout the labour.
[51] *ML* (n 7) [90].
[52] ibid.
[53] ibid.

On the basis that SL was less than coherent at the relevant time, as a result of the usual and expected pain of labour, the court found that it would be inappropriate to have the kind of conversation which would be necessary to ensure that she made a voluntary and informed choice as to whether to have a Caesarean section.

> It would in fact be impossible to have the kind of discussion of risk and benefit envisaged by ... the NICE guidelines with a woman who is not wholly coherent and thinking straightforwardly and logically because of the extreme pain she was in and could be regarded as irresponsible for a midwife or obstetrician to attempt to have such a discussion with a woman before her pain had been addressed.[54]

The decision in *ML* is to be welcomed in so far as it recognises the existing rules on informed consent and that information communication can prove challenging in the context of labour where the woman is in pain, perhaps feeling vulnerable, and therefore may not be in a position to engage in the same kind of reasoning or questioning as she would be in a different context. This acknowledgement of the gap between the theory of consent and practice is important. However, this is something of a double-edged sword because at the same time this characterisation of the pain of labour as somehow rendering a labouring woman less competent can be seen as feeding into the broader narratives of pregnant women as inherently incapable. The use of the word 'coherent' by SL in her evidence was unfortunate in this context as it provided a hook for the court to focus the discussion on competence and capacity. Perhaps a more useful approach by the court would have been to recognise that the pain SL was experiencing impacted on her decision-making ability without framing that in terms of competence. Also, having recognised the impact of pain in labour on decision-making, the court then placed the onus on SL, once her pain had been addressed, to raise the issue of a Caesarean section again. An argument could be made that those involved in caring for SL should have checked in with her again, once the pain relief had taken effect, to see if the possibility of a Caesarean section was something that she still wished to discuss. Such an approach would be more in line with a model of childbirth that prioritised and respected the autonomy of labouring women and supported them in decision-making.

IV. Conclusion: Challenges and Solutions

The issue of vaginal examinations in labour without consent requires us to consider the legal framework on consent from a new perspective. The focus on the impact of pain in labour on decision-making ability and consent shines a light on some of the troubling issues with the current model of consent. Because the legal framework for consent is constructed around a series of binaries, any suggestion that

---

[54] ibid.

the decision-making ability of women in labour might be affected by pain and pressure has the potential to be fraught. This is because of the implication that it moves labouring women from the capable to the incapable category, and all of the consequences for autonomy that are associated with that shift. It also appears to affirm the existing stereotypes and narratives of the pregnant woman as a less than fully autonomous subject. The cause of the difficulty here is not that pregnant women in labour do not fit the otherwise serviceable model of consent, but rather that the model of consent on which the legal framework is based is not sufficiently flexible to be effective for women in labour. This needs to change, because the shortcomings of consent in this context apply in respect of all interventions in labour, including vaginal examinations, and while this model remains women will continue to experience a range of harms in pregnancy and childbirth, particularly in relation to autonomy.[55]

A. Stretching the Temporal Context

One potential solution is a more flexible legal model of consent that moves away from the rigid binary divisions that underpin the current framework. For consent to be meaningful for women in labour the temporal context for consent needs to be stretched. One aspect of this would be more clear and effective communication in advance of labour about all aspects of labour and birth.[56] This is in accordance with the emphasis in *Montgomery* on the importance of communication in ensuring effective consent. This should include an open discussion about the possibility of vaginal examinations during labour, the purpose of these examinations, what is involved, any potential downsides to not having a vaginal examination, and the fact that this is something that the woman can refuse if she so wishes, even if she has consented to a vaginal examination at an earlier point in labour.[57] The

---

[55] For a discussion of harm in childbirth and the importance of developing vocabularies of harm in response to systemic experiences of violation see F Aoláin, 'On Being the Subject of Law: Feminist Reflections on Gender, Harm and Violence in Northern Ireland' delivered as the Stephen Livingstone Lecture 2018 at www.youtube.com/watch?v=yb92m12_hus.

[56] O'Donovan and Madden, in the context of a discussion on the difficulties faced by members of the public who submit complaints to medical professional regulators in having those complaints taken seriously and referred on for further inquiry, note that 'Time and time again, poor communication with patients and their families has been found to be at the core of what goes wrong in medicine': O O'Donovan and D Madden, 'Why do Medical Professional Regulators Dismiss Most Complaints from Members of the Public? Regulatory Illiteracy, Epistemic Injustice, and Symbolic Power' (2018) 15 *Bioethical Inquiry* 469, 477. They reference the Report of the Parliamentary and Health Service Ombudsman, *Listening and Learning: The Ombudsman's Review of Complaint Handling by the NHS in England 2010–11* (London, The Stationery Office, 2011) in support of this.

[57] It is worth noting that in some instances the term vaginal examination is not even used when healthcare professionals are attending women in labour, with phrases such as 'an internal' or 'a VE'. being used instead. M Stewart, '"I'm Just Going to Wash You Down": Sanitizing the Vaginal Examination' (2005) 51 *Journal of Advanced Nursing* 587, conducted a study which included interviews with midwives and at 592 suggested that 'they might feel uncomfortable using terminology that makes

importance of clear communication about vaginal examinations was highlighted by Mary Stewart, who notes that 'midwives need to consider how they discuss vaginal examinations with women during pregnancy in order to inform them of their purpose and rationale so that women, in turn, can become involved in decisions about how and when they should be done'.[58]

Such an approach would allow women to have the space and time needed, away from the intensity of labour, to make decisions, if they wish with the input of others, and to indicate preferences at this earlier stage.[59] This is closely linked to the importance of effective and realistic birth planning, which again should include references to vaginal examinations in labour if this is something that is important to the woman.[60] Outside of the labour context the benefits of advance healthcare planning are recognised in situations where there is a concern that decision-making may be affected in the future.[61] None of the above is to ignore the reality that complications can arise in labour and emergency situations can develop which may require reassessment of previously expressed preferences in challenging circumstances, but that does not undermine the value of those earlier discussions and planning which are crucial to a woman-centred model of childbirth. Increased continuity of care throughout pregnancy and labour is also important in building relationships of trust which are helpful in ensuring effective communication during periods of labour which may be more challenging for the woman.[62]

From the judgment in *ML* we see the importance of ensuring that whenever possible decision-making in labour should occur at times where the woman is not in significant pain. That may require those caring for women to pay close attention to the rhythms of labour and where possible discuss interventions or seek consent

explicit reference to women's genitalia and use abbreviations as a means of overcoming this discomfort'. This contributes to women being unsure exactly what is involved in the proposed examination.

[58] Stewart (n 57) 593. While some failures in communication on this topic may be attributable to embarrassment discussing vaginas, there is a more worrying explanation as well, with Stewart at 592 suggesting that failure to communicate clearly can also sometimes be an example of power strategies 'where midwives decide what information will be given to women and what will be withheld'.

[59] For a discussion of a 'rich' understanding of consent, which recognises the relational nature of consent and highlights the importance of understanding consent within context, see Herring (n 6).

[60] This may include advance refusals of vaginal examinations, or the woman may wish to outline the circumstances in which she is willing to consent to a vaginal examination in labour.

[61] See discussion in M Donnelly, 'Developing a Framework for Advance Healthcare Planning: Comparing England and Wales and Ireland' (2017) 24 *European Journal of Health Law* 67.

[62] L Dixon et al, 'Women's Perspectives of the Stages and Phases of Labour' (2013) 29 *Midwifery* 10 at 15 noted that in the New Zealand context where women have a midwife they know, and who provides all of their intrapartum care, women were less anxious and unsure in relation to the onset of labour. The women involved in this study also did not express any negative feelings towards vaginal examinations, in contrast with other studies. See HG Dahlen et al, 'Vaginal Examination during Normal Labor: Routine Examination or Routine Intervention?' (2013) 3 *International Journal of Childbirth* 142 and D Lewin et al, 'Women's Experiences of Vaginal Examinations in Labour' (2005) 21 *Midwifery* 267. For the importance of continuity of care see also S Clement, 'Unwanted Vaginal Examinations' (1994) 10 *British Journal of Midwifery* 368 and Royal College of Midwives (n 2).

during lulls in pain.[63] In some cases, as in *ML*, pain relief may need to be provided before other requests or options are discussed.

Before concluding, it is important to recognise the risks associated with the arguments outlined above. Acknowledging the impact of pain and pressure on decision-making in labour in isolation, without also rejecting the binary model of consent, has the potential to further reinforce the existing stereotypes of pregnant women as not fully autonomous subjects. This occurred to an extent in *ML*. It also risks labour being characterised as an unusually traumatic or damaging process, which is unhelpful in respect of the normalisation of the pregnant subject.[64] The process of reimagining consent is not something that can be achieved in the short term and is unlikely to occur without set-backs and challenges. However, it is important to begin to have these kinds of conversations if the ultimate objective is a legal framework on consent that works in practice for pregnant women in labour.

---

[63] The Royal College of Obstetricians and Gynaecologists (n 2) 6 states 'When consent has to be obtained from a woman during painful labour, such as to perform a vaginal examination, episiotomy, operative delivery or to site an epidural, information should be given between contractions'.

[64] See the judgment in *Re (A Minor) and Others v Calderdale and Huddersfield NHS Foundation Trust* (n 28) where, in the context of a claim for psychiatric injury by a mother and grandmother resulting from a birth where the baby suffered injury, childbirth was characterised as a sudden, shocking and horrifying event. J Lindsey, 'Psychiatric Injury Claims and Pregnancy: *Re (A Minor) and Others v Calderdale and Huddersfield NHS Foundation Trust* [2017] EWHC 824' (2017) 26 *Medical Law Review* 117, 122 notes that 'Characterisations that frame childbirth as shocking and horrifying could have a wider impact on how pregnant women are treated and undermine the struggle to ensure a pregnant woman's autonomy is respected'.

12

Redressing Unauthorised Vaginal Examinations through Litigation

ANDREA MULLIGAN

I. Introduction

A vaginal examination during pregnancy or labour involves a healthcare professional inserting his or her hand into a woman's vagina to carry out checks on
the cervix, the foetal membranes and foetal presentation. Clearly, this is a medical examination that requires consent and if it is carried out without consent,
the woman in question has suffered a legal wrong. However, seeking redress for
that legal wrong is rather complex. This chapter explores how a woman who has
experienced unauthorised vaginal examination might go about seeking redress
through civil proceedings.[1] The fact pattern in focus in this chapter involves either
a situation where a woman expressly refuses consent to a vaginal examination,
and despite this, is subjected to one, or a situation where no consent is sought
for a vaginal examination in advance of it taking place, despite the woman being
capable of providing that consent.[2] This is described as unauthorised vaginal
examination.[3] This chapter focuses on the jurisdictions of England and Wales, and
Ireland, jurisdictions which bear some important similarities but also some very
significant differences.

When embarking upon litigation a central concern is the matter of remedies.
In short, what does the litigant hope to attain? Does she want an award of damages
or is she more concerned with recognition that a wrong was done? Does she want
a public acknowledgement of the harm she suffered or is a settlement equally, or
even more, attractive? What if that settlement contains a confidentiality clause?

---

[1] For criminal offences, see Chapter 8, by C Sjölin, 'Including the Victim's Perspective: Can Vaginal
Examinations Ever be Sexual Assaults?'.

[2] Meaning that the woman is formally competent to make a decision in respect of the examination,
pursuant to the Mental Capacity Act 2005 (in England and Wales) or the test in *Fitzpatrick v FK* [2008]
IEHC 104, [2009] 2 IR 7 in Ireland.

[3] While the chapter will touch on questions of informed consent, cases of inadequately informed
consent are not the primary focus.

What if it is made with no admission of liability or wrongdoing? These questions are deeply personal. Redress means different things to different people, and so the desired remedy is a very significant factor in identifying the best litigation strategy. As this chapter demonstrates, the available remedies vary greatly between different types of action.

This chapter will begin in section II by exploring tortious actions that may be pursued by a woman who has experienced unauthorised vaginal examination, namely the torts of negligence and battery. It will be argued that the concept of 'relevant damage' in negligence poses a significant hurdle for many women who have experienced such an examination, and that at the level of principle the more appropriate tortious cause of action is battery. Section III will explore fundamental rights actions arising from unauthorised vaginal examination. It will be argued that in the English context such an examination constitutes a breach of Article 8 of the European Convention on Human Rights, which may be litigated via the Human Rights Act 1998. It will then be argued that unauthorised vaginal examination constitutes a breach of fundamental rights under the Irish Constitution, which grounds an individual action for breach of constitutional rights against the healthcare professional or hospital in question. Mechanisms of redress for unauthorised vaginal examinations are broadly similar in both jurisdictions in so far as tortious actions are concerned, but the fundamental rights dimension is very different, especially in so far as the interaction of tortious and fundamental rights actions is concerned.

II. Actions in Tort

The first potential avenue of redress is through the law of tort, the law of civil wrongs.[4] There are two principal torts that seem most capable of accommodating unauthorised vaginal examination: negligence and battery.

A. Negligence

Negligence is by far the most litigated tort.[5] Its broad, flexible nature means that it provides an avenue for redress in a diversity of factual contexts, making it the natural starting point for a claim in respect of unauthorised vaginal examination. A successful claim in negligence requires: the existence of a duty of care owed

---

[4] See generally P Cane, *The Anatomy of Tort Law* (Oxford, Hart Publishing, 1997); J Oberdiek (ed), *Philosophical Foundations of the Law of Torts* (Oxford, Oxford University Press, 2018); J Steele, *Tort Law: Text Cases and Materials*, 4th edn (Oxford, Oxford University Press, 2017); S Deakin and Z Adams, *Markesinis and Deakin's Tort Law*, 8th edn (Oxford, Oxford University Press, 2019); N McBride and R Bagshaw, *Tort Law*, 6th edn (London, Pearson, 2018).

[5] For example, Steele comments that it 'dominates the modern law of tort', ibid 115.

by the defendant to the claimant; breach of that duty; that the breach caused the claimant to suffer damage of a type recognised as compensable; and that the damage caused is not too remote, or alternatively that the damage is within the scope of the defendant's duty.[6] Crucially, negligence is only actionable on proof of damage. In the medical context, the existence of a duty of care between a healthcare professional and his or her patient is generally relatively straightforward. Where an unauthorised vaginal examination occurs, the healthcare professional would clearly owe a duty of care to the patient to avoid causing her physical damage during the vaginal examination but duties in respect of psychological injury are less straightforward. There is no duty of care to avoid causing psychological damage that does not amount to a recognised psychiatric injury, and such injuries do not constitute actionable damage. The question of the scope of the duty of care intersects with the question of what type of damage is compensable, as explored below.

In the medical context the standard of care inquiry is governed in England and Wales by the test in *Bolam v Friern Hospital Management Committee* as qualified by *Bolitho v City and Hackney Health Authority*.[7] In effect, *Bolam* and *Bolitho* establish a two-stage test whereby the Court asks first whether the healthcare professional was acting in accordance with a practice accepted as proper by a responsible body of medical opinion. If the defendant establishes that he or she was acting in accordance with such opinion, then the claimant can argue, under *Bolitho*, that the body of medical opinion relied on is not 'capable of withstanding logical analysis'. If unauthorised vaginal examination is to be analysed by reference to standard *Bolam/Bolitho* principles, this inquiry would depend on the evidence to be led in a particular case. There is little doubt that a claimant would be able to find experts to say that good clinical practice requires that consent be obtained to vaginal examination in the course of labour. By contrast, it is difficult to conceive of an expert in obstetrics, nursing or midwifery who would give evidence of a responsible body of medical opinion that did not require consent to vaginal examination in labour, or who would say that vaginal examination without consent could be justified.

It is possible however, that the *Bolam/Bolitho* tests have no application to the requirement of consent to treatment, within the standard of care. As Clare Murray explores in this collection, the importance of consent in the specific context of labour has been affirmed by the case of *Montgomery v Lanarkshire Health Board*, a case which concerned the requirement of informed consent in respect of the choice between vaginal birth and Caesarean section.[8] Lady Hale confirmed in *Montgomery* that the general requirement of consent was not qualified because the patient was pregnant. Citing the earlier case of *St George's Healthcare NHS Trust v S*,

---

[6] *Lochgelly Iron and Coal Co v McMullan* [1934] AC 1.

[7] *Bolam v Friern Hospital Management Committee* [1957] 1 WLR 582; *Bolitho v City and Hackney Health Authority* [1998] AC 232.

[8] See Chapter 11, by C Murray, 'Troubling Consent: Pain and Pressure in Labour and Childbirth', text at note 5; *Montgomery v Lanarkshire Health Board* [2015] UKSC 11.

she commented: 'Gone are the days when it was thought that, on becoming pregnant, a woman lost, not only her capacity, but also her right to act as a genuinely autonomous human being'.[9] If the requirement of consent is unchanged in the context of a necessary Caesarean section with an imminent risk of death to the foetus, as was in issue in *St George's*, there can be no doubt that consent is required to vaginal examination in labour. On the standard of care question, *Montgomery* concluded that in respect of disclosure of information to secure informed consent, *Bolam* does not represent the correct legal test. Instead, the doctor is subject to a freestanding requirement to disclose 'material risks' involved in proposed treatment, and to offer the patient reasonable alternative treatments.[10] *Montgomery* represents a move away from *Bolam* where informed consent is concerned. The unauthorised vaginal examination fact pattern does not concern a flaw in informed consent, but rather a lack of *any* consent. The requirement for consent, surely, is an even more basic requirement than the requirement of disclosure. It may be that – following the approach in *Montgomery* – the requirement of consent does not fall to be analysed under *Bolam* at all, but rather is a freestanding aspect of the standard of care. Accordingly, even if there was a body of medical opinion that believed it was legitimate to conduct a vaginal examination in the absence of consent, this conduct could nonetheless be found to be negligent.

Application of the relevant legal principles in Irish law would lead to much the same result. In Irish law, professional negligence including medical negligence is governed by the test established in *Dunne v National Maternity Hospital*,[11] which in substance is not unlike a combination of *Bolam* and *Bolitho*. The requirement to obtain consent from the patient is universally acknowledged, and is an aspect of the standard of care.[12] Disclosure is governed by a separate body of case law.[13]

Whether or not *Bolam/Bolitho* and *Dunne* apply, there can be little doubt that in both jurisdictions the standard of care would be found to include a requirement to obtain consent from a competent patient to vaginal examination in the course of labour, and that proceeding with an examination in the absence of that consent would be a breach of the duty of care. The far more complex aspect of building a negligence case is demonstrating that the breach caused the claimant a harm of a relevant type, and thus fulfils the damage requirement that is essential to the tort of negligence. The tort of negligence deems only certain forms of damage to be damage of a 'relevant' type.

---

[9] *St George's Healthcare NHS Trust v S* [1998] 3 WLR 936 (CA); *Montgomery* (n 8) [116].

[10] 'Materiality' depends on whether 'in the circumstances of the particular case, a reasonable person in the patient's position would be likely to attach significance to the risk, or the doctor is or should reasonably be aware that the particular patient would be likely to attach significance to it': *Montgomery* (n 8) [87].

[11] *Dunne v National Maternity Hospital* [1989] IR 91.

[12] *In the Matter of a Ward of Court* [1996] 2 IR 73, [1995] 2 ILRM 401; *Fitzpatrick* (n 2).

[13] *Walsh v Family Planning Services Ltd* [1992] 1 IR 496; *Geoghegan v Harris* [2000] 3 IR 536; *Fitzpatrick v White* [2008] 3 IR 551; *Healy v Buckley and Another* [2015] IECA 251.

The general duty of care recognised in *Donoghue v Stevenson* applied to the personal safety and health, and to the property interests of the claimant.[14] Historically, mental or psychiatric injury was regarded as falling outside of that duty, and thus as not constituting a relevant form of damage. The tort of negligence now recognises psychiatric injuries as compensable, but draws a sharp distinction between recognised psychiatric conditions and emotional distress.[15] While emotional distress may be compensated if it accompanies personal injury or injury to property, standalone mental injury is only compensable where it constitutes a recognised psychiatric condition. The same rule applies in Irish law.[16]

In English law an important distinction is also drawn between primary and secondary victims. Where a person is a secondary victim, recovery is subject to the additional requirements of: (1) sufficient closeness both in terms of love and affection to the person injured or killed and being in sight or sound of the directly injurious event giving rise to the tortious liability; and (2) the induction of psychiatric illness by an identifiable shocking event.[17] It would appear that the woman who is subjected to an unauthorised vaginal examination is a primary victim, as she is the person who is the subject of the medical treatment, and of the alleged negligence. This can be contrasted with circumstances where it might be argued that the foetus is the subject of the medical intervention and thus the primary victim, and the woman's psychiatric injury arises secondary to that. In any event, the English courts have on occasion taken the view that the woman is a primary victim where the insult/act occurs when the woman and the foetus are the same legal entity.[18]

So, what is the damage arising from unauthorised vaginal examination? Many women who experience it describe feelings of shock and extreme distress. Some of them also can point to the development of post-traumatic stress disorder (PTSD).[19] For the purposes of a negligence action, those women who can prove that they have suffered PTSD will meet the requirement of proving actionable damage, so long as they can show that the PTSD is attributable to the examination.[20] It may be possible, furthermore, to show that the PTSD interferes with the woman's ability to access medical treatment in the future, whether during routine gynaecological

---

[14] *Donoghue v Stevenson* [1932] AC 562. See discussion in Deakin and Adams (n 4) 105.

[15] *McLoughlin v O'Brien* [1983] 1 AC 410; *Alcock v Chief Constable of South Yorkshire* [1992] 1 AC 310; *Vernon v Bosley (No 1)* [1997] 1 All ER 577.

[16] *Mullally v Bus Éireann* [1992] ILRM 722; *Kelly v Hennessy* [1995] 3 IR 253; *Hegarty v Mercy University Hospital Cork* [2011] IEHC 435.

[17] *Mcloughlin* (n 15); *Alcock* (n 15); *Page v Smith* [1996] AC 155.

[18] *RE v Calderdale & Huddersfield NHS Foundation Trust* [2017] EWHC 824 (QB); *Wells v University Hospital Southampton NHS Foundation Trust* [2015] EWHC 2376 (QB); *Farrell v Merton, Sutton and Wandsworth Health Authority* (2001) 57 BMLR 158.

[19] See Chapter 2, by R Brione, 'Non-Consented Vaginal Examinations: The Birthrights and AIMS Perspective', text at note 33. For the purposes of this chapter, it is assumed that unauthorised vaginal examination does not cause the women a physical injury.

[20] The law also draws a distinction between primary victims and secondary victims. As the physical contact leading to the injury happened directly to the woman, it would seem that she is a primary victim.

examinations or examinations in the course of pregnancy or labour. This would further exacerbate the damage and fits squarely within the negligence rubric as it raises the possibility of future physical damage resulting from an aversion to medically necessary examinations.

The woman who has not suffered PTSD, or any other recognised psychiatric condition, is in a far weaker position from the perspective of the tort of negligence. The emotional distress, the feelings of shock, and any future discomfort with physical examinations are not actionable harms, no matter how upsetting they are, so long as they fall short of a recognised psychiatric condition. This reality demonstrates the fundamental difficulty in using negligence to tackle unauthorised vaginal examinations: to a large extent, negligence is not concerned with what really makes the examinations problematic. Women who experience these unauthorised examinations suffer distress, but equally importantly, they are denied their lawful entitlement to refuse an examination. They may be harmed by unauthorised vaginal examination, but more importantly they are wronged by it. Negligence, however, is not driven primarily by the objective of redressing wrongs, but rather by the objective of remedying loss or damage. As has so often been observed, damage is 'the gist' of negligence.[21]

Certain commentators, including Tony Weir and Jason Varuhas, argue that some torts are driven by a loss model, while other torts are driven by a rights-based model.[22] Negligence, Varuhas argues, is the quintessential example of a tort which aims to compensate loss.[23] This aspect of negligence is further demonstrated by the fact that the primary remedy available in negligence is an award of damages, rather than declaratory relief. The fact that negligence is fundamentally concerned with damage creates a serious problem for litigating unauthorised vaginal examination. A woman who experiences such an examination may not necessarily feel that she has suffered a loss. To the extent that she feels she has suffered an injury, this may not be one that the law of negligence will deem actionable. Notably, the English courts have also rejected the idea that loss of or interference with autonomy could be deemed to be a standalone head of actionable damage, thus precluding the impact of unauthorised vaginal examination from being characterised as 'loss of autonomy'.[24]

---

[21] *Sidaway v Board of Governors of the Bethlehem Royal Hospital* [1985] SC 871 [883].

[22] See also the analysis of T Weir, *A Casebook on Tort*, 10th edn (London, Sweet and Maxwell, 2004) 322–23; J Varuhas, *Damages and Human Rights* (Oxford, Hart Publishing, 2016) 23. Note that Varuhas and Weir take a median position in this debate, arguing that different torts have different functions, whereas other commentators argue that tort law as a whole is motivated by the need to vindicate rights, or to compensate loss. See discussion of the opposing views in R Stevens, *Torts and Rights* (Oxford, Oxford University Press, 2007) 1–2. See also D Nolan and A Robertson, 'Rights and Private Law' in D Nolan and A Robertson (eds), *Rights and Private Law* (Oxford, Hart Publishing, 2012); E Descheemaeker, 'Unravelling Harms in Tort Law' (2016) 138 *Law Quarterly Review* 595.

[23] Varuhas (n 22) 23.

[24] *Shaw v Kovak* [2017] EWCA Civ 1028. In the earlier case of *Rees v Darlington Memorial Hospital NHS Trust* [2004] 1 AC 309, the court made an award of a conventional sum in recognition of the

Finally, in addition to these hurdles there is a further problem that may affect even the woman who can show she developed a recognised psychiatric condition. Calculating damages in negligence requires the claimant to show that she is entitled to compensation that would restore her to the position she would have been in had the tort not occurred. This necessarily involves proving a counterfactual: the claimant must identify what she says should have happened, and how she would have been better off in that scenario. The difference between that situation and her present one constitutes the actionable damage, and the basis on which an award of damages is calculated. The woman who alleges negligence arising from unauthorised vaginal examination must explain what she says should have happened, had the tort not been committed. This could be problematic if the woman's position is that she would never have given consent to examination and that one should never have taken place, and if the medical evidence demonstrates that this would have caused her serious medical complications. Many very dangerous and unpleasant counterfactual scenarios could be imagined. In effect, it might be that the examination was wrong and unlawful because consent was absent, but it could be that ultimately the woman was better off because some very serious complication in the course of labour was avoided. This does not render the unauthorised vaginal examination any less wrong, but it makes it even more difficult to conceptualise it in terms of loss. The tort of negligence copes very badly with such nuances.[25]

B. Battery

The tort of battery is committed when a defendant directly and intentionally brings about contact with the body of the claimant, where the contact exceeds what is lawful. The necessary intention is to bring about the physical contact rather than the intention to commit the tort of battery.[26] Crucially, battery is actionable per se, meaning that it does not require proof of damage, though claimants may be limited to nominal damages only if they cannot show damage.[27] Importantly, a claimant may seek and obtain a declaration that the conduct was unlawful. The physical contact is unlawful and amounts to a battery where it cannot be

---

denial of an important aspect of the plaintiff's personal autonomy, namely the right to limit the size of their family. While *Rees* is often described as an example of vindicatory damages, the conventional appears to be limited to very specific contexts: Stevens (n 22) 77; H Varuhas, 'The Concept of Vindication in the Law of Damages' (2014) 34 *Oxford Journal of Legal Studies* 253, 270. For a discussion of the relevance of the conventional award in the context of assisted human reproduction see A Mulligan, 'A Vindicatory Approach to Tortious Liability for Mistakes in Assisted Human Reproduction' (2020) *Legal Studies* (forthcoming).

[25] It may be that elements of the same problem arise in respect of calculating damages in battery. See the discussion of the counterfactual analysis in *R (Lumba) v Secretary of State for the Home Department* [2011] UKSC 12 below.

[26] *Wong v Parkside* [2003] 3 All ER 932. See F Trindade, 'Intentional Torts: Some Thoughts on Assault and Battery' (1982) 2 *Oxford Journal of Legal Studies* 211.

[27] See discussion below concerning *Lumba* (n 25).

justified by reference to consent, necessity, or self-defence. While at one time it was suggested that the contact had to be 'hostile' to be regarded as battery, it is now clear that this is not the case.[28] As Lord Goff commented in *Re F (Mental Patient: Sterilisation)*: 'everybody is protected not only against physical injury but against any form of physical molestation'.[29]

Battery seems rather well suited to addressing unauthorised vaginal examination. The contact involved is physical, direct, intentional and not consensual. In the fact pattern in focus, the woman has either refused consent, or not been asked to provide consent. Thus, the only potential justification for the unauthorised examination is that of necessity, a recognised defence to battery.[30] It might be asserted that the vaginal examination is necessary to protect the foetus from complications arising in the course of labour that would compromise its life or health. The case of *St George's Healthcare NHS Trust v S* suggests, however, that such an argument would not succeed.[31] This case concerned a pregnant woman who was suffering from a medical condition that posed a risk to her life and to that of the foetus. She was advised to undergo a Caesarean section but refused her consent. While an order dispensing with her consent was granted at first instance, this was overturned on appeal. Concern for the right to life of the foetus was found not to justify such a profound interference with the woman's right to physical autonomy.

The Court's detailed discussion of this issue is of note in the context of unauthorised vaginal examinations. The Court was careful to say that the foetus was 'not nothing' and to acknowledge that where 'human life is at stake' the pressure to authorise unwanted medical intervention was very great.[32] It concluded, however, that despite these natural urges, the principle of autonomy had to be respected. The Court stated:

> In our judgment while pregnancy increases the personal responsibilities of a woman it does not diminish her entitlement to decide whether or not to undergo medical treatment. Although human, and protected by the law in a number of different ways set out in the judgment in *In re MB (An Adult: Medical Treatment)* [1997] 2 FCR 541, an unborn child is not a separate person from its mother. Its need for medical assistance does not prevail over her rights. She is entitled not to be forced to submit to an invasion of her body against her will, whether her own life or that of her unborn child depends on it. Her right is not reduced or diminished merely because her decision to exercise it may appear morally repugnant. The declaration in this case involved the removal of the baby from within the body of her mother under physical compulsion. Unless lawfully justified this constituted an infringement of the mother's autonomy. Of themselves the perceived needs of the foetus did not provide the necessary justification.[33]

---

[28] *Collins v Wilcock* [1984] 1 WLR 1172, *Wilson v Pringle* [1987] QB 237, *Re F (Mental Patient: Sterilisation)* [1990] 2 AC 1.

[29] *Re F* (n 28) [72].

[30] ibid, *Re A (Children) (Conjoined Twins: Medical Separation)* [2001] Fam 147 (CA).

[31] *St George's Healthcare NHS Trust* (n 9).

[32] ibid [46].

[33] ibid 50.

The Court's analysis seems to resolve any question of necessity in the context of unauthorised vaginal examinations. If necessity cannot justify a forced medical treatment where the life of the foetus is at stake, then it surely cannot provide a defence to an unauthorised vaginal examination.

A central reason why battery is better suited to redressing unauthorised vaginal examination than negligence, is because it is actionable per se. Varuhas argues that the vindicatory purpose of the law of torts is clearest in torts which are actionable per se, because these are torts which afford 'strong protection from outside interference to fundamental personal and proprietary interests'.[34] Battery is actionable per se, Varuhas observes, in recognition of the fundamental nature of the interest in physical integrity. For the same reason, it requires no proof of malice. Returning to the 'wrong' of the unauthorised vaginal examination, it is clear that redressing that wrong sits more comfortably in the tort of battery, than in loss-oriented negligence. While a woman may suffer consequential loss as a result of the examination, it is significant that the tort of battery is committed even if she does not. Some difficulty may arise, however, in practically obtaining an award of damages for battery without proof of loss.

Because battery is actionable per se, one would expect to be able to recover a certain quantum of damages for simply showing that the tort has been committed. This has, however, been called into question by the decision of the UK Supreme Court in *R (Lumba) v Secretary of State for the Home Department*.[35] This decision concerned a claim for false imprisonment arising from unlawful detention by a public authority in circumstances where the claimants would have remained in prison even if the lawful policy had been applied. To use the language of the counterfactual, it was undisputed that if the tort had not been committed, the claimants would have been imprisoned in any event. *Lumba* is a complex nine-judge decision, involving different splits between judges on different aspects of the claim, ultimately leading to a majority accepting that false imprisonment had occurred but rejecting the claim for damages.

Lumba can be read therefore as finding that torts which are actionable per se allow only for an award of nominal damages, in the absence of proof of harm. This is a surprising outcome, given the history and purpose of torts that are actionable per se. *Lumba* has been the subject of much criticism,[36] and has not been consistently applied.[37] Furthermore, *Lumba* may not necessarily be found to apply to battery. Even if it did, a woman who had suffered an unauthorised vaginal examination could characterise her reaction to and experience of it as harm or loss. She would certainly be able to distinguish herself from the claimants in *Lumba*,

---

[34] Varuhas (n 24) 254.

[35] *Lumba* (n 25).

[36] A Ruck Keene and C Dobson, 'At What Price Liberty? The Supreme Court Decision in *Lumba* and Compensation for False Imprisonment' [2012] 4 *Public Law* 628; Varuhas (n 24) 279–81.

[37] See *R (Sessay) v South London and Maudsley NHS Trust* [2011] EWHC 2617 (QB), in which damages were found to be payable in respect of false imprisonment without a specific finding of harm.

because there is no lawful authority under which she could have been subjected to vaginal examination in the absence of consent, looking to the counterfactual analysis.

Even if *Lumba* does apply, a defendant could not assert that the claimant would have been subjected to unauthorised vaginal examination, even if the tort had not been committed. In addition, the calculation of damages in battery may not necessarily be subject to the 'recognised psychiatric condition' requirement of negligence. Finally, it is important to recall that even if a claimant was confined to nominal damages by *Lumba*, it would still be open to her to seek a declaration that the conduct in question was unlawful, a remedy that many women may consider to be as important as monetary relief.[38]

C. Conclusion on Tortious Causes of Action

The law of torts appears to provide a reasonable prospect of redress in cases of unauthorised vaginal examination, and potentially a substantial remedy in damages where medical evidence can demonstrate the causal development of a recognised psychiatric condition. The vindicatory charge of battery is instinctively more appropriate and more attractive than loss-focused negligence, allowing as it does for recognition of the fact that unauthorised vaginal examination fundamentally interferes with a woman's rights to physical autonomy and bodily integrity. This observation begs the question, however, of whether such an examination is more properly framed as a breach of rights, rather than as a civil wrong – meaning, perhaps, that it may be better tackled outside of the law of tort altogether.

III. Fundamental Rights Litigation

This section considers the potential for seeking redress for unauthorised vaginal examination via actions for breaches of fundamental rights. As is explored elsewhere in this collection, unauthorised vaginal examination entails a serious interference with the pregnant woman's fundamental rights, conceived of as the rights to bodily integrity, autonomy, or self-determination. In England and Wales, the fundamental rights action must proceed under the Human Rights Act 1998, while in Ireland, the more fruitful source of rights protection is the Constitution, *Bunreacht na hÉireann*.

---

[38] The Irish law on battery is much the same as that of England and Wales. B McMahon and W Binchy, *Law of Torts*, 4th edn (Dublin, Bloomsbury Professional, 2013) [22.11]–[22.19].

A. England and Wales: Actions under the Human Rights Act 1998

The Human Rights Act 1998 (HRA 1998) provided the European Convention on Human Rights 1950 (the Convention) with a radically expanded role in English law.[39] For present purposes, the most important aspect of this change is contained in the HRA 1998, sections 7 and 8. These create an individual cause of action where a person's Convention rights are breached by a public authority. It should be noted that this is a standalone cause of action which is separate to any tortious action that may lie. Importantly, this action should be distinguished from situations where Convention rights are referred to as a basis or reason for developing the law of torts. For example, in *Montgomery*, the UK Supreme Court referred to Convention protections in the context of discussing changing social and legal developments in understandings of the doctor-patient relationship. This is a separate question, and beyond scope of this chapter.[40]

i. Relevant Case Law from the European Court of Human Rights

For a section 7 cause of action to lie, there must in the first instance be a breach of a person's Convention rights. The first question, therefore, is whether unauthorised vaginal examination constitutes a breach of the Convention. It is well established that medical treatment carried out against the will of a patient constitutes an interference with the right to respect for private life, as protected by Article 8 of the Convention.[41] In addition, certain forms of forced medical treatment will constitute an interference with Article 3 of the Convention, which protects torture and inhuman and degrading treatment. The crucial distinction between Article 8 and Article 3 is that interferences with Article 8 may be justified, while in general interferences with Article 3 may not. There is a body of case law from the European Court of Human Rights addressing the issue of gynaecological examinations carried out without consent.[42]

---

[39] See HRA 1998, ss 6, 3 and 2. See discussion in D Hoffman et al, 'Introduction' in D Hoffman (ed), *The Impact of the UK Human Rights Act on Private Law* (Cambridge, Cambridge University Press, 2011).

[40] A rich debate surrounds the question of whether tort law should be developed to vindicate human/fundamental rights. For some important contributions to this debate see D Nolan, 'Negligence and Human Rights Law: The Case for Separate Development' (2013) 76 *Modern Law Review* 286; F du Bois, 'Social Purposes, Fundamental Rights and the Judicial Development of Private Law' in D Nolan and A Robertson (eds), *Rights and Private Law* (Oxford, Hart Publishing, 2012); R Bagshaw, 'Tort Design and Human Rights Thinking' in Hoffman (n 39).

[41] *Storck v Germany*, App no 61603/00 (European Court of Human Rights, 16 June 2005).

[42] W Buelens et al, 'The View of the European Court of Human Rights on Competent Patients' Right of Informed Consent. Research in the Light of arts 3 and 8 of the European Convention on Human Rights' (2016) 23 *European Journal of Health Law* 481.

In the case of *YF v Turkey* the applicant alleged a violation on behalf of his wife, who had (with him) been held in police custody on suspicion of aiding and abetting an illegal terrorist organisation, the PKK (Workers' Party of Kurdistan).[43] The applicant alleged that his wife, Mrs F, had been subjected to physical abuse in the course of which she was forced to undergo a gynaecological examination in the absence of consent.[44] The police authorities, and the Turkish government in turn, maintained that she had consented to the examination. Before resolving the factual dispute, the court found that an unconsented to examination of this nature would constitute an interference with Article 8. It commented:

> The Court observes that Article 8 is clearly applicable to these complaints, which concern a matter of 'private life', a concept which covers the physical and psychological integrity of a person (see X and Y v. the Netherlands, judgment of 26 March 1985, Series A no 91, p. 11, § 22). It reiterates in this connection that a person's body concerns the most intimate aspect of private life. Thus, a compulsory medical intervention, even if it is of minor importance, constitutes an interference with this right.[45]

This passage acknowledges the important principle that an unconsented to examination, as well as an unconsented to treatment, constitutes an interference with Article 8. Effectively the Court's view was that there is no principle of de minimis where interventions with bodily integrity are concerned: even a minor intervention interferes with Article 8.

To some extent, the Court sidestepped the factual dispute, appearing to accept the argument of the Turkish government that it would not have been possible to carry out the examination without the consent of Mrs F – an argument that is surely unsustainable – but concluding that it would not have been reasonable to expect Mrs F to resist examination, given her vulnerability. In effect the Court treated the case as one where either the consent was coerced, or where consent was not sought. The Court concluded there had been an interference with Mrs F's rights under Article 8(1) and proceeded to consider whether the interference could be justified under Article 8(2).

The Turkish government's defence fell at the first hurdle: it could not argue that the interference had been 'in accordance with the law'. It was clear that under Turkish law, interferences with physical integrity in the absence of consent were confined to emergency situations, and circumstances defined by law, which did not apply in Mrs F's case. Furthermore, the law providing for examinations of a detainee only permitted them to be carried out at the request of a public prosecutor.[46] Though the Court accepted that medical examination of detainees could

---

[43] *YF v Turkey*, App no 24209/94 (European Court of Human Rights, 22 July 2003). There was no dispute that the applicant could make a complaint on behalf of his wife.

[44] The ostensible purpose of the examination was to investigate whether the applicant's wife had had sexual intercourse while in custody.

[45] *YF* (n 43) [33].

[46] While this is not clear from the judgment or the domestic law cited, one assumes this refers to non-consensual examinations.

provide an important safeguard against false accusations of 'sexual molestation' or ill-treatment, these were only acceptable where provided for by law and where carried out with the consent of the person.[47] The Court concluded that there had been a breach of Mrs F's Article 8 rights.

Similar circumstances generated the case of *Juhnke v Turkey*.[48] The applicant was a German national who was detained in connection with involvement with the PKK. She alleged violations of both Article 8 and Article 3 of the Convention arising from her period in detention, which included an allegation that she had been subjected to a forced gynaecological examination.[49] As in *VF*, the Turkish government argued that the applicant had consented to the examination, and that it was justified by reference to the need to protect police officers from false allegations of sexual violence. On the factual dispute the Court took a similar approach to *VF*, concluding that the applicant's allegation that she was forced to undergo a gynaecological examination was unsubstantiated but that she had resisted such an examination until persuaded to agree to it and that 'a person in detention cannot be expected to continue to resist submitting to a gynaecological examination, given her vulnerability at the hands of the authorities, who exercise complete control over her throughout her detention'.[50]

The Court further commented that the applicant may not have been adequately informed as to the nature and purpose of the examination and that she may have been led to believe it was compulsory. The Court stated that because the applicant had not established that her express refusal was overridden, this meant that Article 3 of the Convention was not violated. Buelens et al argue that this statement implicitly accepts that a forced gynaecological examination against the express refusal of the woman will constitute a breach of Article 3.[51]

On the facts of *Juhnke* the Court concluded that there was a breach of Article 8(1):

> When account is taken of all the facts above, it cannot be concluded with certainty that any consent given by the applicant was free and informed. The Court, therefore, considers that the imposition of a gynaecological examination on the applicant, in such circumstances, gave rise to an interference with her right to respect for her private life, and in particular her right to physical integrity.[52]

As in *VF*, the Court found the examination not to be in accordance with law under Article 8(2), noting that the legal context was the same as in the earlier case. It observed that the examination was not carried out within a legal structure, but

---

[47] *YF* (n 43) [43].

[48] *Juhnke v Turkey*, App no 52515/99 (European Court of Human Rights, 13 May 2008).

[49] Article 3 prohibits torture and inhuman and degrading treatment. Violations of Art 3 cannot be justified. Only the element of the claim pertaining to the gynaecological examination was found to be admissible.

[50] *Juhnke* (n 48) [76].

[51] Buelens et al (n 42).

[52] *Juhnke* (n 48) [77].

rather was a discretionary decision made by the detaining officers. Interestingly, in *Juhnke* having found the violation the Court proceeded to go on to consider the subsequent prong of Article 8(2), whether the interference was 'necessary in a democratic society'. The Court did not express a definite view on whether or not the protection of the security forces from false allegations of sexual assault was a legitimate aim, but stated that even if it was, the carrying out of such examinations would not be proportionate to this aim. It opined that a gynaecological examination in a case of alleged sexual assault should not be carried out without the consent of the woman, and observed that in this case there had been no such allegation. Thus the examination was neither in accordance with law, nor necessary in a democratic society and thus was not justified under Article 8(2).

In the subsequent case of *Yazgul Yilmaz v Turkey* the applicant was 16 years of age when she was arrested by the Turkish authorities on suspicion of assisting the PKK.[53] She alleged that she had been subjected to a forced gynaecological examination while in custody and claimed that this had breached her rights under Article 8 and Article 3.[54] On the facts the Court found that there was no evidence that that either the applicant or her guardians had ever given their consent to the examination. The Court observed that special measures should have been taken to ensure that consent was given, in view of the fact that the prisoner was a minor. Furthermore, the Court was critical of the justification advanced by the Turkish government, which was the same justification as in the earlier cases: the protection of police officers from false accusations of sexual assault. The Court took a significantly stronger line on this issue than it had in earlier cases, finding that a general policy of this nature was inappropriate. The totality of the features of the applicant's case meant that the applicant had been subjected to degrading treatment in breach of Article 3.

These cases are clearly highly relevant to the fact pattern of the unauthorised vaginal examination. In the first instance, it should be noted that where this fact pattern arises in England and Wales, the woman will in the great majority of cases be under the care of the National Health Service, a state body, so no question of horizontal application of the Convention arises.[55] *VF* and *Juhnke* clearly establish that a gynaecological examination carried out in the absence of consent, or in circumstances of inadequately informed consent constitutes an interference under Article 8(1). *Yazgul Yilmaz* goes further than the earlier cases and demonstrates that forced gynaecological examination may violate Article 3.[56] Buelens et al argue that *Yazgul Yilmaz* confirms the implicit conclusion in *Juhnke* that forced gynaecological examination will always breach Article 3, commenting that this is

---

[53] *Affaire Yazgul Yilmaz c Turquie* Requête no 36369/06 (Cour Européenne des Droits de l'Homme 1er février 2011). Note that this case was never reported in English.

[54] She also alleged breaches of Arts 6 and 13.

[55] A Young, 'Mapping Horizontal Effect' in Hoffman (n 39); G Phillipson and A Williams 'Horizontal Effect and the Constitutional Constraint' (2011) 74 *Modern Law Review* 878.

[56] Buelens et al (n 42).

especially clear where the woman is a minor. Unauthorised vaginal examination involves forced rather than coerced or persuaded consent, meaning that it may in fact fall within the Article 3 instead of within Article 8. If it does reach the Article 3 threshold of severity, the interference cannot be justified. Admittedly, the typical position of a woman experiencing unauthorised vaginal examination is quite different from the facts of *Yazgul Yilmaz*, in that she will be in a hospital, and there will be at least an argument that the procedure is medically necessary. This clearly differs significantly from the position of a minor prisoner subjected to medical examination where there is a legal rather than medical necessity.

Even if unauthorised vaginal examination constitutes an interference with Article 8 and not Article 3, it is very difficult to see how it could be justified pursuant to Article 8(2). As discussed, there is no plausible argument that gynaecological examination in the absence of consent is permissible under the law of England and Wales, never mind provided for by law. The decision in question is not only discretionary, but also unlawful. In such circumstances there is no need to consider whether the interference is necessary in a democratic society but one may do so for argument's sake, following the approach of the Court in *Junhke*.

The only conceivable justifications for proceeding with vaginal examination in the absence of consent are: (1) protection of the foetus; and (2) protection of the woman herself. The European Court of Human Rights has definitively refused to take a position on the question of foetal life, according the Member States a wide margin of appreciation in the sphere of abortion.[57] Thus it is quite possible that protection of the foetus in labour could be found to be a legitimate aim on the part of a Member State. However, that wide margin of appreciation has been applied in circumstances where the legitimate aim is evidenced and pursued in legislation, not where the activity in question is in fact unlawful, as unauthorised vaginal examination is.[58] Similarly, it is difficult to see how a measure could be found to be proportionate to that aim if the 'measure' in question is allowing medical practitioners the discretion to act unlawfully.

It is important to note that there is Convention case law that acknowledges that the fact that medical treatment was provided in an emergency context is relevant to the necessity inquiry.[59] Unauthorised vaginal examination is not, however, a situation of true emergency. Following the approach in domestic English law whereby the need for an emergency Caesarean section does not remove the requirement for consent, it is difficult to see how the need for a vaginal examination could constitute a true emergency. Furthermore, there does not appear to be any basis on which it could be alleged that the Convention permits medical interventions

---

[57] The Court declined to apply Art 2 (right to life) to the foetus in *Vo v France* App no 53924/00 (European Court of Human Rights, 8 July 2004). In *A, B and C v Ireland* App no 23379/05 (European Courts of Human Right, 16 December 2010) the Court found that a wide margin of appreciation applied to Member State legislation on abortion.

[58] eg in *A, B and C* (n 57).

[59] *Glass v UK* App no 61827/00 (European Court of Human Rights, 9 March 2004).

to protect the patient herself in the absence of consent, outside of an emergency situation.[60] In short, there appear to be strong grounds for saying that unauthorised vaginal examination constitutes a breach of both Article 3 and Article 8 of the Convention.

ii. Actions under the HRA 1998

The action under the HRA 1998, section 7 is confined to actions against public authorities.[61] As noted, the great majority of unauthorised vaginal examination cases that arise in England and Wales will occur in a public context, because the woman will be in the care of the NHS.[62] This leads to the question of whether a woman who is subjected to such an examination would be entitled to sue the relevant NHS trust as a public authority, in circumstances where the act alleged to breach her Convention rights is carried out by one or more individual healthcare professionals employed by that trust. General speaking in cases of unauthorised vaginal examination, the trust has not sanctioned the conduct, nor recommended it as a matter of policy.

The question of what constitutes a public authority has generated substantial debate in other contexts, such as housing.[63] While the housing context raises complex issues in respect of quasi-private actors being deemed to be public authorities, it is more straightforward in so far as the act alleged to have breached a person's Convention rights is more likely to be a clear policy on the part of the relevant housing body, rather than a situation where an employee of the housing authority has independently carried out a rights breach.[64] For this reason, the better analogy may be with human rights-based claims against the police.[65] In such cases the actions constituting the rights breach are carried out by an individual or group of individual employees. However, there is generally an allegation of 'operational' failures against the organisation itself, and an allegation of a failure to carry out an effective investigation as required by Article 3 of the Convention, which contrasts with the fact pattern of the unauthorised vaginal examination.

Where there have been human rights claims against NHS trusts, these have generally arisen in the mental health context. In *Rabone v Pennine Care NHS Foundation Trust* the claimants alleged both negligence and breach of Article 2 of the Convention in circumstances where their daughter had been released from

---

[60] *Jehovah's Witnesses of Moscow v Russia* App no 302/02 (European Court of Human Rights, 10 June 2010).

[61] HRA 1998, s 6.

[62] See graphic explanation of NHS structure at www.kingsfund.org.uk/audio-video/how-new-nhs-structured.

[63] *YL v Birmingham City Council* [2007] UKHL 27; *R (on the application of Weaver) v London & Quadrant Housing Trust* [2009] EWCA Civ 587; Health and Social Care Act 2008, s 145.

[64] H Quane, 'The Strasbourg Jurisprudence and the Meaning of a "Public Authority" under the Human Rights Act' (2006) *Public Law* 106.

[65] *Michael v Chief Constable of South Wales Police* [2015] AC 1732; *Commissioner of Police of the Metropolis v DSD* [2019] AC 196.

a psychiatric unit, and died by suicide shortly afterwards.[66] The Trust admitted negligence but denied liability under the HRA 1998. The admission of negligence suggests that there was no policy or procedure that justified the actions of the healthcare professionals in question, though this is not discussed in the judgment. The Supreme Court found that an operational duty – not unlike that which applies to the police – existed under Article 2 to protect the life of a voluntary patient who was suicidal, and that the parents of the deceased were entitled to recover damages. Importantly, therefore, this case included an operational duty element, which would not necessarily arise in unauthorised vaginal examinations.[67]

In *R (Sessay) v South London and Maudsley NHS Trust* the claimant, who had at the time of the incident been suffering from a mental illness, succeeded in her claims for both false imprisonment and breach of Article 5 of the Convention against the defendant Trust.[68] In that case, the claimant had been detained for a 13-hour period without a proper legal basis. The Court rejected a separate claim that the Trust's policy on mental health detention was not Convention compliant. This policy permitted periods of detention for up to eight hours. There was no suggestion, however, that the detention which actually took place was in compliance with the Trust's policies. This fact pattern may be more in line with the unauthorised vaginal examination example, as it does not appear to engage an operational duty element, but rather a situation where the course of action that was followed was expressly in violation of the Trust's policies.

It seems, therefore, that some degree of uncertainty exists as to whether a claim would definitively lie against an NHS Trust *qua* public authority, in cases of unauthorised vaginal examination. While there appears to be an absence of decided cases which are precisely on point, it is important to note that there can be little doubt that a NHS Trust would be vicariously liable in negligence for the actions of a healthcare professional who engaged in an unauthorised vaginal examination.[69] As such, there do not appear to be strong policy reasons for absolving Trusts of liability under the HRA 1998. Finally, it is of note that in its report on the meaning of a public authority, published in 2004, the Joint Committee on Human Rights noted that during parliamentary debates at the time of the passage of the HRA 1998 the Lord Chancellor commented: 'Doctors in general practice would be public authorities in relation to their National Health Service functions, but not in

---

[66] *Rabone v Pennine Care NHS Foundation Trust* [2012] UKSC 2. For commentary on this case see J Varuhas, 'Liability under the Human Rights Act 1998: The Duty to Protect Life, Indirect Victims and Damages' (2012) 71 *The Cambridge Law Journal* 263; N Poole, 'Rabone v Pennine Care NHS Foundation Trust: Claiming Damages under the Human Rights Act' (2012) 2 *Journal of Personal Injury Law* 127.

[67] See also *Savage v South Essex Partnership Foundation Trust* [2009] 1 All ER 1053.

[68] *Sessay* (n 37).

[69] See generally the principles in *Catholic Child Welfare Society v Various Claimants* [2012] UKSC 56; *Cox v Ministry of Justice* [2016] UKSC 10; *Mohamud v WM Morrison Supermarkets plc* [2016] UKSC 11; *Armes v Nottinghamshire County Council* [2017] UKSC 60.

relation to their private patients'.[70] This suggests at least some basis for saying that the intention of the legislature was that human rights claims would operate in the clinical setting.

Assuming that a HRA 1998 action can be maintained against a Trust, an important distinction between HRA 1998 actions and tort actions is the approach to remedies. Section 8 of the HRA 1998 provides that courts may make awards of damages for breach of the Convention, but the court is required to take account of any other relief granted in respect of the breach, and the consequences of the decision in respect of the breach, and no award of damages is to be made unless, taking into account these factors, an award of damages is necessary to guarantee 'just satisfaction' to the claimant.[71] It is clear, therefore, that a court will not necessarily make an award of damages even where there has been a breach of the Convention. This is premised on the assumption that the finding of a breach is, in and of itself, a valuable relief to the claimant.

Furthermore, courts are required to take into account the principles applied by the European Court of Human Rights in relation to the award of damages.[72] The approach of the courts to the process of calculating HRA 1998 damages is still unfolding. In the years immediately following the passage of the HRA 1998, damages under the Act were rarely considered by the courts and when they were addressed, a very restrictive approach was taken.[73] Steele observes that this approach has changed over time, with more recent years seeing the courts more willing to make awards of damages under the HRA 1998, especially in circumstances where tort law does not afford a remedy.[74] Awards remain quite low, and lower than awards in tort law, but they are not insubstantial.[75]

Importantly, a claimant is entitled to maintain an action both in tort and under the HRA 1998 arising from the same facts. As discussed, in the case of *R (Sessay) v South London and Maudsley NHS Trust* the claimant successfully established that she had been subject to the tort of false imprisonment, and that she had suffered a breach of her Article 5 Convention rights due to her detention at psychiatric hospital.[76] The court found that she was entitled to both tortious and HRA 1998 damages, which would be assessed by the court if not agreed by the parties.

---

[70] House of Lords, House of Commons, Joint Committee on Human Rights, *The Meaning of Public Authority under the Human Rights Act* (Seventh Report of Session 2003–2004) 10; Lord Chancellor, HL Deb, 24 November 1997, col 811.

[71] HRA 1998, s 8(3).

[72] HRA 1998, s 8(4).

[73] *Anufrijeva v Southwark LBC* [2003] EWCA Civ 1406; *R (on the application of Greenfield) v Secretary of State for the Home Department* [2005] UKHL 14; R Clayton, 'Damage Limitation: The Courts and the Human Rights Act Damages' (2005) *Public Law* 429; J Hartshorne, 'The Human Rights Act 1998 and Damages for Non-Pecuniary Loss' (2004) 6 *European Human Rights Law Review* 660.

[74] Steele (n 4) 557–59, considering the cases of *OOO v Commissioners for the Metropolis* [2011] EWHC 1246 (QB); *R (Waxman) v Crown Prosecution Service* [2012] EWHC 133 (Admin); *R (Faulkner) v Secretary of State for Justice* [2013] UKSC 23; *R (Sturnham) v Parole Board and Another* [2013] UKSC 23.

[75] See further discussion of the recent case law in M Andenas et al, 'A Fair Price for Violations of Human Rights?' (2014) 130 *Law Quarterly Review* 48.

[76] *Sessay* (n 37).

It seems, therefore, that a woman who was subjected to unauthorised vaginal examination in an NHS hospital would have a reasonable prospect of maintaining a claim for breach of Article 8 of the Convention in the English courts, and of achieving a declaration that the breach had happened. Depending on her particular circumstances, she might also be entitled to an award of damages in line with the Strasbourg case law and the evolving English jurisprudence. Notably, the court would be entitled to look to the severity of the breach in calculating damages, and not only to the harm caused to the claimant.[77]

B. Ireland: Actions for Breach of Constitutional Rights

The fundamental rights context in Ireland is quite different to that in England and Wales. Ireland has a written constitution, *Bunreacht na hÉireann*, ratified in 1937, which protects a wide range of fundamental rights and allows for strong-form judicial review. Legislation that breaches constitutional rights is void, and can be declared so by the courts.[78] In addition the Constitution allows for individual, private actions for breach of constitutional rights. The Irish Constitution is horizontally applicable, meaning that actions for breach of constitutional rights may be taken by one private individual against another.[79] This is significant in the context of Irish healthcare, which involves significantly more private providers than are found in the English system.[80]

The central limiting principle for the breach of constitutional rights action is that an individual is only entitled to bring an action for breach of constitutional rights where that right is not otherwise protected by private law.[81] Irish law operates on the basis that the private law vindicates constitutional rights.[82] It is only where the private law does not adequately vindicate a constitutional right that a litigant can rely directly on the Constitution. For example, the tort of defamation protects the constitutional right to a good name, so one would not be entitled to sue for breach of that right in reliance directly on the Constitution. Due to this doctrinal structure, actions for breach of constitutional rights are relatively rare, but very significant when they do occur.

A recent affirmation of the importance of the action for breach of constitutional rights can be seen in the case of *Simpson v Governor of Mountjoy Prison*.[83]

---

[77] As discussed, this approach may also be available in the tort of battery, subject to the above discussion of *Lumba* (n 25).

[78] Articles 15.4 and 34.3.2 *Bunreacht na hÉireann*; *Buckley v Attorney General* [1950] IR 67.

[79] *Byrne v Ireland* [1972] IR 241; *Meskell v CIE* [1973] IR 121; *Glover v BLN* [1973] IR 388.

[80] L Geary et al, *The Irish Healthcare System: An Historical and Comparative Review* (Dublin, The Health Insurance Authority, 2018).

[81] *Hanrahan v Merck Sharp Dohme (Ireland) Ltd* [1988] 1 ILRM 629; *McDonnell v Ireland* [1998] 1 IR 134.

[82] See eg *Grant v Roche Products* [2008] 4 IR 679, where the Supreme Court of Ireland acknowledged that part of the function of the tort of negligence is to vindicate constitutional rights.

[83] *Simpson v Governor of Mountjoy Prison and Others* (Supreme Court, 14 November 2019, awaiting neutral citation).

The Supreme Court found that being subjected to the practice of 'slopping-out' while in prison constituted a breach of the plaintiff's constitutional rights.[84] 'Slopping out' meant that prisoners were held in cells with no toilet or washing facilities and forced to rely on chamber pots and buckets which they 'slopped-out' daily into a sluice. The plaintiff was awarded the sum of €7,500 in damages for breach of his constitutional rights. As was reiterated in *Simpson*, in Irish law the Constitution takes precedence over the Convention on fundamental rights issues. The Convention is only indirectly applicable in Irish law, subject to the European Convention on Human Rights Act 2003.[85] Resort to the Convention is only permissible where no other remedy is available, and it does not apply horizontally.[86] Accordingly, Courts consider the constitutional issue first in any proceedings, and given the significant role of private providers in Irish healthcare, the Constitution is by far the more important source of fundamental rights protection in respect of unauthorised vaginal examination.

A woman who is subjected to unauthorised vaginal examination in Ireland could successfully take an action for breach of constitutional rights against the healthcare professional and/or the hospital in question, if she could show that: (1) her constitutional rights have been breached; and (2) the constitutional right is not otherwise vindicated by the private law. The latter qualification is important: if a woman was or would be successful in negligence or battery, she would not be able to rely on the standalone action for breach of constitutional rights. This would not, however, prevent a litigant from pleading both causes of action and pursuing them in the alternative.

The Irish Constitution provides robust protection for the right to refuse treatment. In the seminal case of *In Re a Ward of Court* the Irish Supreme Court found that medical treatment provided in the absence of consent was 'a trespass against the person in civil law, a battery in criminal law, and a breach of the individual's constitutional rights'.[87] In addition, the Irish Constitution protects the right to bodily integrity.[88] While this right seems to be limited to protecting the person against interferences with bodily integrity that pose a threat to the person's life or health, this would appear to encompass unauthorised vaginal examination, which at the very least poses a risk of significant distress.[89]

A third right which may protect against unauthorised vaginal examination is the right to person, an express right under the Constitution which has gained currency in recent years.[90] In his concurring judgment in *Simpson*, O'Donnell J elaborated on the content of this right, observing that it encompassed not just a

---

[84] The term 'plaintiff' rather than 'claimant' is used in Ireland.

[85] The limited incorporation of the Convention is at least in part due to the rich fundamental rights jurisprudence in Irish law.

[86] European Convention on Human Rights Act 2003, s 3(2).

[87] In *Re a Ward of Court* [1996] 2 IR 79, 156. The existence of this right has been confirmed many times by the courts including in *Fitzpatrick* (n 2).

[88] *Ryan v AG* [1965] IR 294.

[89] ibid. As opposed to interferences with a person's body *simpliciter*: *State (C) v Frawley* [1976] 1 IR 365; *State (Richardson) v Governor of Mountjoy Prison* [1980] ILRM 82.

[90] art 40.3.2 *Bunreacht na hÉireann*. D Kenny 'Recent Developments on the Rights of the Person in art 40.3: Fleming v Ireland and the Spectre of Unenumerated Rights' (2013) 36 *Dublin University Law*

prohibition on physical intrusion but also that it protected the personal space and psychological wellbeing of the individual.[91] This right to person, read alongside the constitutional rights and/or values of privacy, autonomy, and dignity, protected the individual from detention in the appalling conditions the plaintiff had experienced. Importantly, the right to person encompasses concepts of both physical and psychological integrity, both of which are clearly engaged and seriously compromised in unauthorised vaginal examination.

In general, constitutional rights are subject to legitimate limitation by reference to a proportionality test.[92] In theory, therefore, a breach of these rights in the context of unauthorised vaginal examination could be justified if shown to be proportionate.[93] It is virtually impossible to see, however, how an intervention that is itself unlawful could ever be regarded as a proportionate restriction of constitutional rights. As such, there seem to be quite good grounds for arguing that unauthorised vaginal examination could provide the basis for a successful breach of constitutional rights action, so long as it could not be demonstrated that the rights were otherwise vindicated.

If such an action is successful, this raises the question of whether damages will be awarded, and if so, what the quantum of damages would be. Because actions for breaches of constitutional rights are relatively rare, the principles on which such damages are awarded have until recently been somewhat opaque. In an interesting contrast to the Strasbourg and HRA 1998 positions, there is case law in which the Irish courts have specifically acknowledged that a mere declaration that there has been a breach of constitutional rights is not adequate vindication of constitutional rights.[94]

There is some basis for arguing, therefore, that a plaintiff who succeeds in establishing a breach of constitutional rights will generally be entitled to some award of damages. That said, in the Irish context the award of €7,500 made in *Simpson* is a very small award when compared with standard awards in personal injuries cases.[95] This suggests that the Supreme Court is signalling that while breaches of constitutional rights are certainly actionable, they are not necessarily going to generate significant awards of damages.

Journal 322; O Doyle and T Hickey, *Constitutional Law: Text, Cases and Materials*, 2nd edn (Dublin, Clarus Press, 2019). Note that the right to refuse treatment and the right to bodily integrity are unenumerated rights.

[91] *Simpson* (n 83) O'Donnell J [10].

[92] Where the legislature balances two competing constitutional rights in legislation, this is subject to a higher degree of deference contained in the rationality test: *Tuohy v Courtney* [1994] 3 IR 1 [47].

[93] The version of the proportionality test that applies in Irish law requires that 'The objective of the impugned provision must be of sufficient importance to warrant overriding a constitutionally protected right. It must relate to concerns pressing and substantial in a free and democratic society. The means chosen must pass a proportionality test. They must: (a) be rationally connected to the objective and not be arbitrary, unfair or based on irrational considerations; (b) impair the right as little as possible, and (c) be such that their effects on rights are proportional to the objective': *Heaney v Ireland* [1994] 3 IR 593, 607.

[94] Henchy J commented in *Hanrahan v Merck Sharp Dohme (Ireland) Ltd.* [1988] 1 ILRM 629 that a declaration was not an adequate mechanism of 'implementation' of constitutional rights.

[95] On variations in damages for personal injuries between England and Wales and Ireland see C Brennan, 'Our Payouts Are Three Times That of the UK, So Why Wouldn't Whiplash Legislation Work Here?' *The Journal* (Dublin, 22 April 2018) at www.thejournal.ie/whiplash-legislation-ireland-3968982-Apr2018/.

The Supreme Court in *Simpson* is to be commended for taking the opportunity to clarify the principles that apply to that calculation where damages are awarded. The Court commented that this calculation should seek to put the claimant back in the position he would have been in had the rights breach not occurred, that the approach should be an equitable one that has regard to the particular facts and the seriousness of the violation, and that the traditional heads of common law damages should be used, where necessary, namely: 'non-pecuniary loss including pain, suffering, psychological harm, distress, frustration, inconvenience, humiliation, anxiety, and loss of reputation'.[96] These comments suggest that the calculation of damages for breach of constitutional rights has both a compensatory and a vindicatory component. In cases of unauthorised vaginal examination, there would seem to be good grounds to argue that there should be an award of damages and to justify the award by reference to both vindication of constitutional rights and what is undoubtedly a serious breach, and to the need to compensate the plaintiff for loss suffered which can include pain, suffering and distress, falling short of a recognised psychiatric condition.

C. Conclusion on Fundamental Rights Causes of Action

Under both the Convention and the Irish Constitution there are strong arguments to say that unauthorised vaginal examination constitutes an interference with fundamental rights, and not one that is justifiable by reference to standard concepts of proportionality. A crucial distinction between the jurisdictions is that in England and Wales the litigant could succeed in both the tortious action and the HRA 1998 claim, whereas the Irish litigant could argue both the breach of constitutional rights and the tortious claim but could ultimately only succeed in one. The possibility of dual success in England and Wales is very significant, and should provide a reason for lawyers to look to the HRA 1998 in the personal injuries context as well as the public law context.[97] In both jurisdictions it appears that fundamental rights claims generally lead to lower awards than those found in tortious actions, and this would inevitably influence a litigant's preference as to which kind of action to pursue.

IV. Conclusion

Unauthorised vaginal examination is an unusual phenomenon, in that it appears to be incontrovertibly unlawful as a matter of civil law, and yet seeking redress for

---

[96] *Simpson* (n 83) McMenamin J [125].

[97] It has been argued that personal injuries lawyers as well as public lawyers need to be concerned with the HRA 1998: Poole (n 66).

that legal wrong presents challenges. This chapter has argued that so far as tort law actions are concerned, battery rather than negligence accommodates unauthorised vaginal examination better because it does not require evidence of a recognised psychiatric condition. Pursuing a case in battery alone, however, would be rather daunting. Though the theoretical framework for the action is secure, battery is far less litigated than negligence and indeed may be perceived as only being relied upon where the well-established requirements of negligence cannot be fulfilled. These problems are compounded by the decision in *Lumba*. The cautious lawyer would probably feel more comfortable proceeding in negligence, and if supportive reports demonstrated a recognised psychiatric condition, this tort would almost certainly be preferred. But even for the woman who has suffered a recognised psychiatric condition, proceeding in negligence is unsatisfactory. At a fundamental level, negligence is a tort that is not designed to redress the core wrong entailed in unauthorised vaginal examination. If she succeeds in her negligence claim, and recovers damages for her psychiatric injury, arguably the examination has not been fully addressed because there is generally no recognition of the wrong – as opposed to the loss – involved.

These challenges in the law of torts demonstrate the need for unauthorised vaginal examination to be addressed through the rubric of fundamental rights, as well as in tort. Though such actions tend to yield lower awards, they should do a better job of recognising wrongs, and vindicating rights. As was noted at the outset of this chapter, the question of remedies is central in litigation, and preferences as between different remedies are deeply personal. The doctrinal limitations and opportunities afforded by the various causes of action must ultimately be assessed by reference to the individual judgment of the woman who has experienced unauthorised vaginal examination, and her personal understanding of redress.

Afterword: Unauthorised Intimate Examinations as/and Sexual Violence: Some Epistemic and Phenomenological Considerations

SARA COHEN SHABOT

The collection you hold in your hands is the first to tackle from a theoretical perspective the specific issue of unauthorised intimate examinations within the broader discussion of non-consensual practices in childbirth and obstetric violence in general. The chapters of this book establish a new point of departure for further debates on the role of the law in cases of obstetric violence and the problematic meaning of 'informed consent' in labour – especially regarding intimate examinations performed during medicalised labour. These non-consensual practices result in loss of dignity, loss of autonomy, and trauma, converting birthing subjects into objects of medical scrutiny without agency. The various chapters of this volume demonstrate, however, that non-consensual intimate examinations in childbirth are distinct from other forms of obstetric violence, at least partially because of their clear similarities with certain forms of sexual violence. Thus, even if we agree that obstetric violence in general is gender violence, this specific practice calls for an analysis and thematisation through the specific framework of the study of sexual violence.

One particularly interesting question within the present discussion concerns the epistemic problem of recognising violence within systems that have normalised that violence. Is it possible to recognise practices as violent when those practices have been thoroughly normalised and the harm done has become invisible to the law, to medical institutions, and to society more broadly? In what sense is violence still violence when it is not epistemically framed as such (even by its own victims)? The lack of hermeneutical resources for recognising normalised violence as violence plays a central role in the theoretical discussion of sexual violence – and thus must also be firmly present within the theorisation of (non-consensual) intimate examinations in labour. My bracketing of 'non-consensual' is intentional: these problems fundamentally erode the very notion of consent.

In 'Why "Normal" Feels So Bad', I argue that many labouring women lack the epistemic resources to recognise vaginal examinations as violent, unnecessary, or declinable.[1] The unrecognised violence of vaginal examinations in childbirth constitutes part of a more general problem: that women, ourselves, frequently do not fully recognise obstetric violence as such. But vaginal examinations are more specifically related to childbirth's sexual dimension and sexuality in general. Many reports of 'birth rape' emphasise vaginal examinations or other vaginal procedures (such as episiotomies). Shea Richland's narrative of 'birth rape' reads: 'I was drugged and knocked unconscious. I was sexually assaulted: My vagina was cut and a man's tool (forceps) was inserted into my body'.[2] See also the now-infamous 'Kelly's Story', a terrifying case of 'birth rape' caught on camera in its entirety.[3] I address vaginal examinations during childbirth as a special case of obstetric violence, where women frequently lack the epistemic resources to recognise the practice as violent not only because of the inherent difficulty of recognising violence in an 'essentially benevolent' setting such as the medical one but, even more so, because of the pervasive sexual reification of women under patriarchy and the pervasive shame to which women are subjected.

'Why "Normal" Feels So Bad' argues that vaginal examinations are indeed bodily apprehended as violent by many women, but that their full epistemic recognition as violence is often obstructed because the experience perfectly coincides with women's normal phenomenological situation within patriarchy and thus cannot really be framed as violent. A phenomenological analysis presenting women's embodied experience under patriarchy as always already tied to sexual availability and commodification, and to shame, explains this epistemological impairment.

Diana Taylor used Judith Butler's framework to show how sexual violence against women is not truly recognised as violence (neither by the perpetrators nor, all too frequently, by the victims).[4] Taylor argues that because patriarchy constructs women's bodies as ambivalent – both 'inviting sex' (available for others' sexual pleasure) and vulnerable, needing constant surveillance – sexual violence against women is framed not as violence but as an expected, legitimate response

---

[1] S Cohen Shabot, 'Why "Normal" Feels So Bad: Violence and Vaginal Examinations during Labor – A Feminist Phenomenology' *Feminist Theory* (2020), 4464700120920764.

[2] S Richland, 'Birth Rape: Another Midwife's Story' (2008) 85 *Midwifery Today* 42, 43.

[3] H Hayes-Klein, 'Forced Episiotomy: Kelly's Story' (Open Democracy, 10 September 2014) at www.opendemocracy.net/en/transformation/forced-episiotomy-kellys-story/. For a more detailed analysis of birth rape and the feminist questions it raises, see S Cohen Shabot, 'Making Loud Bodies "Feminine": A Feminist-Phenomenological Analysis of Obstetric Violence' (2016) 39 *Human Studies* 231, 238–39. In the cases referred to above, vaginal manipulations were fully recognised as sexual violence, but in my paper, as noted, I deal with the absence of recognition.

[4] D Taylor, 'Are Women's Lives (Fully) Grievable? Gendered Framing and Sexual Violence' in C Fischer and L Dolezal (eds), *New Feminist Perspectives on Embodiment* (Cham, Palgrave Macmillan, 2018), citing J Butler, *Frames of War: When Is Life Grievable?* (London, Verso, 2009).

to women's 'nature', at least when the victim violates gendered bodily regulations.[5] She writes:

> With respect to sexual violence against women, the normative distinction at stake is not so much whether sexual violence is morally acceptable or reprehensible, but rather whether sexual violence is or is not properly violence at all … If simply being embodied as a woman is 'to ask for it', then any degree of male sexual attention directed at women cannot by definition be unwanted and, hence, a violation. This in turn calls into question whether such attention can be the sort of forcible and injurious action that constitutes violence.[6]

It is not only sexual violence that goes unrecognised as violence: crucially, medical (and specifically obstetric) violence is also difficult to frame, at least prima facie, as violence. Violence is frequently conceptualised as requiring intention, as oxymoronic in spaces seen as essentially benevolent or involving practices understood to be in the individual's best interest. Human childbirth is culturally constructed, and part of its medicalised construction is that it is a highly risky event that necessitates rescuing by medical authorities.[7] Therefore, defining what medical authorities do in childbirth as violence can seem puzzling, at the least. An important difference between obstetric violence and sexual violence is that obstetric violence occurs exclusively within one of the most essentially benevolent spaces we can imagine – the hospital – and at the hands of people whose central role is to heal and make us well. Conversely, sexual violence that happens within insecure or violent contexts is much more readily identifiable. However, the fact that sexual violence is often performed within familiar or other seemingly 'protected' contexts definitely blurs this difference.[8]

---

[5] ibid. Taylor (at 157) reminds us, though, that these strict gender norms are impossible to satisfy; thus, even when the victim appears not to have 'deserved' violence, sexual violence elicits no authentic surprise: 'Sexual violence against women who adhere to traditional gender norms and, consistent with neoliberalism, surveil their own behavior and actions may be recognized as a violation and therefore produce a level of moral outrage. That the violation of even "good victims" fails to produce *surprise*, however, illustrates the degree to which sexual violence against women has become uncritically accepted as simply inevitable'.

[6] ibid 155.

[7] R Chadwick and D Foster, 'Negotiating Risky Bodies: Childbirth and Constructions of Risk' (2014) 16 *Health, Risk & Society* 68; B Rothman, *In Labour: Women and Power in the Birth Place* (London, Junction Books, 1982); B Rothman, 'Pregnancy, Birth and Risk: An Introduction' (2014) 16 *Health, Risk & Society* 1.

[8] The feminist theorisation of violence has worked to uncover the integral and essentially masculine elements that structure and form violence as we understand it. For instance, see J Butler, *Precarious Life: The Power of Mourning and Violence* (London, Verso, 2004); Butler (n 4); J Butler, *Notes toward a Performative Theory of Assembly* (Cambridge, Harvard University Press, 2015); J Butler, 'Rethinking Vulnerability in Resistance' in J Butler et al (eds), *Vulnerability in Resistance* (Durham, Duke University Press, 2016) 12; S Karhu, 'Judith Butler's Critique of Violence and the Legacy of Monique Wittig' (2016) 31 *Hypatia* (8) 27; R Schott, 'War Rape, Natality and Genocide' (2011) 13 *Journal of Genocide Research* 5. This theorisation makes it clear that many forms of gender violence are misrecognised or remain invisible, since they do not correspond to mainstream concepts of violence. See D Bergoffen, *Contesting the Politics of Genocidal Rape: Affirming the Dignity of the Vulnerable Body* (New York, Routledge, 2012). Feminist theory has done much to broaden the spectrum of what is considered violence and illuminate how state violence is normalised or made invisible, for instance see J Lokaneeta, 'Violence' in L Disch

There are two issues that I would like to explore more deeply in this regard. The first is the relation between privilege and epistemic power in the context of sexual or/and obstetric violence. While working on 'Why "Normal" Feels so Bad', I came to realise that many epistemic questions regarding the possibility of recognising obstetric violence as such are connected, first, to the specific type of obstetric violence being performed and, second, to the specific birthing persons towards whom this violence is directed. The 'too much too soon' type of obstetric violence[9] appears to be much harder to identify as violence; due to the construction of childbirth as risky and requiring medical intervention, more intervention in childbirth is less recognisable as violence than is less or no intervention. My paper thus led me to a somewhat paradoxical conclusion: privileged women receiving advanced technologies and care may be more lacking in the epistemic resources needed to fully identify and possibly resist violence than are marginalised, poor, or mistreated women, because of the strong illusion of choice and of fair, evidence-based care and treatment in wealthy Western hospitals and maternity wards. Carine Mardorossian, for instance, argues that in her own birthing experience' the illusion of choice and of the medical institution's essential benevolence and nonviolence (which prevails within medicalised childbirth in the United States) prevented her from seeing – until much later – how violent her labour actually was.[10]

Birth experiences are grounded in a concretely sexist, patriarchal reality and in particular operations of power (including ones that present medical settings as essentially benign). This is crucial in explaining why certain populations are better suited to recognising obstetric violence: when medical attention is already recognised as threatening and untrustworthy, obstetric violence is more easily recognised as violence. Women who suffer blatant disrespect in childbirth and poor medical care may be able to articulate more clearly what is wrong with medicalised childbirth, and with vaginal examinations in particular. Women with previous

---

and M Hawkesworth (eds), *The Oxford Handbook of Feminist Theory* (Oxford, Oxford University Press, 2016). Nevertheless, much more needs to be done.

[9] Obstetric violence has been recognised as being experienced very differently by white, Euro-American, middle-class women (like myself) than it is by marginalised, poor, or minority populations, see S Miller et al, 'Beyond Too Little, Too Late and Too Much, Too Soon: A Pathway towards Evidence-Based, Respectful Maternity Care Worldwide' (2016) 388 *The Lancet* 2176. 'Too much too soon' refers to medicalisation and the overuse of technology in labour, which has been shown to diminish labouring women's self-image and sense of control and agency, see R Behruzi et al, 'Understanding Childbirth Practices as an Organizational Cultural Phenomenon: A Conceptual Framework' (2013) 13 *BMC Pregnancy and Childbirth* 205; A Smeenk and H ten Have, 'Medicalization and Obstetric Care: An Analysis of Developments in Dutch Midwifery' (2003) 6 *Medicine, Health Care and Philosophy* 153; J Wolf, *Deliver Me from Pain: Anesthesia and Birth in America* (Martland, Johns Hopkins University Press, 2012). 'Too little too late' refers to a lack of technology and basic medical attention. Initially, this was understood as a distinction between affluent and low-to-middle-income countries. Miller et al (2176), however, propose that the two extremes coexist globally because of social and health inequities within countries. Thus, they argue: 'A global approach to quality and equitable maternal health, supporting the implementation of respectful, evidence-based care for all, is urgently needed'.

[10] C Mardorossian, *Framing the Rape Victim: Gender and Agency Reconsidered* (New Brunswick, Rutgers University Press, 2014) 87–89.

childbirth experiences outside of medicalised facilities also come equipped with a broader perspective on what is or is not 'normal', often allowing them to articulate how various obstetric practices might be wrong, sexually violent, or unnecessary and even giving them the power to refuse and resist those practices.[11]

Thus, paradoxically, privilege does not always coincide with access to better epistemic resources, and marginalised populations may be more epistemically able to recognise obstetric and gender violence. This does not mean that they are better off – it just says something about how epistemic mechanisms develop. I want to explore this idea under two aspects: first, as an example of feminist standpoint theory, according to which the socially disadvantaged might in fact be epistemically privileged and the most capable of spotting oppressive patriarchal structures.[12] Second, as challenging some recent scholarship on epistemic injustice, especially Fricker's notion of hermeneutical injustice, which contends that oppressed groups frequently lack the interpretative resources to comprehend and communicate meaningful aspects of their collective experience, implying that social privilege generally guarantees more epistemic power.[13] Such concepts as 'testimonial injustice' and 'hermeneutical injustice' are useful for theorising the epistemic difficulties involved in identifying obstetric violence: birthing persons are so oppressed and domesticated by institutions that they cannot recognise the violence they are treated with. Nevertheless, the opposite also seems to be true: as posited in Hartsock's standpoint theory, the more oppressed birthing subjects are, the epistemically better equipped they may be to recognise obstetric violence.

The second point I would like to develop involves the problem of consent in childbirth in relation to the subject's non-linear, changing, ambiguous self. Ellie Anderson writes about this in the context of sexual ethics and sexual violence,[14] quoting Linda Alcoff[15] and Rebecca Kukla[16] – among others – in order to emphasise that consent is necessary but not sufficient for demarcating the true limits of a positive sexual experience. She explains that there is such a wide spectrum between 'not being raped' and having a satisfactory sexual experience that the consent/non-consent binary is clearly inadequate for understanding the complexity of sexual interactions. Anderson discusses many reasons why the concept of consent falls short: consent may develop into non-consent; consent presupposes

---

[11] B Bradby, 'Like a Video: The Sexualisation of Childbirth in Bolivia' (1998) 6 *Reproductive Health Matters* 50.

[12] N Hartsock, 'The Feminist Standpoint: Developing the Ground for a Specifically Feminist Historical Materialism' in S Harding and M Hintikka (eds), *Discovering Reality: Feminist Perspectives on Epistemology, Metaphysics, Methodology, and the Philosophy of Science* (Dordrecht, Kluwer Academic Publishers, 1983).

[13] M Fricker, *Epistemic Injustice: Power and the Ethics of Knowing* (Oxford, Oxford University Press, 2007).

[14] E Anderson, 'The Limits of Consent in Sexual Ethics' (Blog of the APA, 24 April 2019) at blog.apaonline.org/2019/04/24/women-in-philosophy-the-limits-of-consent-in-sexual-ethics/?fbclid=IwAR028JEerJn2BuPYez5vKr0cm-UImkBkOPiQb5pi0gm4VKGh8X1Z0qm_lz4.

[15] L Alcoff, *Rape and Resistance* (Cambridge, Polity Press, 2018).

[16] R Kukla, 'Sex Talks: Consent and Refusal are not the Only Talking Points on Sex' (*Aeon Essays*, 4 February 2019) at aeon.co/essays/consent-and-refusal-are-not-the-only-talking-points-in-sex.

'a proprietary notion of selfhood derived from social contract theory' and thus that 'I can sign away my body'; heterosexual relations are constructed assuming that consent is almost always something for women to deliver and men to ask for; and 'consent fails to register the temporally unfolding nature of sexual encounters'. This is all relevant to the discussion of consent within medicalised childbirth and obstetric violence. However, what interests me the most in this context is that the conceptualisation of the subject as 'relational' – constructed through interpersonal relations and thus never completely finished nor clearly delineated once and for all (a conceptualisation explored in different ways throughout this collection as well as in my paper 'We Birth with Others')[17] – contests the possibility of 'clear consent', because such a subject changes during the experience itself and is never completely 'transparent' to herself. This is Anderson's main theme, and it poses important questions regarding consent within childbirth. Anderson also suggests that consent is insufficient because

> consent presumes a level of self-knowledge that individuals often lack. Many of us are often ignorant of our own desires, so suggesting that we can know what we want the moment we are asked overlooks historically coded forms of behavior, the effects of past experiences, and the relative power of differing social locations.[18]

This does not imply, however, that paternalistic protection should follow (ie that if we are ignorant of our own desires, maybe others know better what's best for us), but rather that we need to develop more complex understandings of consent, taking into account a complex, dynamic self that is never crystal-clear, either to the subject herself or to those surrounding her. In Anderson's words:

> Within the context of sex, the idea that self-relation is not different in kind from relations to other beings does not give free license to paternalism, but rather suggests that we apply the same complex interpretive frameworks for negotiating our behaviour with others to self-relations. Rather than taking my desires to be immediately transparent to myself, I might look at the ways they are revealed in various registers, including my behavior toward others and patterns of thought.[19]

These important insights into consent in sexual encounters may be key to rethinking consent in the birthing room: so far, obstetric violence has been discussed using a very straightforward notion of consent. But the experience of labour recalls that of a sexual encounter in several ways, and it seems vital not to oversimplify our understandings of consent in the labour room. Anderson's conclusion (in the context of sexual encounters) reveals much about what such a complexification of consent might achieve:

> In suggesting that we focus on the felt dimensions of our sexual subjectivity, I do not mean to suggest a turn to 'raw' emotion at the expense of other dimensions of lived

---

[17] S Cohen Shabot, 'We Birth with Others: Towards a Beauvoirian Understanding of Obstetric Violence' *European Journal of Women's Studies* (2020), 1350506820919474.

[18] Anderson (n 14).

[19] ibid.

experience. The problem with the traditional view of consent is not that it overthinks sexual encounters, but rather that it underthinks the way that our feelings exist in relation to social scripts, relations of power, and the like. It presumes that people are rational agents with transparent desires that they may freely communicate to others. By conceptualizing sexual ethics on the basis of the heterogeneous self, we may better account for its complex intersubjective character. We may envision modes of self-fashioning that deepen our relations to others by recognizing that we are others to ourselves. This project takes us into still-uncharted territory, but I think it holds more promise than continuing to try building sexual ethics around a notion of selfhood inherited from social contract theory that feminist theory has proven wrong.[20]

Will this also prove to be true for the labour room? This collection gives us a number of resources for beginning to ponder this and other urgent questions.

[20] ibid.

INDEX